Pulpit and Nation

Jeffersonian America

JAN ELLEN LEWIS, PETER S. ONUF,
AND ANDREW O'SHAUGHNESSY, EDITORS

Pulpit and Nation

Clergymen and the Politics of Revolutionary America

SPENCER W. MCBRIDE

University of Virginia Press

CHARLOTTESVILLE AND LONDON

University of Virginia Press
© 2016 by the Rector and Visitors of the University of Virginia
All rights reserved
Printed in the United States of America on acid-free paper

First published 2016
First paperback edition published 2018

ISBN 978-0-8139-3956-8 (cloth)
ISBN 978-0-8139-4192-9 (paper)
ISBN 978-0-8139-3957-5 (ebook)

9 8 7 6 5 4 3 2 1

Library of Congress Cataloging-in-Publication Data is available for this title.

Cover art: Detail of *Battle of Springfield, N.J. (Give 'em Watts, Boys) 1780* by John Ward Dunsmore, oil on canvas, 1908. (Fraunces Tavern® Museum, New York City)

To Lindsay

Contents

Acknowledgments

At times, writing a history book seems a very solitary process. Yet, as I look back on the years of research, writing, and revision that went into this book's creation, I am profoundly grateful for the assistance and encouragement I received from numerous friends, family members, colleagues, and trusted advisors. As a graduate student at Louisiana State University, I benefitted immensely from the expertise of my dissertation advisor, Andrew Burstein. He encouraged me when my research was headed toward new discoveries and reigned me in when it appeared that I was headed down tangential detours. He was always generous with his time; as mentors and friends go, he is one of the very best. Nancy Isenberg was similarly generous with her time and talents. A brilliant scholar, she lent her historical expertise and experience as an author to help me shape this project from its earliest stages. Michael Pasquier was also an extremely helpful guide, particularly in navigating the intersections of two related, but at times quite different, disciplines: history and religious studies.

In the Department of History at LSU, I discovered a vibrant academic community that proved an ideal setting in which to conduct the research that informs this book. Several faculty members went above and beyond their responsibilities to assist and encourage me, including Gaines Foster, Christine Kooi, Carolyn Herbst Lewis, Suzanne Marchand, Paul Paskoff, Charles Shindo, and Victor Stater. My fellow doctoral candidates in that department became invaluable colleagues and friends, particularly Geoffrey Cunningham, Terry Wagner, and Andrew Wegmann, as well as Jonathan Awtrey, Ashley Allen Baggett, Tom Barber, Nathan Buman, Chris Childers, Rebecca Bond Costa, Michael Frawley, Erin Halloran, Zach Isenhower, Andrew Johnson, Adam Pratt, Kat Sawyer Robinson, Michael Robinson, and Stu Tully.

At the Joseph Smith Papers Project, I have been able to further explore themes of religion and its impact on American political culture. Several of my colleagues there read part or all of this manuscript and offered meaningful feedback, including Mason Allred, Christopher Blythe, Matthew Godfrey, Matthew Grow, Reid Neilson, and Brent Rogers. In the wider world of academia, several other able historians read either part or all of the book manuscript—or provided feedback on portions I presented in academic settings—and saved me from several errors, including Thomas Bullock, Benjamin Carp, Matthew Dennis, Kevin Doyle, Sara Georgini, and Tara Strauch. Dick Holway and the capable editorial staff at the University of Virginia Press have been indispensable guides as I navigated the numerous steps involved in publishing a monograph. All the individuals I have mentioned above helped me make this book what it is today. However, the work is ultimately mine, and I alone am responsible for its content.

I presented aspects of this book at a variety of history conferences and in other academic settings. These presentations helped shape my thinking on the subject of religion and early American political culture in important ways. I will not list them all, but three occasions were particularly influential on the shape this project eventually took. A conference on national fasts and thanksgivings at Durham University in Durham, England, inspired me to think more deeply about the political ramifications of religious rites. The annual meetings of the Society for Historians of the Early American Republic provided ideal settings for scholars such as me to begin to engage with a wider academic audience. Lastly, I returned from a 2015 speaking engagement at the Kinder Institute on Constitutional Democracy with constructive feedback on how to further develop my understanding and explanation of the role clergymen played in the ratification debates of 1787–88.

Financial support for this project was provided in part through grants and fellowship from various institutions. The Department of History and Graduate School at LSU each offered generous funding for travel to archives and conferences throughout the country and overseas. The Department of History's T. Harry Williams Dissertation Fellowship afforded me the time and resources necessary to complete the dissertation upon which this book is based. Additionally, an Andrew W. Mellon fellowship from the Virginia Historical Society resulted in key discoveries in its vast collections.

Lastly, but most importantly, I could not have written this book without the support and encouragement I received from my family. My parents, Monroe and Laurie McBride, raised me in a home that was full of books, as well as engaging conversation about the past and its significance to the present. Knowing that some parents express dismay when their children choose a major in the humanities, I consider myself very fortunate indeed to have parents who rejoiced when I told them I would major in history and pursue graduate degrees in the same. My parents-in-law, Kris and Gail Budinger, made no objections to their daughter marrying an erstwhile historian and have continually cheered me on in my academic endeavors. I thank my children, Erik, Laney, Joshua, and Thomas, who motivate me to be my best in a way that is difficult to articulate. Instead, I will simply state here that they never hesitated to play with me while I was writing this book, even if my mind was, at times, seemingly stuck in the eighteenth and nineteenth centuries. And then there is my wife, Lindsay. More than anybody else, this book exists because of this incredible woman. For reasons too numerous to list, I have dedicated this book to her.

Pulpit and Nation

Introduction

Parents instruct their children to avoid discussing two topics in polite company: religion and politics. With apologies to "polite company" everywhere, this book is immersed in both. It examines the way America's first national political leaders, in partnership with Protestant Christian clergymen, politicized religious language and biblical symbols.

The alliances American political leaders forged with politicized clergymen during the Revolution and in the early republic are misunderstood and underappreciated aspects of United States history. Historians have frequently relegated clergymen to the margins of the American past—presenting them as cheerleaders who merely urged on revolutionaries from the sidelines, or as the subjects of human interest stories tangential to the central narratives of early America. Many of the most widely read histories of the Revolutionary era omit them altogether. Such portrayals are inadequate because they do not capture the complex interplay between religion and politics in the founding of the United States. Politicized clergymen played an essential role in the American Revolution and in the era of nation building that followed. They are not an interesting side story; they are a crucial part of *the* story.[1]

American clergymen were involved in politics long before the Revolution, but the Revolution changed the nature of their political activity. Prior to the imperial crisis that arose in the 1760s, clergymen typically limited their political voices to local issues. But when acts of Parliament such as the Stamp Act and the Intolerable Acts roused the colonies to united, continental action, American clergymen expanded the scope of their political activity accordingly. The creation of the Continental Congress in 1774 and its reprise in 1775 signaled the creation of a national political stage. From the outset of the Revolution, Congress explicitly encouraged clergymen to preach national politics from their pulpits, and partisan politicians continued the practice during the early republic. In the process, clergymen became essential intermediaries between would-be national leaders and average Americans.

The clergy's intermediary role helps to explain how the fight for independence and the process of state formation became popular movements and not undertakings confined to society's elite. Revolutionary leaders bombarded American readers with pamphlets and newspaper essays explaining the justness of the patriot cause in terms of international law and the philosophy of natural rights. Early national leaders used a similar vocabulary to contend for competing visions of how they should govern the United States. In both cases, these arguments were best suited for the colonies' most educated citizens, not their general populations. The Revolution amounted to a violent transfer of power from England's ruling elite to the aggrieved colonial elite. Despite celebratory depictions of the Revolution opening government to "the many," the reality is that, in the war's immediate aftermath, power was still largely restricted to "the few." Politicized clergymen helped to mobilize "the many" into this elite power struggle by translating the legal and philosophical justifications for revolution into religious terms. They appealed to emotions and homegrown religiosity, effectively creating and mobilizing a moral community that included far more than the colonies' wealthiest and best educated. The Revolutionary leadership and their clerical allies succeeded in framing religious commitment in terms of political commitment and vice versa. However, patriot clergymen were not pawns; the anxieties they expressed reflected broader anxieties shared by their parishioners. The lives and activities of clergymen are therefore central to any understanding of American political culture and the sense of a collective identity forged during the Revolution and in its aftermath.[2]

These clergymen preached sermons and published essays that became mechanisms of political mobilization and later encouraged Americans to view partisan battles in national terms. Without these influential men, America's first constitutionally elected leaders would have been hard-pressed to persuade Americans to look and think beyond the boundaries of local interests and prejudices. Political leaders looked to the persuasive powers of their ecclesiastical counterparts to reach where politicians and newspaper editors could not. Clergymen in turn used their new political role to shore up their social and cultural authority, an authority that was otherwise eroding in the late-eighteenth and early-nineteenth centuries. It is not an exaggeration to state that Americans began to think of themselves as members of a new imagined community in large part because their trusted spiritual leaders told them that they were.

Many scholars have overlooked the political significance of the religious language and symbolism early national leaders used in their public appeals; others have overemphasized the same. This study intends to accomplish something more, to introduce persuasive evidence of the actual role religion played in American political culture at the time of the country's founding and to explain both the impact and limitations of that role. By exploring the interplay of politicized religion and religiously infused politics—and paying close attention to local, state, and regional idiosyncrasies in the process—we uncover the important relationship between American religion and Revolutionary-era political culture. We discover that while religion mattered to Americans at this time, it meant different things to different people. Its significance to Americans, individually and collectively, varied according to context. Revolutionary Virginia provides an instructive example. In the early stages of the war, the Anglican establishment negotiated the extent of its religious hegemony in order to ensure support for the patriot cause among the state's sizable population of Protestant dissenters. Did this willingness to part with certain religious privileges mean that religion mattered very little to Virginia's patriot Anglicans? No. It simply demonstrates that although religion was important to these Revolutionaries, it was not the final determinant in their political struggle. American Revolutionaries were willing to negotiate and reorder religion's priority in the long list of principles they claimed to be fighting for in their struggle for independence.[3]

As a meditation on religion and clergymen in the politics of Revolutionary America, this book examines the impact of religious language and symbols on the political and martial mobilization of the American people, as well as their place in the creation of an American national identity. The nature of the Revolutionary War was deeply influenced by clergymen and religious rhetoric, and the development of Americans' national identity was informed in many ways as a direct result of clerical participation in that conflict. Through their political activism, clergymen helped transform a limited struggle over what British sovereignty entailed into a full-fledged continental revolution by helping mobilize common people to face bullets for what we might consider rather esoteric considerations. Though they had drawn men into violent conflict, in the war's aftermath, clergymen helped facilitate a process of state formation that was contentious but relatively nonviolent.

The American Revolution was not a religious event, but the very nature of the Revolution was determined in significant ways by the religious rhetoric employed by secular and clerical leaders alike.

outline starts here

This fresh look at religion and politics in Revolutionary America focuses on pivotal national events and developments between 1775 and 1800 in which religious language and symbolism helped shape public discourse. In the six chapters that follow, this book examines the religious dimensions of mobilizing Americans to the Revolutionary cause and sustaining their revolutionary fervor. It also explains the entanglement of clerical allegiances during the fight with Great Britain and the plurality of religious interests involved in factional-turned-partisan debates that helped bring the Revolution to its contentious, but nonviolent, close.

Chapter 1 describes the political motives behind the Continental Congress's proclamations of national days of fasting and prayer in the interest of colonial unity. Instead of demonstrating congressional concern for Americans' commitment to Christian morality or proving the collective piety of the delegates, the language of congressional fast day proclamations reveals a complex web of political motives and measured results. What kinds of public responses did these proclamations generate? Were fast days the effective vehicle of political mobilization Congress thought they were? In Philadelphia, we discover fast days were almost entirely successful. What about other American cities? What about rural or backcountry communities? The diaries and letters of Americans and their clergymen demonstrate that fast days elicited a mixed popular response, one that sheds new light on both the effectiveness and limitations of religion as a nationalizing theme and as a means of political mobilization.

The Revolutionary leadership's dependence on clergymen to serve as chaplains, both in the army and in Congress, is the focus of chapter 2. Congressional delegates and the army's officers placed expectations on their chaplains that went far beyond those traditionally associated with chaplaincies in other Western armies and legislative assemblies. There were political, symbolic, and pragmatic reasons Revolutionary leaders relied on chaplains. At times, soldiers and chaplains had different expectations of each other, and the same can be said of congressional delegates and the chaplains they employed to open meetings with prayer. But ultimately, the army used chaplains to keep Americans in the war, while Congress used chaplains to promote civil discourse in congressional debates and to symbolically unite Americans of different religious denominations under a national government.

Chapter 3 juxtaposes the Revolutionary experiences of three different clergymen from three different regions of the country: Bishop Samuel Seabury of Connecticut, Bishop James Madison of Virginia, and the Reverend John Joachim Zubly of Georgia. All three men have largely disappeared from historical memory. Their reintroduction is meant to do more than supply biographical portraits. Taken separately, the experiences of Seabury, Madison, and Zubly demonstrate the provocative ideas clergymen expressed and the situations in which they found themselves in the midst of war. But collectively, they present a reliable perspective of what it meant to be a politicized clergyman during the Revolution. Seabury was a staunch loyalist, while Madison was a devoted patriot. Both men went on to ecclesiastical prominence in the war's aftermath. But Zubly, who switched midwar from patriotism to loyalism, had a more ignominious fate. Their combined experiences effectively and dramatically illustrate the tension many Americans felt between patriotism and loyalism. The politicization of clergymen, and of Americans in general, is more accurately depicted as a process than as a singular instance in which individuals chose between joining the patriot cause or remaining loyal to Great Britain. Navigating the domestic civil war created by the "international" dispute with Great Britain was far more consequential than the mere act of choosing sides.

The long-overlooked participation of clergymen in the ratification debates of 1787–88 is the subject of chapter 4. Though the Constitutional Convention focused on drafting a wholly secular document for stabilizing American society, a sizable contingent of clergymen and other religious Americans expressed concern in these debates over the effect the Constitution would have on America's religious landscape. When we examine the activity of clergymen as recorded in the documentary history of the ratification debates, three major themes emerge. First, both Federalists and Anti-Federalists spoke of the clergy as a special interest group, a political force to be reckoned with. This classification suggests that in the 1780s, many Americans accepted the clergy's recently enlarged political influence, while others were fearful of clerical hegemony in the secular sphere and tried to curtail it. Second, the language of American providentialism figured prominently in the appeals both lay and clerical Americans made either for or against the Constitution. Clearly, the rhetorical tool once used by Congress to unite thirteen disparate colonies had been appropriated by Federalists and Anti-Federalists alike and served as a trigger for factional division, an ideological shift that challenged enduring conceptions of the United States as God's "chosen land"

and "chosen people." The notion of a "chosen people" living in a "chosen land" was a constant theme in late colonial protonationalism. By presenting competing visions of America's national future, Federalists and Anti-Federalists assigned significant national importance to the Constitution as a document that would either bolster or destroy the foundation of American nationalism—and, by extension, a nascent form of American exceptionalism. Third, the aspect of the ratification debates most concerned with the pragmatic association of religion with the new national government surrounded the prohibition of religious tests as a prerequisite for federal office holding. Clergymen were divided on the subject. In part, the question was whether the federal government would establish a national religion. But its broader implications addressed the ongoing debate as to whether religion was severable from public morality. Though clergymen and religion were noticeably absent from the Constitutional Convention—no clergymen participated in the convention, and its members rejected motions to open their daily meetings with prayer—the people's spiritual leaders had a strong presence in the ratification debates.[4]

Chapter 5 explains the significance of clerical participation in the formation of America's first party system during the 1790s. Some historians have written about the New England clergy's role in this process and the way Congregationalist ministers in particular used the Federalist Party to regain—or at least shore up—a cultural authority that had started to erode amid the social disruption of the Revolution. Did ecclesiastical self-interest similarly motivate Federalist clergymen south of New England and Republican clergymen throughout the country to preach party from their pulpits? Many ministers from established churches (and those recently disestablished) became Federalists because of the party's message of hierarchy and social order, believing the party's success would help them to retain or regain their traditional voice in American society. Similarly, many ministers from dissenting Protestant denominations became Republicans because of the party's opposition to elite, monarchical-like control over society and government, believing that the party's success would further the influences of their respective denominations in the new national religious landscape. However, sermons, pamphlets, and newspapers demonstrate that religious affiliation did not necessarily determine the party a politicized clergyman endorsed. Local power dynamics and cultural idiosyncrasies created too many exceptions to make these trends hard and fast rules. To understand patterns of clerical politicization, we must understand the challenges they were facing in different localities. By doing so, it becomes clear that in the 1790s politicized clergymen helped build political parties *nationally* in order to maintain their cultural authority *locally*.

The sixth chapter is a search for the historical origins of an extraconstitutional expectation embraced by millions of twenty-first-century Americans, namely that the president must be a Christian. Accordingly, we must look to the first manifestations of this mythic requirement in the elections of 1796 and 1800 between John Adams and Thomas Jefferson. Why did Federalists lean so heavily on the strategy of contesting Jefferson's candidacy based upon his personal religious beliefs? What were the long- and short-term effects of this strategy on the way Americans conceived of the presidency? Records that illuminate local political conditions during the national elections of 1796 and 1800 reveal that the expectation that the American president must be a Christian did not come from the nation's founding documents or from some unspoken rule generally accepted by the country's founders. Instead, the Christian president fantasy originated in the partisan political battles of the early republic; it was created by desperate Federalists exploiting the intuitive prejudice held by a portion of the public in favor of Christian leaders. Later generations of Americans crystallized the myth in American political culture with their skewed retellings of the nation's founding era. One of the most overlooked legacies of the elections of 1796 and 1800 is the way these elections linked the religious identity of the president to that of the burgeoning American nation at large.

Where American nationalism is concerned, religion is a theme with great potential but real limitations. There were moments in the founding era when religious symbols, rituals, and language effectively spurred Americans to begin conceiving of themselves as part of a new national community. Yet there were moments when such nationalizing tools fell short. Religion plays an important role in the story of early American nationalism, but it is important to remember that it did not function in exclusion of other factors. Religion alone did not generate an American nation, nor should it be viewed as the chief characteristic upon which Americans first imagined their community. We must examine it in the fuller context of American political culture.

To restate, this book addresses a curious interrelationship: the political utility of religion and the religious utility of politics. We should not assume that any instance in which early national leaders participated in religious rituals, referenced religious symbols, or spoke of the country in religious language is evidence of genuine religious belief. A more critical approach reveals several other possible explanations and an additional layer of analytical depth.

An assortment of fears and aspirations motivated the founders' invocation of the religious for the promotion of the secular. In 1775, for instance, deists in Congress supported the motion for a continental fast day even though they dismissed from their personal creeds the idea of supernatural intervention in the affairs of humankind. In the ratification debates of 1787–88, the devoutly Christian Samuel Adams conceded his support of the Constitution despite its omission of any reference to God. Then, in the election of 1800, clerical and lay Federalists alike used extreme language to warn their fellow Americans that elevating Thomas Jefferson to the presidency would spell spiritual doom for the country. We see in these instances that in the political arena, a person could use religious language for its political utility without necessarily believing in the theological implications of such language. Or, in the case of Samuel Adams, people could put aside their religious scruples for a political vote without disavowing their faith. Some of America's first national leaders used religious language for solely political reasons; others used it for genuinely religious reasons. In some instances, leaders were motivated by a combination of the two. We should not take the religious utterances of men waging fierce political battles at face value. When power is at stake, we should always question motives.

The political utility of religious language in early American political discourse sheds light on a related historical theme: the ways in which politics altered Protestant Christian theology. Until now, the inverse has been the dominant theme among historians of religion and politics who focus on instances in which changes to the American theological landscape had a direct impact on the political developments of the American Revolution and early republic, arguing that theological developments either preempted or caused political change. The most notable examples of this frame of thinking are depictions of the Great Awakening as the direct precursor to the Revolution—that as churchgoing Americans began to challenge the patriarchal authority of established denominations they were inspired to challenge unjust patriarchy elsewhere. Taking this trope of theology as the harbinger of secular transformation even further, some historians privilege evangelical Christians in historical relief wherever they are found in the events of the Revolution and the process of nation building. Often, such studies rely on the application of a vague definition of evangelicalism to men in the founding generation who would never have conceived of themselves under such a label. While there are certainly moments in American history when theological change strongly influenced political transformation, we cannot assume that this was always a one-way street. We need to explore alternative explanations and even turn traditional constructs on their heads.[5]

There are, after all, numerous instances in which politics transformed Protestant Christian theology in American churches. We find a prime example of this process in the public debate over the country's alliance with France during the Revolutionary War. A decade earlier, American colonists fasted and prayed communally for victory over their imperial rival, a country that Protestant ministers depicted as an extension of the Pope's influence and an agent of the antichrist. Yet in 1777 Congress proclaimed a fast, urging all to pray for their French allies. In essence, Congress extended the favor of Providence to Catholic France by civil decree, a clear departure from traditional Protestant beliefs. Instances in which politics were the agent of theological change are an understudied aspect in the history of religion and America's political system, an aspect with the potential to reshape the way Americans understand the place of religion in the nation's creation story.

Beyond exploring the nature of the American Revolution and the construction of a distinct national identity within the Atlantic world, this book challenges long-standing assumptions about the Enlightenment and the formation of the American political system. The participation of clergymen in national politics highlights a growing point of disagreement among Americans during this era: whether or not public morality could exist without religion. Public morality is defined here as people dealing honestly and virtuously with each other in the public sphere, including the dealings of public officials with their constituents. This question of severing public morality from religion was not new, nor was it distinctly American. But the establishment of new governments in the aftermath of independence injected the question with a greater sense of urgency. When the colonists seized their chance "to begin the world over again," they did so under the influence of more than two centuries of Enlightenment philosophy and empiricism that had challenged once firmly entrenched political ideas such as the divine right of kings and the exclusively divine origins of civil society.[6]

America's experiment with republicanism was informed in part by an Enlightenment that was neither wholly religious nor entirely secular. While republicanism was an attractive political philosophy for many Americans, they disagreed on the surest way of guarding a republican society from corruption. With the rapid revolt against monarchy and the institution of republican governments in the 1770s and 1780s, what had long been a favorite topic of European philosophers conversing in luxurious salons became the actual undertaking of American politicians legislating in austere statehouses. The American Revolution made the question of whether or not public morality could be severed from religion far less abstract than it had hitherto been; the early American republic was where the metaphorical rubber met the road. Some Americans maintained that religion was essential to the virtue and morality of public officials and insisted that religious tests and religiously charged oaths were essential to guard public office from the nonreligious. Other Americans argued that religious tests and oaths were ineffective and only served to exclude religious minorities and oppress the American mind.

The issue of public morality's connection to religion was so prominent in the early republic that George Washington weighed in on the ongoing debate in his farewell address, insisting that "reason and experience both forbid us to expect that National morality can prevail in exclusion of religious principle." But Washington's claims were neither the first nor the last word on the subject; his was merely one of numerous opinions on the matter.[7]

In fact, there has never been a consensus among Americans or their elected leaders on the proper place of religion in political culture. America's founders were ambitious men who recognized the political value of religion and utilized it to their advantage. At times their actions were examples of astute political persuasion. At other times, their actions were examples of calculated political manipulation. Most of the time, however, their use of religion in the political sphere lay on an ambiguous plane somewhere in between. Unceasing disagreement and debate on the place of religion in American politics is one of the most enduring legacies of the country's founding era. Even Alexis de Tocqueville observed as much during his 1831 tour of the United States, after which he remarked, "The organization and establishment of democracy in Christendom is the great problem of our times. The Americans, unquestionably, have not resolved this problem, but furnish useful data to those who undertake to resolve it."[8]

ONE

Congress and the Courtship of Providence

In June 1775, the American colonies had done little to justify the name "United Colonies." Despite their common grievance with Parliament, each colony jealously guarded its autonomy, counting on local militia to protect its borders while relying on local officials to make and enforce laws. When Americans formed the Continental Congress to coordinate resistance to the imperial policies of Parliament, unifying the inhabitants of the disparate colonies instantly became the measure of its success. One of the first attempts by Congress to foster colonial unity was its proclamation of a day of fasting and prayer. John Adams envisioned "millions on their knees at once before their Great Creator, imploring . . . his Smiles on American Councils and Arms." He believed the fast day would prompt the clergy to "engage with a fervor that will produce wonderful effects."[1]

Ostensibly, these fast days were instances in which a secular government promoted religious rituals. As historians examine the significance of such occasions, the easy explanation is that fast days are indicative of the founders' personal religious beliefs and demonstrate a congressional concern for citizens' moral conduct, highlighting the belief that Americans' sins had brought on the imperial crisis and could yet work against the cause of independence. This approach, however, is far too narrow and misleading. America's Revolutionary fast days were not simply religious acts recommended to the public by a political body. Certainly the religious implications of such occasions are important and should not be dismissed. Yet a more careful examination reveals these fast days' full context and ultimate significance as instruments of nation building that brought the clergy into the emerging national political arena.[2]

This chapter explains how and why the Continental Congress appropriated the fast day tradition and deployed the language of American providentialism for its own ends during the Revolution. It also explains how popular fast day observance varied from colony to colony and from urban to rural settings. Congress stood to gain clear political advantages from the widespread observance of fast days. By uniting the colonists in religious worship, these occasions would create for Congress an effective channel of communication with constituents by mobilizing an "army" of clergymen to more effectively lead their congregations to acknowledge resistance to Great Britain as just. Clergymen, who had long been active participants in local politics, would be urged by Congress to preach politics from a "national," or at least "continental," perspective. But the most important advantages to be gained were ideological. To encourage participation by as many colonists as possible, the fast days had to be publicized in terms that transcended the doctrinal differences of denominations. Toward this end, Congress utilized the language of American providentialism, effectively framing the war with Great Britain in religious terms that made American success synonymous with the realization of "the great Governor of the World's" plan for the moral redemption of mankind. America's Revolutionary fast days were much more than mere religious acts proclaimed by a political body. They were a mechanism for the political mobilization of Americans and a means of authorizing the political legitimacy of Congress.[3]

"The Clergy, This Way, Are But Now Beginning to Engage in Politicks"

American days of fasting and prayer were rooted in the political and religious culture of England. Puritans immigrating to North America in the early seventeenth century brought with them the practice of community-wide fasting and prayer. Seventeenth-century English theologians taught that fasting enhanced prayer's efficacy. In addition to numerous biblical examples of fasting generating spiritual power, contemporary English theologians offered physiological explanations of the benefits produced by its practice. Reverend William Perkins preached in 1608 that fasting "causeth watchfulness, & cuts off drowsiness, and so makes a man more lively and fresh in prayer. . . . It makes us feele our wants and miseries, and so brings us to some conscience of our sinnes, whereupon the heart is more humbled and so stirred up more frequently to call for mercie." Similarly, in 1625 Reverend Henry

Mason argued that "fulnes of bread, and the pampering of flesh . . . more immediately and directly breede matter for unchaste and fleshly lusts. . . . On the contrary side, fasting, and the pinching of the body, and putting it to hardnesse, they are means to cool the bloud, and tame the spirits, and pull down the pride of the flesh." Such teachings were applied to both individual and community-wide fasting by the Puritans at the time of their immigration and thereafter. Community-wide fasts, then, were an example of sacrificing comfort for the higher good, an appeal frequently made by the American Revolutionary leadership to patriots in the 1770s.[4]

Fast days rested upon the idea of providentialism, most simply defined as a belief in God's intervention in the affairs of mankind. But in seventeenth- and eighteenth-century America, providentialism became a complex and malleable trope. As demonstrated below, the American colonists sometimes used providentialism as an ideology or worldview, while at other times they used it as a sociopolitical rhetoric to assign divine approbation to an event, cause, or idea. If it seems that historians are too loose with the term providentialism, it is in large part because early Americans used it loosely and its connotations and implications varied with context. From the early colonial era to the eve of the Revolution, Americans could use providential language as a vague and diluted version of Christian theology, as an invocation of the biblical jeremiad tradition in current affairs, or as a veil for deist views. Or its use could entail all of the above at once. Though providentialism was not inherently political or national, it was easily molded to fit such categories.[5]

The community-wide observance of fast days also fit perfectly with the Puritans' Calvinist faith, particularly its covenant theology and millennialism. The Puritans' belief that America would play a crucial role in ushering in the millennium combined with their belief that they were God's "chosen" people to create a distinctly American form of providentialism. Whereas many in Europe similarly believed that the affairs of mankind were directed by God for his own purposes, these colonists projected the idea that they had been cast in the starring role for the final act in the history of mankind. Though these colonists were on the *periphery* of the British Empire, they saw themselves at the *center* of God's Kingdom.

American providentialism remained a viable worldview and rhetorical tradition among colonists in New England even amid the theological and cultural changes that occurred during the seventeenth and eighteenth centuries, including the rise of other religious sects in the region. The resilience of this idea of a special purpose for America is exhibited by the regular observance of fast days in the years leading up to and during the American Revolution. In most New England colonies, fast days were observed each spring, though some communities made short-lived attempts at monthly or even weekly fast days. Historians have suggested the annual observances became mundane rituals, losing the zeal that initially accompanied the practice. For instance, the fast days routinely observed to mark the change in seasons rarely warranted much more than a brief mention in diaries, letters, and church records. Yet, at times of crisis, during waves of sickness or religious dissension, fast days acquired a sense of urgency and social potency. In these instances, the sense of danger and hope for deliverance fully occupied the community's attention. Hence, we cannot understand the full meaning of fast days if we ignore context. As illustrated below, colonists had a clear sense of "moment" in the 1770s when they turned to fast days.[6]

Until the middle of the eighteenth century, however, fast days and the adoption of American providentialism were still primarily features of the New England colonies. Yet some Englishmen made unsuccessful and fleeting attempts at assigning providential missions to the establishment of colonies outside New England in the seventeenth century. The Virginia Company provides one such example. In an attempt to differentiate its goals of wealth from those of the Spanish colonies in North America, the company attempted to persuade would-be colonists reading its pamphlets that by moving to Virginia, they would be fulfilling England's providential mission of spreading Protestantism to the Americas and protecting Native Americans from the "cruelty" and "false" religion of Catholic Spain. However, there is no evidence that this providential rhetoric convinced anyone to leave England for Virginia. It was not until the Great Awakening of the mid-eighteenth century that providentialism experienced greater acceptance in the middle and southern colonies. Through the widespread revivals that characterized this movement, many of the providential ideas long held in New England were adapted to and embraced by other Protestant denominations, particularly the Presbyterians, Baptists, and Methodists. These revivals also fueled the belief that a "concert of prayer" would not only win the support of Providence, but could accelerate God's plans to bring about the second coming of Christ. To this end, ministers such as Jonathan Edwards communicated with ministers in Scotland, attempting, albeit unsuccessfully, to coordinate transatlantic group prayer to enhance its potency. Because the "concert of prayer" was inherent to fast day observance, such occasions remained significant in American providential thought.[7]

Nonetheless, the practice of fast days did not spread as quickly as the providential ideology supporting it. By the time of the Seven Years' War, providential explanations were advanced throughout the colonies to underscore the necessity and inevitability of a British victory over the French and their Native American allies. Fast days so dedicated were held in several of the middle and southern colonies, but still occurred most frequently in New England. It was not until the imperial crisis that arose on the heels of this war that fast days made real headway in the middle and southern colonies.[8]

In one notable instance before the Revolution, the Virginia House of Burgesses declared a fast day in May 1774. This act was meant as a show of support for Virginia's "Sister Colony of Massachusetts Bay" after King George III and Parliament declared its ports closed to trade and virtually annulled the colony's charter as a consequence of the Boston Tea Party. As Thomas Jefferson explained in his autobiography, "We were under conviction of the necessity of arousing our people from the lethargy into which they had fallen as to passing events; and thought that fasting and prayer would be most likely to call up and alarm their attention." The last time the House of Burgesses had declared a fast day was 1755, during the Seven Years' War. But, as Jefferson explained further, since then "a new generation had grown up." He and his collaborators on the fast day proclamation were unsure of the protocol surrounding such an occasion, and therefore looked to the histories of the English Civil Wars (1642–51) and "rummaged over . . . the revolutionary precedents and forms of the Puritans of that day . . . [and] cooked up a resolution, somewhat modernizing their phrases." The motion was unanimously passed by the House of Burgesses, and on June 1, 1774—the date the Boston Port Act took effect—"the people met generally, with anxiety and alarm in their countenances, and the effect of the day, through the whole colony, was like a shock of electricity, arousing every man, and placing him erect and on his centre."[9]

Jefferson's description of Virginia's 1774 day of fasting is significant to the history of fast days in America for several reasons. First, the nineteen years separating the observances of such days in Virginia shows the infrequency of the practice outside of New England. Second, the fact that the burgesses felt compelled to review the Puritans' fast day proclamations and protocol reveals their awareness of the English (and subsequently New England Puritan) origins of this tradition and acceptance of the practice despite the different denominational tendencies of the two regions. In the 1770s, New England and the colonies to the south had negative views of each other, views that Virginians were attempting to set aside—at least for the moment—to address their common grievances. By proclaiming a fast day, they signaled colonial unity in resisting the Coercive Acts.

Colonists south of New England were especially critical of that region's manners and politics. For instance, Edward Rutledge of South Carolina expressed his opinions of the "Eastern Provinces" (New England) in a letter to John Jay of New York. "I dread their low Cunning," Rutledge wrote, "and those leveling Principles which Men without Character and without Fortune in general Possess, which are so captivating to the lower Class of Mankind." Such prejudices seemed to be confirmed by George Washington when he assumed leadership over an army of New Englanders at Boston in 1775. "I daresay the Men would fight very well (if properly officered) although they are an exceeding dirty & nasty people," the general wrote to his distant cousin Lund Washington. A week later, Washington further criticized the New Englanders in another letter back to Virginia, insisting that their indifference to military discipline proceeded from "an unaccountable kind of stupidity in the lower class of these people, which believe me prevails but too generally among the Officers of the Massachusetts part of the Army, who are nearly of the same kidney, with the Privates." In fact, the exploitation of these sections' differences and perceptions of each other became a key component of British strategy during the Revolutionary War. Although these regional prejudices largely amount to stereotypes, their prevalence in the colonies makes Virginia's 1774 fast day all the more significant. In this instance, the dissimilar colonies were searching for common methods in their common cause. By the middle of the eighteenth century, fast days were no longer exclusively Puritan or Congregationalist affairs. Nor were they exclusively religious.[10]

In stating that the fast day's primary purpose was to rouse people from their "lethargy," Jefferson displayed a newfound belief that heightened patriotism could be achieved through religious rhetoric connected to group fasting and prayer. Just as theologians believed that fasting sharpened the senses of the physical body to better discern spiritual matters, Jefferson apparently believed it would have a comparable effect on the body politic in promoting patriotism in anxious circumstances. Upon the outbreak of war one year later, the Continental Congress exhibited this same belief, but on a much larger scale.[11]

The resolution of the Continental Congress in June 1775 to appoint a day of fasting and prayer throughout the colonies represented one of the earliest acts of Congress to give direction to all of its constituents. Other than the 1774 Articles of Association, most of the letters and proclamations Congress composed in the first months after convening were addressed to parties in England, Canada, the Caribbean, or individual colonies. Proclaiming a day of fasting *throughout* the colonies was a pivotal moment in which this representative body sought to govern at once all those it represented. Arguably, this was the first step toward practical unification. That Congress was at this moment concerned with establishing its legitimacy as a governing body is supported by the British politics surrounding such observances. As historians David Waldstreicher and Benjamin H. Irvin have each observed, the proclaiming of fast days (with the exception of those observed in individual towns and cities) was a right reserved for colonial governors, assemblies, and the English monarch. By assuming the right to proclaim a continental fast, Congress was sending a deliberate message about its role as a governing body.[12]

It is impossible to know all the factors leading to the motion in Congress to declare its first fast day, but some glimpses into the weeks preceding the decision are recoverable. The private correspondence of delegates reveals additional clues to the discussion and debate over this fast day. The day before the motion was made, John Adams wrote to his wife, Abigail, that he had thoroughly enjoyed the sermons he had heard while in Philadelphia. Adams made particular mention of a sermon he had attended earlier that morning from Reverend George Duffield, "a Preacher in this City whose Principles, Prayers and Sermons more nearly resemble, those of our New England Clergy than any that I have heard. . . . [He] applied the whole Prophesy [of Isaiah chapter 35] to this Country, and gave us, as animating an entertainment, as I ever heard. He fill'd and swell'd the Bosom of every Hearer." Adams recognized the political merits of providentialism, and in the words of Isaiah, the tactical advantage of persuading the "deaf" to hear. With this letter Adams enclosed a copy of a published sermon in order to demonstrate how "the Clergy, this Way, are but now beginning to engage in Politicks, and they engage with a fervour that will produce wonderfull Effects."[13]

The political tenor of the Philadelphia clergy in the summer of 1775, then, appears to have been a primary influence on the timing of the first fast day. Adams's enthusiastic response to Duffield's sermon occurred the day before Congress passed the motion to declare the fast. Possibly, Adams himself made the motion, or at least was one of its strongest supporters. There is every indication that he believed a congressionally appointed fast day would give colonial clergymen both license and occasion to preach Revolutionary politics from their pulpits.

Creating such an alliance with the clergy throughout the colonies offered a partial solution to problems Congress faced at the time of its inception. As mentioned earlier, the Continental Congress had not firmly established its legitimacy and effectiveness. Also, at this time there were relatively few "national" figures, men whose reputations were known and respected throughout the thirteen colonies. Average Americans tended to be familiar with the political leadership of their own colonies and perhaps that of neighboring colonies. However, a farmer in South Carolina was unlikely to know of Adams at this time, just as a fisherman in Rhode Island was unlikely to know of Jefferson. Hence, congressional communications sent through local committees of correspondence would lack the established authority of known local politicians. Through fast days, Congress was attempting to bridge this gap by reaching out to the people's clerical leaders. By urging the clergy to lead fast day observations and preach to their congregations on the spiritual justification and necessity of resisting Great Britain's imperial policies, Congress was delivering its message through individuals known and trusted by local audiences. Fast days turned participating clergymen and churches into political forums—adjuncts of and advocates for Congress.[14]

Looking back, it is not surprising that America's Revolutionary leadership reached out to the clergy to forge a political alliance. The clergy were among the most educated men in colonial society, typically well read and trained to speak persuasively. Many clergymen educated at American colleges witnessed firsthand the politicization of college faculties in the 1750s and 1760s, as the curricula of those institutions became increasingly concerned with preparing students to better serve the state. Furthermore, several clergymen had displayed a willingness to speak out on political matters affecting the entire continent during the Stamp Act crisis of 1765. These moments of political activism did not result in an enduring participation in the political sphere at this time, but they allowed secular leaders to see the potential effectiveness of the clergy therein. Hence, it was both reasonable and realistic for Congress to expect the clergymen who accepted their invitation to preach politics on fast days to become potent extensions of Congress and its protests.[15]

It was also reasonable for Congress to predict that the day of fasting would unite the colonists as a people. Modern nations have frequently used public rites to nurture a common identity, and the public observance of a fast day was no different. Though fast days were not particularly festive, they still served the purpose of a public holiday. By collectively taking a break from life's ordinary events to focus for an entire day on the extraordinary, people in each colony would share the same experience: abstaining from food and drink, engaging in a concert of prayer, and listening to their respective ministers preach on the providential mission of America. While not every colonist would participate in the fast, the appearance of consensus was crucial to the ritual's efficacy in establishing a common identity. In this case, providentialism was a ready-made idea upon which Congress could help build a collective American identity, because it bypassed denominational and regional barriers. Congress, however, was not necessarily envisioning an enduring American "nation" at this time. Many delegates were still calling for a plan of reconciliation such as Joseph Galloway's "Plan of Union," which had been tabled by Congress in September 1774. Galloway's plan proposed a constitutional status within the empire similar to Scotland: the United American Colonies would have domestic self-government without forfeiting the trade benefits and protection of the empire. Whether during the Revolution's early stages when Congress was seeking reconciliation or during the later stages when it sought separation, colonial unity was essential. Providentialism was a versatile idea, creating a dialogue that was simultaneously national and imperial.[16]

The use of a providential ideology and rhetoric as a unifying tool was by no means the invention of American Revolutionary leaders operating in a cultural vacuum. As historian Linda Colley has shown, the task of uniting the three separate kingdoms of England, Wales, and Scotland into one United Kingdom of Great Britain was aided greatly by the idea of Protestantism in general. The people of these three kingdoms could boast a common heritage that unified them against the Catholic Counter-Reformation on the European continent. Colley concludes that this British form of providential thought, from which the American version was largely descended, "was the foundation that made the invention of Great Britain possible." There is tremendous irony in this statement: it means that as Americans were defining themselves as a distinct people, they were employing a *British* strategy for asserting national identity.[17]

"That All America May Soon Behold a Gracious Interposition of Heaven"

Though the official congressional record does not go into great detail about the debate surrounding the motion to declare a fast, a letter from Benjamin Rush to John Adams over thirty years later helps fill the gap. Rush recalled to Adams that "Mr. Jefferson not only opposed [the fast day], but treated it with ridicule, and hinted some objections to the Christian religion. You arose and defended the motion, and in reply to Mr. Jefferson's objections to Christianity you said . . . it was the only instance you had ever known of a man of sound sense and real genius that was an enemy to Christianity." According to Rush, Adams worried that he had offended Jefferson, but the Virginian "soon convinced [Adams] to the contrary by crossing the room and taking a seat in the chair next to [him]."[18]

Jefferson's support of the Virginia fast day in 1774 and his purported opposition to a continental fast day in 1775 appear inconsistent. Yet, when examined closely, the inconsistency does not lie in Jefferson's actions in the debate over the fast day resolution but rather in Rush's memory of the occasion. Rush's purpose in writing Adams was to rekindle the friendship between the two former presidents. The story served to remind Adams that even when he disagreed with his old ally, in the end they found a way to heal wounds. It is highly unlikely that Jefferson actually spoke out against the fast day because he seldom spoke in congressional debates. Always self-conscious about his poor public speaking skills, Jefferson instead relied on his pen and his work in committees to impact congressional activities. As Adams recalled many years later, "During the whole Time I sat with [Jefferson] in Congress, I never heard him utter three sentences together." In all likelihood, Rush was wrong in recalling Jefferson's objection to the fast day. Yet, even with its inaccuracies, Rush's main point in reviving this memory was to portray Adams as the defender of the fast days, a man of "sound sense and real genius" who understood the spiritual and political efficacy of this traditional ritual.[19]

The three-man committee Congress appointed to write the proclamation consisted of John Adams, William Hooper of North Carolina, and Robert Treat Paine of Massachusetts. Hooper appears to have composed the earliest draft, a resolution described by one historian as "much milder than the final resolve in substance and tone." There are significant political implications in the differing tone and substance of Hooper's draft from the final product approved by Congress that illuminate the different motives behind this continental fast day.[20]

Though he was sent to Congress as a delegate from North Carolina, Hooper had been born in Boston in 1742, the son of an Anglican minister. Upon graduating from Harvard in 1760, he chose a career in law rather than the ministry. Believing that Boston was overrun with lawyers, he moved to North Carolina and quickly established himself. Thus, all three members of the committee were raised and educated in New England and were accordingly quite familiar with traditional Puritan forms of proclaiming days of fasting and prayer.

Hooper's draft set forth the essential information of the fast day but possessed little by way of pomp or literary flourish. It read as follows:

> Resolved that it be and hereby it is recommended to the Inhabitants of the united Colonies in America of all Denominations That Thursday the 20th day of July next be set apart as a day of public humiliation[,] fasting and prayer, that a total Abstenence from Servile labor and recreation be observed[,] and all their religious Assemblies Solemnly Convened to humble themselves before God under the heavy Judgments felt and threatened to confess our manifold Sins, to implore the forgiveness of Heaven, (that a sincere repentance [and] reformation may influence our future Conduct) and that a Blessing may descend on the husbandry, Manufactures & other lawful Employments of this people and especially that the Union of these American Colonies in defence of their Just Rights & priviledges may be preserved, confirmed and prospered, that the Congresses may be inspired with Wisdom, that Great Britain and its Rulers may have their eyes opened to discern the things that shall make for the peace and Happiness of the Nation and all its Connections And that America may soon behold a Gracious interposition of Heaven for the redress of her many Grievances, the restoration of her invaded Liberties, a reconciliation with the parent State upon terms Constitutional and Honourable to them both and the Security of them to the latest posterity.[21]

What did Hooper mean by "Constitutional" and "Honourable" terms of reconciliation? In 1775, Congress was seeking a constitutional independence—not a complete separation from Great Britain, but an exemption from the control of Parliament. The version of the fast day proclamation ultimately approved by Congress also expressed the desire for reconciliation with Great Britain, but changes Congress made to the language preceding the statement significantly transformed the implications of the phrase "terms Constitutional and Honourable to them both." Therefore, an examination of the additions and deletions Congress made to Hooper's draft reveals more plainly the political message Congress eventually agreed to relay to its constituents.[22]

When Congress met as a committee of the whole to consider Hooper's draft, it made substantial changes to the proclamation's language. Though many elements of Hooper's draft remained in the finished product, the final version approved by Congress employed a more eloquent prose style, made bolder claims, and contained more dangerous implications. The approved proclamation was also twice the length of Hooper's draft, and the opening paragraph expressly addressed the general nature of God and his involvement in the events of mankind.

Whereas Hooper's draft began by simply stating the essential information of the appointed fast day, Congress added a preface charged with providential language. The proclamation approved by Congress read as follows:

> As the great Governor of the world, by His supreme and universal providence, not only conducts the course of nature with unerring wisdom and rectitude, but frequently influences the minds of men to serve the wise and gracious purposes of His providential government; and it being at all times our indispensable duty devoutly to acknowledge His superintending providence, especially in times of impending danger and public calamity, to reverence and adore his immutable justice as well as to implore His merciful interposition for our deliverance:
>
> This Congress, therefore, considering the present critical, alarming and calamitous state of these colonies, do earnestly recommend that Thursday, the 20th day of July next, be observed, by the inhabitants of all the English colonies on this continent, as a day of public humiliation, fasting and prayer; that we may, with united hearts and voices, unfeignedly confess and deplore our many sins; and offer up our joint supplications to the all-wise, omnipotent, and merciful Disposer of all events; humbly beseeching him to forgive our iniquities, to remove our present calamities, to avert those desolating judgments, with which we are threatened, and to bless our rightful sovereign, King George the third, and inspire him with wisdom to discern and pursue the true interest of all his subjects, that a speedy end may be put to the civil discord between Great Britain and the American colonies, without farther effusion of blood: And that the British nation may be influenced to regard the things that belong to her peace, before they are hid from her eyes: That these colonies may be ever under the care and protection of a kind Providence, and be prospered in all their interests; That the divine blessing may descend and rest upon all our civil rulers, and upon the representatives of the people, in their several assemblies and con-

ventions, that they may be directed to wise and effectual measures for preserving the union, and securing the just rights and priviledges of the colonies; That virtue and true religion may revive and flourish throughout our land; And that all America may soon behold a gracious interposition of Heaven, for the redress of her many grievances, the restoration of her invaded rights, a reconciliation with the parent state, on terms constitutional and honorable to both; And that her civil and religious priviledges may be secured to the latest posterity.

And it is recommended to Christians, of all denominations, to assemble for public worship, and to abstain from servile labour and recreations on said day.[23]

The added preface is important because it became the premise upon which the rest of the proclamation was based. By using the intervening nature of God as the reason for proclaiming a day of fasting and humiliation, Congress explicitly couched the declaration of a continental fast day in providential thought. Whereas Hooper's draft never used the term "Providence," the approved proclamation used it four times. This is not to say that Hooper did not make providential references in his draft, but that the references to Providence Congress added to the final version were substantially more pronounced. The invocation of Providence in the fast day proclamation was intended to equate resistance to Great Britain's imperial policies with the colonies' compliance to God's will, and to present the entire conflict as more than just a battle between two conflicting views of taxation and representation—it was, in effect, a fight between good and evil. Congress was saying that it was God's will that the colonists' "many grievances" and "invaded rights" should be redressed. Such language suggested that the fate of America would no longer be determined by a distant Parliament, but by an omnipresent Providence.

If reconciliation "on terms constitutional and honorable to both" sounded conciliatory, it still referred exclusively to the colonists' objectives; only now, the terms and conditions were presented as synonymous with those of God. By asking the colonists to pray that George III might be "inspired with wisdom to discern and pursue the true interest of his subjects," Congress was implying—if not leaping to the dangerous conclusion—that his actions had hitherto been in opposition to God's grand plan. Added to this implication was the warning that if the British nation did not begin to "regard the things that belong to her peace," Providence would hide them "from her eyes." It was not just the future of America but the future of the world that hung in the balance. Moral progress was being attached to a still largely unexplored, uncivilized continent that stood as a testing ground for godly purposes. The distance from Puritan principles—and fearful rhetoric—may not have been as vast as the more skeptical texts of the Enlightenment advertise. Where the broader public was concerned, extreme language had a place.[24]

Other subtle providential phrases were added to the fast day proclamation, including references to God as a political figure. By identifying God as "the great Governor of the World," Congress reasserted the belief that God governed all human events. More particularly, by assigning political titles to God, Congress presented the image of America's political affairs being directed by an omniscient and omnipotent "Ruler" who was operating *through* Congress and the assemblies of the individual colonies. Congress used such phrases to help legitimize itself as a political body authorized by God to advance America's providential destiny. So when Congress referred to God as "the great Governor," "the Ruler of the Universe," or even "his Most Christian Majesty," it was to argue that God's wisdom superseded that of Parliament and even the king.[25]

The foregoing examination of the revisions Congress made to Hooper's draft reveals that the addition of providential language was intentional, that in this instance, the invocation of providence was not a mere platitude. Clearly, to call a fast day was not the only purpose of the proclamation. If it was, then Hooper's draft would have been more than adequate. The addition of more direct providential rhetoric allowed the fast day proclamation to serve as a piece of political propaganda. This is not surprising, as America's Revolutionary leaders have long stood out in modern history as an especially gifted group when it came to eloquently making their case in published writings.[26]

For instance, the writing and editing of the Declaration on the Causes and Necessity of Taking Up Arms in the summer of 1775 provides a meaningful example of Congress insisting that its published declarations use purposeful language. After a committee of four delegates presented its draft to Congress on June 24, Congress debated the document for two days before wholly rejecting it. Congress added Thomas Jefferson and John Dickinson to the committee with instructions to begin the declaration anew. Dickinson and Jefferson had a strained partnership, but the result was a Declaration on the Causes and Necessity Congress could enthusiastically publish. Dickinson was the primary author of the finished document, and he included therein many of the Quaker principles that influenced his political theory along with several appeals to Providence. This collaboration and the inclusion of Quaker principles in the Declaration on the Causes and Necessity is also important because it demonstrates how congressional delegates brought together different religious values and constructed different religious frameworks to solve problems and make persuasive appeals to the general public.[27]

The drafting of the Declaration of Independence nearly a year after the proclamation of the first fast day further points to the delegates' readiness to seize opportunities to gain public support by using bold, purposeful language in justifying their actions. Their revision of Jefferson's Declaration shows that the delegates were very particular about the words that expressed common purposes, shared motivations, and a more or less uniform ideology. They were well aware of the implied meanings in the Revolutionary vocabulary. It is not accidental that language in Jefferson's draft of the Declaration that blamed George III for perpetuating the slave trade in America was removed. The ideological implications of the slavery passages threatened the unity of Congress and the erstwhile colonies. Furthermore, some delegates were aware of the hypocrisy of claiming "inalienable rights" for "all men" while enslaving millions of African slaves. In a document designed to assign blame to the king, the inclusion of the slavery passages invoked the colonists' complicity in the slave trade, thus weakening their argument against the monarch. Another example of this sensibility is the inclusion of two additional references to God by Congress. Though Jefferson referred to God in his draft as "nature's god" and man's "Creator," Congress inserted stronger references to "the supreme judge of the world" and included an appeal to "the protection of divine providence" in order to appeal to a broader religious constituency. Just as a comparison of Jefferson's initial draft of the Declaration with the final version provides insight into the workings of Congress, so too does a comparison of Hooper's draft of the fast day proclamation with the final version of that document. Like the Declaration on the Causes and Necessities and the Declaration of Independence, the first Revolutionary fast day proclamation was a pragmatic document turned carefully by Congress into an expression justifying resistance to British authority.[28]

An even more applicable example of the ways Congress utilized a religious vocabulary to achieve political ends is John Adams's speech in defense of the resolution for independence on July 2, 1776. No verbatim account of his speech exists, but historians have reasonably speculated that Adams's letters written around this time that specifically address the resolution for independence provide probable clues as to the contents of his speech. Adams's letter to Abigail on July 3 is especially insightful in this regard, as it was written the day after the resolution was passed and for the express purpose of celebrating the profound effect his speech had on the momentous vote. Using the same biblical language of the Jeremiad, Adams alluded to Isaiah 48:10: "Behold, I have refined you, but not with silver; I have chosen you in the furnace of affliction." Applying the verse to the crisis at hand, Adams declared, "It may be the Will of Heaven that America shall suffer Calamities still more wasting and Distresses yet more dreadful. . . . The Furnace of Affliction produces Refinement, in states as well as Individuals. And the new Governments we are assuming, in every Part, will require a Purification from our Vices, and an Augmentation of our Virtues or they will be no Blessings." In this instance, Adams used religious language to inspire civic virtue: declaring independence would certainly prolong America's calamitous struggle for its rights, but the states would emerge from this "furnace of affliction" as more virtuous republics. Adams's speech also demonstrates that biblical symbolism could inspire the delegates in their civic activities much like they used it to inspire their constituents. Adams believed his speech and the resulting vote for independence would enshrine the "day" (July 2) for ritualized observation in the new country's future; it would serve as a kind of secular fast day.[29]

As the war proceeded, Congress proclaimed days of fasting every spring and usually a corresponding day of thanksgiving in the fall. This continued until the end of the war. On each occasion, a new committee was appointed to write the proclamation. As the events of the war and the morale of the colonists changed, so did the specific application of providential language. For instance, in the spring of 1779, there was no end to the war in sight. The British army had taken Savannah, Georgia, during the winter and began restoring royal civil government in that southernmost colony. Rates of desertion by enlisted men and resignation by officers remained high. Americans were discouraged; their patriotic fervor was waning. At this pivotal moment, Congress recognized the desperate need for a new infusion of revolutionary enthusiasm, the *rage militaire* that had swept the country in 1775. The delegates attempted to utilize the approaching fast day for this precise purpose. In the fast day proclamation of that year, Congress attempted to explain to its constituents why the American victory assured them by Providence had not yet occurred: "His divine Providence hath, hitherto, in a wonderful manner, conducted us, so that we might acknowledge that the race is not to the swift, nor the battle to the strong."[30]

The 1779 fast day proclamation also offered a providential perspective on the newly negotiated alliance with France. The proclamation appealed to the people to pray that Providence would "give to both Parties of this Alliance, Grace to perform with Honor and Fidelity their National Engagements." This is a significant development because just twenty years earlier, Americans were using providentialism to portray France and their Catholic beliefs as the work of the Antichrist, a country working to impede the fulfillment of God's foreordained plan for the world. But once France was aligned politically with the Americans, Congress was willing to overlook France's religious disposition that had threatened God's work on the earth just twenty years earlier. Because the extension of providential favor to France by Congress was inconsistent with fundamental tenets of Protestantism, we can conclude that it was above all else a political gesture.[31]

Fast day proclamations issued by Congress after it declared independence no longer portrayed Great Britain merely as a parent state guilty of mistreating its colonies. Rather, British tyranny was portrayed as antiprovidential, deliberately seeking to destroy Americans' freedom and thus prevent the realization of God's master plan. In one such proclamation, Congress explained why Providence required so much "innocent" blood to be spilt for America to be delivered from British oppression. George III was compared to Pharaoh, whose refusal to free the Israelites from bondage was used by God "as a scourge . . . to vindicate [His] slighted Majesty." This biblical allusion not only cast the British government as an institution seeking to thwart God's plan for his chosen people but depicted Americans as parallel to God's chosen people.[32]

This same imagery of the Israelites' exodus from Egypt arose in congressional deliberations over the new country's seal. Benjamin Franklin's proposal for the seal was an image of Pharaoh's army being swallowed by the Red Sea, encircled by the words "Rebellion to Tyrants is Obedience to God." John Adams submitted another proposed design for the seal that featured the allegorical engraving by Simon Gribelin *The Judgment of Hercules*. This image, well known by contemporary Americans, depicted Hercules choosing between the easier path of self-indulgence and the more rugged path of duty and honor. While the New Englander pushed for a classical trope, the canny, and deistical Pennsylvanian opted for the biblical symbol.[33]

Such references to the Exodus invoked the theme of deliverance. In the context of the War for Independence, deliverance carried three important implications. First, it turned Americans into victims. From this view, British oppression was not the result of American wrongdoing but arose wholly from the unjust acts of a tyrannical king and parliament. Second, deliverance conjured up images of slavery. Throughout the imperial crisis, patriot spokesmen had accused the British of conspiring to "enslave" their American brethren. The hypocrisy that many of the men who considered the British colonial policy akin to slavery were themselves slaveholders was not lost on many contemporary Britons. Still, this rhetoric resonated with many Revolutionary Americans and compelled them to take up arms against the British.[34]

Third, Congress used the biblical theme of deliverance to declare the Revolution's historical significance before the war was even won. According to many biblical scholars, the Exodus was the impetus of Israel's formation as a nation, transitioning from *people* united by a common lineage (Jacob), to *a people* forged by a common experience. More specifically, these same scholars identify the Israelites' escape from Pharaoh's armies through a supernaturally parted Red Sea as the moment when "the division between Israel and Egypt becomes definite." Just as the Exodus was a pivotal event in the biblical understanding of the Judeo-Christian worldview and in the creation of the nation of Israel, Congress was implying that the American Revolution would possess a similar historical distinction. The Revolution was both the moment of definite separation from Great Britain and the formation of a distinct American "people."[35]

Even in their boldest uses of biblical imagery, congressional delegates carefully avoided raising dissension among their constituents' denominational and theological differences. Delegates omitted from fast day proclamations the most extreme and damning biblical symbolism then circulating throughout the colonies by some of the most radical patriot clergymen. In published sermons dating back as far as the Stamp Act crisis in 1765, many theologically and politically radical ministers utilized the images of dragons and beasts in the book of Revelation, which they claimed referred "to 'all the tyrants of the earth' and 'to every species of tyranny.'" These images soon found their way into political cartoons and political speeches pertaining to the imperial crisis.[36]

For the American clergy, depicting British tyranny as a sign of the apocalypse—in this case the dragons and beasts found in Revelation—represented a notable break with their ecclesiastical counterparts in England. The use of these apocalyptic figures to historicize Revelation (interpreting them as representative of events or individuals immediately preceding the commencement of the millennial era) was a prominent feature of Reformation England and, thereafter, Anglican theology. Initially used to justify the break with Rome,

English theologians persisted in identifying all of England's enemies and rivals with these eschatological symbols, promoting the belief that England (and subsequently Great Britain) was an elect nation. When radical patriot clergymen—many of whom were New Englanders—depicted British tyranny as one of these signs of the apocalypse, these individuals were declaring both their spiritual independence from Great Britain and that nation's fall from providential favor.[37]

Congress did not make these direct apocalyptic comparisons. Surely the delegates were aware of such damning claims being circulated by Americans outside the statehouse walls. Maybe they considered adopting this extreme language in their own proclamations but feared that doing so could easily have alienated potential patriots unwilling to jump to such drastic theological conclusions. Whether or not this was the case, it is clear that they were conscious of how the public perceived their religious activities. In observing their appointed fast days, delegates made a point to attend worship services together, alternating between different sects to avoid the impression that one denomination was preferred by Congress over all others. Whether or not the theological differences of denominations were really so pronounced as to represent the source of a potentially catastrophic schism among religiously sensitive patriots, enough delegates clearly thought that they were. As a result, they consciously used religious expressions in denominationally neutral ways.

The British government naturally saw the war differently and similarly utilized providential language in appointing fast days as counterpoints to those proclaimed by Congress. Like the American proclamations, the British versions included pleas for the pardon of sins. These pleas were usually followed by requests that all subjects fast and pray for God to open the eyes of the treasonous and rebellious Americans to the errors of their ways, while delivering "loyal subjects . . . from the Violence, Injustice, and Tyranny of the daring Rebels who have assumed to themselves the Exercises of Arbitrary Power." Both sides were courting a providential favor they claimed already existed in order to persuade their countrymen that their effort was destined for victory. The British were depicting American loyalists as the real victims deserving deliverance and condemning the arrogance of Congress for its egregious sin of bringing the pestilence of war upon the colonies. Neither the king's fast day proclamations nor those made by Congress can be viewed simply as religious expressions. This is not to discount entirely the presence of religious considerations among those who took part in proclaiming fast days but rather to highlight the more significant intention of consciously crafting a political strategy.[38]

The tradition of the Continental Congress appointing national days of fasting and prayer continued until American independence was achieved. Afterwards, several states continued to proclaim fast days, but these occasions did not return to the national stage until the adoption of the new federal government in 1789. At this point in the country's history, America's Revolutionary fast days had the short-term effect of helping to establish the political legitimacy of Congress and providing the delegates a tool for persuading Americans to support the Revolution. However, these days of fasting had an enduring impact as well. Congress was not merely continuing the colonial tradition of politicizing providential language; it was seeking to politicize American clergymen in an entirely new way. These religious leaders had long been involved in local politics, but a permanent stage for national politics was created only with the Revolution. By proclaiming fast days, Congress was inviting American clergymen to engage with the public on this new national campaign to forge a sense of unity. Public rituals such as fast days had become national in scope, reducing the differences among regions and among denominations and thus serving a more secular agenda of civil religion. These occasions reveal far more than a congressional concern for the morality of its constituents, as too many historians have incompletely tried to explain them.[39]

"For They Abominate This Fast"

Examining the political motivations behind congressionally proclaimed fast days during the Revolution raises questions of whether or not these occasions had the effect that Congress intended. Did people flock to their places of worship on the appointed days to hear political sermons? Did fast day sermons inspire greater revolutionary fervor among those listening in the pews? Did Americans' responses to these events vary by location? In short, we need to examine whether or not fast days were the effective mechanisms of political mobilization Congress thought them to be.[40]

In general, measuring the response of the eighteenth-century American public to rhetoric and propaganda is a difficult task because the proportion of eighteenth-century Americans who recorded events with their corresponding thoughts, feelings, and beliefs is relatively small. Hence, accurately discerning Americans' response to the religious language and symbolism of fast days is a difficult task, but not an impossible one. By closely reading a broad collection of church records, clergymen's diaries and letters, newspapers, pamphlets, court records, and the minutes of local Revolutionary committees, a clearer—albeit still incomplete—picture comes into view of the real effect fast days had on Americans.

Congress drafted its fast day proclamations with language it felt was most likely to elicit a patriotic public response. But once distributed outside the confines of the Pennsylvania State House, Congress relinquished control of its carefully crafted propaganda campaign to local governments and ecclesiastical bodies. There is no evidence that fast days persuaded a single loyalist to take up the patriot cause, but we can still argue that fast days served the purposes of all revolutionary rituals: forcing Americans to declare their political opinions by participation in a public act and pushing fence-sitters toward one side of the conflict or the other. Fast days were simultaneously instruments of unification and division, uniting patriotic Americans in chapels while dividing them from their loyalist neighbors. In this sense, they were a forerunner to the more coercive loyalty oaths demanded by councils and committees in the different states during the war's later stages.[41]

"The Fast was observed here with a Decorum and solemnity, never before seen ever on a Sabbath," John Adams wrote to Abigail from Philadelphia after the first fast day in 1775. "The Clergy of all Denominations, here preach Politicks and War in a manner that I never heard in N. England. They are a Flame of Fire. It is astonishing to me, that the People are so cool here. Such sermons in our Country would have a much greater Effect." Clearly Adams approved of the way in which Philadelphia clergymen assumed their new role as spokesmen for the Revolution, but he still complained of what he perceived as a subdued political fervor among the population.[42]

This is classic Adams hyperbole, a rhetorical strategy he frequently employed to declare the correctness of his ideas and the successful implementation of his plans. Others, however, gave conflicting reports of the fast day observance in Philadelphia. The Quakers in the city refused to participate in the appointed fast in keeping with their doctrine of pacifism. Many Philadelphia Quakers kept their businesses open on the appointed day, defiant acts that went expressly against the measures proposed by Congress. Enthusiastic patriots viewed this as a declaration against the American cause and accordingly smashed the windows of the Quaker shopkeepers. Surely this was not the "Decorum and solemnity" Adams observed, nor was it the act of a politically "cool" population. The smashing of store windows amounted to a politically charged fast day riot. While fast days united Philadelphians in the city's churches, it divided them on its streets.[43]

The attack on Philadelphia's Quaker businesses associated with the 1775 fast day illustrates the way in which American Revolutionaries could hypocritically persecute political and religious dissenters under the banner of liberty and providentialism. In this instance, many of Philadelphia's elite used the fast day to further scapegoat the city's Quaker population, constituting yet another episode in a long-running local power struggle between Philadelphians allied with the Penn family and the city's small but influential Quaker population and its allies. Though city leaders urged citizens on subsequent fast days to "forebear from any kind of insult to [Quakers], or any others who may . . . refuse to keep the said fast," the city's anti-Quaker temperament demonstrated in the 1775 fast day riot did not dissipate.[44]

Recent immigrants to Philadelphia such as Thomas Paine tapped into this local power struggle, recognizing that its polarizing effect could be used to promote a continental revolution. Paine became an especially harsh critic of the Society of Friends, despite the strong Quaker influence on his early education. As historian Jane E. Calvert persuasively argues, Paine used the Quakers as "a convenient foil and the means of rallying the non-Quaker Pennsylvanians against Great Britain." He consistently equated the Society's pacifism with passivity and at other times conflated it with loyalism; both were gross mischaracterizations of the Quakers' political stance. His anti-Quaker diatribes in popular pamphlets such as *Common Sense* and *The Crisis* fit into the "common cause" rhetoric with which Revolutionary spokesmen vilified dissenters. American patriots were standing up for their liberties while denying the same to their neighbors with different opinions. Thus, fast days did not occur in a political or cultural vacuum. Instead, they presented patriot opportunists an additional avenue to pursue their political ambitions, local or national.[45]

In New York, the Reverend Samuel Seabury chose not to participate in the first congressionally proclaimed fast day and took his nonobservance to another level by locking the doors of the church to prevent patriot parishioners from congregating there. Seabury was an ardent loyalist from the beginning of the conflict, and locking the church was a clear public statement of his political opposition to Congress. When arrested by a militant party of the Sons of Liberty in 1776, Seabury was accused of subverting the American cause and forced to stand trial. Among the accusations the impromptu court brought against him was his refusal to open his church to Americans desiring to observe the fast. In his own defense, Seabury pled ignorance, insisting that he had not been informed of the fast day. The credibility of his defense is questionable, however, as the fast day proclamation appeared in newspapers throughout the colony and was distributed as a broadside in the area as well. Surely Seabury was well aware of the fast. In the spirit of Revolutionary rituals, his refusal to participate amounted to a public statement of his loyalty to Great Britain and his dismissal of congressional legitimacy.[46]

In Massachusetts, where patriot fervor reached fever pitch early in the conflict, congressionally appointed fast days were typically well observed. In his diary, Reverend Ebenezer Parkman noted each fast day in the town of Westborough along with the topics of the morning and evening sermons. On such occasions, his congregation of patriots flocked to the pews. Yet these events do not appear to have generated the same riotous interaction between the colony's patriot and loyalist populations that attended fast day observance in Philadelphia. Prior to the outbreak of war, clergymen abstaining from fast days appointed by the Massachusetts Provincial Congress faced fierce backlash. For instance, in 1774 patriots in Pownalborough (now Dresden, Maine) deemed Anglican clergyman Jacob Bailey "a malignant Tory" and "severely threatened" him for refusing to preach a fast day sermon. But by the time Congress appointed its first fast in June 1775, the British army already occupied Boston. Therefore, the first fast day was not kept in the city, while anxious patriots in towns throughout the colony observed the ritual while waiting for George Washington and his troops to recapture Massachusetts's capital. When Washington and his soldiers drove the British out of Boston early in 1776, large numbers of the city's loyalists fled as well. The exodus of many of the region's staunchest loyalists certainly helped to keep the well-attended fast days relatively civil and unremarkable.[47]

Looking at broad trends, fast day observance varied based on location and demographics. In rural areas, Americans often observed the fast and thanksgiving days associated with major events in the war but continued about their usual daily routines on those proclaimed when the war was not going well or was uneventful. The diary of Reverend John Newton is especially telling on this matter. Newton was an itinerant preacher primarily working in the rural backcountry regions of Virginia, the Carolinas, and Georgia. A fastidious diarist, Newton's personal record reveals that with the exception of the fasts and thanksgivings marking major events in the war, he and those around him largely ignored the fast day proclamations. On the 1783 thanksgiving day appointed by Congress to celebrate the Treaty of Paris, Newton wrote that he preached to a sizable group on America's "being delivered out of the hands of our enemies." Yet, on congressionally appointed fasts and thanksgivings between 1777 and 1782, the clergyman was nowhere near a church. Instead, he spent these days gardening, combing the countryside for ore deposits to support his metallurgy hobby, or experimenting with medicinal concoctions he pedaled to his neighbors. Inasmuch as Newton's experience provides insight into popular fast day observance (or nonobservance), by and large the participation of rural Americans in such rituals did not fit consistently with John Adams's hyperbolic description of the 1775 fast day's "Decorum and solemnity, never before seen ever on a Sabbath."[48]

Urban southerners had very different fast day experiences. In large southern cities, such as Charleston, these occasions were widely observed. A prominent Baptist preacher and fervent patriot in that city, Oliver Hart, recorded the observance of every such occasion in his diary of sermons. According to his record, on each fast day appointed between 1775 and 1779, Hart preached two political sermons to his patriotic congregation and others who filled the pews on each particular occasion. The only event that interrupted Charleston's otherwise consistent annual fast day observance was the British occupation of the city beginning in 1780. When General Henry Clinton's army entered Charleston, Hart was among the many Revolutionaries who fled to the North. The many patriots of all religious denominations who remained were soon banished by the British to St. Augustine in Spanish Florida "for refusing to become a King's subject." Charleston patriots clearly embraced the Revolutionary fast day tradition, as only the presence of redcoats could quiet the ringing of church bells in the city on each of the congressionally appointed occasions.[49]

Fast day participation was similarly high in Newport, Rhode Island, but some patriots questioned their neighbors' sincerity. "It has been a serious & solemn & I hope sincere Fast!" Ezra Stiles wrote in his journal, describing the 1775 fast day observance in the city. "I suppose all congregations in town kept it. With Reluctance indeed the Church of England just read prayers at XI o'clock, but without preaching or afternoon service." Stiles was accusing his religious rivals of hypocrisy, claiming that the city's Anglican clergymen were uninterested in the fast day's cause. Instead, their pro forma fast day observance "was rather policy to prevent the church from going to the Meetings [of other denominations]—for they abominate this fast." Stiles's comments were not merely the lamentations of a devoted revolutionary frustrated with his less devoted countrymen. His criticisms were informed by long-standing, latent religious tension within the community. At the time of the Revolution, Newport was one of the most populous cities in the colonies and boasted what was perhaps the most pluralistic religious landscape in New England. Yet the latent interdenominational suspicion and prejudice in the city was uncovered during the Revolution. Fast days became opportunities for religious politics as usual. The rituals enabled Americans such as Stiles to lay the growing loyalist-patriot rift atop long-standing religious rivalries.[50]

The different responses to fast day proclamations from urban and rural Americans can be explained by the general political and demographic differences of the two groups, writ large. In his book on American cities as the premier sites of political mobilization during the Revolution, Benjamin Carp argues that urban Americans had a more direct connection to the British Empire than their rural countrymen and thus had more at stake in the Revolution. Unlike the sprawling urban areas familiar to twenty-first-century Americans, Americans in the 1770s were concentrated in settlements crowded onto islands and peninsulas with populations counted in the tens of thousands. In 1770, the five most populous American cities were Philadelphia (26,789 residents), New York (21,000), Boston (15,520), Charleston (11,500), and Newport (9,000). Carp demonstrates that the largest and most concentrated populations of patriots lived in cities, interacting daily with the largest and most concentrated populations of loyalists. This juxtaposition of demographical extremes often gave the already difficult decision between patriotism and loyalty to king and Parliament an even greater sense of urgency. These arguments illuminate the more constant response of urban Americans to congressionally appointed fast days. It is likely that patriots in America's cities responded in greater numbers and with greater enthusiasm to national fast days because in urban settings the ritual was more urgently needed for publicly separating patriots from loyalists and for stabilizing the seemingly incessant rise and fall of patriotic fervor as the war progressed.[51]

The varied responses to fast days by the local populace also demonstrate the limitations of religious language and ritual in the process of national formation. Revolutionary leaders identified the fast day ritual as a tool for bridging colonial and regional differences by uniting the colonists in a shared communal experience. Like mock funerals for liberty and other forms of street action instigated by groups such as the Sons of Liberty, continental fast days were a necessary step in forging a national polity and national identity because they helped Americans from Massachusetts to Georgia view themselves as part of a larger imagined community. Yet the political and social autonomy of individual colonies was not the only fracture standing in the way of nationalism. These political-religious observances could not universally overcome the urban-rural divide that existed within many of the colonies. Religion's potential to unify Americans nationally is clear, but so are its inadequacies in this regard. Religion alone could not generate an American nation, nor should it be viewed as the chief characteristic upon which Americans formed their imagined community. As later chapters demonstrate, the religious-political community Americans created during the early republic quickly became an instrument for nation building but not the core of the nation itself.

To what extent did Americans adopt the dramatic providential language employed by the spiritual and political leaders of the Revolution? This is an important question, but unfortunately one that historians may never be able to answer conclusively. However, surviving historical records provide glimpses into the adoption of American providentialism by Americans outside the clergy and the Revolutionary leadership. In certain instances, the infusion of religious rhetoric into Revolutionary discourse affected how Americans viewed the war during the conflict and remembered it afterwards. The journal of Samuel Edward Butler is revealing. An aspiring planter traveling through Virginia, the Carolinas, and Georgia in 1786, Butler sought a large tract of land on which to establish his own plantation. In his travels, he took frequent detours to visit sites of Revolutionary War battles. As one of America's earliest battlefield tourists, Butler composed poetic verse infused with providential language and symbolism. Writing about the Battle of Yorktown, Butler declared that "The Great Jehovah" denied the land rain until the "naughty brittons all are slain or bow their stubborn head." He labeled the infamous British colonel Banastre Tarleton one of "Satan's aids" and compared Cornwallis to a fallen Lucifer. According to Butler, God had "raised great Washington to save our bleading land," and France and Spain were to be thanked for their assistance. "But," Butler averred, it was "Christ the lamb who once was slain" who "shall have [Americans'] sacred praise."[52]

Butler's poetry suggests that the providential language and religious symbolism used by the Revolution's spiritual and political leaders influenced the way their audiences remembered the war. Butler was not at Yorktown; he did not witness the unfolding of the battle's events firsthand. But on congressionally proclaimed days of thanksgiving, clergymen recounted the battle to their congregations, denoting American victory the result of divine intervention (and indicative of God's approval). Butler's verses show strong similarities with many of the fast day sermons, particularly the way in which each author used providential language to describe the Revolution and to deride the character of British officers. Butler appropriated dramatic providential language that was central to the religious rituals tied to the politics of the Revolution. Linking British officers to Satan clearly indicated his belief that by fighting against Americans, the British were actively opposing God. The way Butler remembered and assigned significance to the Revolution was influenced by the politicization of clergymen on a national level through fast days and by the Revolutionary leadership's appropriation of religious language as political propaganda.[53]

Congressionally appointed fast and thanksgiving days had the lasting effect of placing patriot clergymen on the newly created national political stage. Despite their elevation on these occasions, fast days did not make Americans more committed to theological beliefs. We will see in chapters 4 and 5 that clergymen in the 1780s and 1790s regularly complained that religious life was weakening. What, then, can we say fast days achieved? By using religious language that resonated with Americans of multiple religious denominations, fast days helped move the country to accept a more religiously neutral space for public participation in shaping a national sense of belonging. Rather than zealously promoting religious doctrine or faith, Congress used providential language and fast days to alter the British language of empire to meet the needs of the young American nation.[54]

TWO

Revolutionizing Chaplains

In the spring of 1775, South Carolina was politically divided. American patriotism ran high in Charleston and throughout the low country, but the colony's backcountry was a different story. Reports of open war between New England colonists and the British army filled Charleston newspapers and generated anxiety that the fighting would soon spread to the southern colony. Charleston patriots believed South Carolina was largely unprepared for such a development owing to their uncertainty as to what side the colony's backcountry residents would support. In this moment of crisis, South Carolina's Provincial Assembly recognized and exploited the political utility of clergymen when it dispatched Christian ministers to accompany an expedition to the colony's backcountry, where they were expected advocate for the patriot cause from local pulpits.

Backcountry loyalism in South Carolina was less the product of deep devotion to the king and Parliament than of long-standing resentment toward the low country's planter elite. Rural settlers in the colony's western region complained of a heavy tax burden and underrepresentation in the Commons House as well as the Provincial Assembly that had recently succeeded it. To these South Carolinians, underrepresentation in the colonial government was more oppressive and had more immediate effects on their daily lives than a total lack of representation in Parliament ever could. To further compound matters, many influential men in backcountry settlements felt overlooked by the Provincial Assembly and exhibited their frustration by rallying their neighbors to oppose the colony's protests against Parliament. If South Carolina was to survive a war with Great Britain, Charleston patriots were convinced that backcountry loyalism had to be diminished, if not outright suppressed. To this end, clergymen became a valuable asset. By licensing preachers to use their religious training and experience as persuasive orators for expressly political ends, the Provincial Assembly transformed Christian ministers into political missionaries.[1]

The Provincial Assembly chose William Henry Drayton, a wealthy planter and eloquent Revolutionary firebrand, to lead the expedition. To help soften potential resentment toward Drayton's class, the Assembly invited Reverend William Tennent, a prominent Presbyterian, to appeal to the backcountry's large Scotch-Irish population, and Reverend Oliver Hart, a prominent Baptist, to appeal to his many coreligionists in the region. Because both Tennent and Hart were Protestant dissenters, assembly delegates believed their presence in the backcountry as spokesmen for the newly formed Continental Association—and the patriot cause in general—could ease that region's animosity toward the strong Anglican establishment centered in Charleston. Furthermore, by including Tennent and Hart on this mission to the interior, South Carolina's Revolutionary leadership displayed confidence that religion could bridge regional, political, and class divides. Thus, Hart and Tennent became itinerant preachers for the American cause.[2]

In some instances, Drayton, Hart, and Tennent convinced local militiamen to sign pledges that they would defend South Carolina against the British if the war reached its borders. In other instances, their impassioned pleas were mocked by local militia men who declared, "No man from Charleston can speak the truth, and . . . all the papers are full of lies." The political missionaries attempted to compensate for these moments of rejection by forming new militia units in neighboring towns dedicated to opposing any pro-British militant force in the area, even if comprised of fellow South Carolinians. The Provincial Assembly thanked Hart and Tennent for their service at the expedition's conclusion, an expression of gratitude that implied that the mission had vindicated the proposition of the clergy's effectiveness in building and maintaining military forces.[3]

South Carolina's Provincial Assembly was not the only Revolutionary group that recognized the clergy's potential as agents of political mobilization. Both the Continental Congress and the Continental Army employed clergymen as chaplains. In part, this was keeping with tradition: chaplains were common components in Western armies, and disparate legislative assemblies throughout the American colonies followed English parliamentary precedents by engaging clergymen to open sessions with prayer. America's Revolutionary leadership may not have invented chaplaincies, but they expanded the traditional role of the office by placing greater significance and higher expectations upon Revolutionary chaplains than were borne by their colonial predecessors or their British counterparts.

Chaplains' main role in the British army was to prepare men to face death. They preached sermons before battles to bolster the men's courage with assurances that life existed after death and spent much of their time administering last rites to dying soldiers or praying with the wounded and otherwise infirm. In addition to these duties, several congressional delegates and military officers expected American chaplains to work as agents of moral reform in turning the Continental Army into a professional force and urged them to further project to soldiers the idea that the new American army was a modern Army of Israel. But perhaps most importantly, Revolutionary leaders expected the chaplains assigned to minister to America's ragtag Revolutionary forces to shoulder a large part of the burden of keeping Americans in the war.[4]

The Continental Congress was similarly convinced that it could manage the war more effectively by expanding the duties and expectations of its chaplains. Delegates in Congress looked to their chaplains to do far more than open each day's legislative meeting with prayer. They expected them to perform a symbolic role and help legitimize Congress in the minds of its constituents. They also regarded prayer as a means to promote civil discourse during congressional debates. This chapter shows that America's Revolutionary chaplains did much more for the patriot cause than offer prayers and preach sermons.[5]

"The Soul of Military Vigour"

In 1777, General Nathanael Greene and John Adams discussed ways of inspiring greater bravery and discipline among American soldiers. Greene suggested that Congress begin issuing medals to soldiers who proved themselves in battle. "Patriotism is a glorious Principle," he wrote to Adams, "but never deny her the necessary aids." Adams responded that though vanity was indeed an "operative Motive to great Action . . . Religion is the greatest Incentive, and wherever it has prevailed, [it] has never failed to produce Heroism." Just as Thomas Jefferson had openly described the effect fast days could have in rousing a lethargic population to political action, Adams and Greene were candid about religion's potential for transforming the "rabble in arms" that made up the Continental Army into a respectable military force.[6]

From the Continental Army's inception in May 1775, Congress and the army's officers were concerned about both the martial and moral discipline of the troops. American soldiers regularly manifested their lack of martial discipline by wasting ammunition to cure boredom, failing to complete even the most basic drills common in European armies, and by maintaining themselves and their camps in a filthy state. The soldiers' lack of moral discipline was marked by widespread profanity, drunkenness, and gambling. In order to instill in the troops the martial discipline expected of a professional army, America's Revolutionary leadership relied on European experts in military strategy and discipline; it enacted numerous forms of corporal and capital punishment. But, in addition to these more common measures, the Revolutionary leadership engaged chaplains as agents of martial and moral reform.[7]

The concern America's Revolutionary leaders expressed over the martial discipline of their soldiers was to be expected. After all, they were waging a war against one of the strongest military forces in the world at that time. But why, exactly, were America's Revolutionary leaders so concerned about the soldiers' moral behavior, and why did they place so much trust in the effectiveness of chaplains in this regard? As in their approach to days of fasting and prayer, Revolutionary leaders desired an alliance with the country's clergymen and insisted that the army enlist as many chaplains as it could recruit. Yet their concerns went beyond the spiritual well-being of the soldiers in the army and a desire to match the professionalism of the British army. American troops were meant to view themselves and to be viewed by the public as Christian soldiers, part of a carefully constructed modern Army of Israel dispatched to protect America's providential destiny. Congress also relied heavily on the persuasive oratory of chaplains to encourage reenlistment and discourage desertion. Ultimately, the most important role America's Revolutionary leadership assigned to chaplains during the Revolution was to keep Americans in the war.

This additional expectation for American chaplains contrasted them with their counterparts in the British army, a contrast explained in part by the differing natures of the two armies. The British ranks primarily consisted of career soldiers. Especially in the latter half of the eighteenth century, enlisted men increasingly came from the rapidly emerging urban working class. Many Englishmen did not enlist for a single conflict but became soldiers for the financial stability a career of military service provided. Though desertion was a problem in the British army, it never approached the epidemic proportions of the American forces, and many enlisted men concluded their military careers as veterans of multiple wars. On the other hand, the Continental Army was primarily made up of citizen-soldiers, volunteers who left home for a defined period of enlistment with the intent of returning to civilian life permanently at the war's conclusion. The prevailing ideology of American Revolutionaries deemed standing armies as characteristic of tyrannical governments, so most believed the army was one of necessity. Whereas the British promoted military service as a career choice, Congress presented it more as a virtuous duty. The dependence of the Continental Army on the citizen-soldier necessitated enlarged responsibility for its chaplains.[8]

Of all the vices present in the Continental Army, General Washington most often addressed profanity and gambling. Both in his letters to Congress and his communications within the army, Washington repeatedly expressed his displeasure with soldiers' use of impious language. He succinctly explained his aversion to profanity in his general orders to the army on August 3, 1776, in which he lamented that "the foolish, and wicked practice, of profane cursing and swearing (a Vice heretofore little known in an American Army) is growing into fashion," adding that "we can have little hopes of the blessing of Heaven on our Arms, if we insult it by our impiety, and folly." Profanity, Washington concluded, was a "vice so mean and low . . . that every man of sense, and character detests and despises it." On the matter of gambling, he ordered that "Gaming of every kind is expressly forbid as the foundation of evil & the cause of many Gallant & Brave Officer's Ruin," though "Games of exercise for amusement may not only be permitted but encouraged." Washington prescribed attendance at religious services as the cure for these vices, and he petitioned Congress for the appointment of more chaplains to minister to the army.[9]

Through this petition, Washington was not necessarily honoring religion for its own sake. His chief concern was vice and its destructive effect on the warrior ethos. By projecting upon American troops the image of a modern Army of Israel, Washington and his fellow officers hoped to inspire the decorum and enthusiasm necessary to defeat the British. But it was a lofty expectation, and maintaining the ideal required the help of persuasive clergymen. In Washington's army, religion was a means to a martial end, not the end itself.

Washington's petition inspired Congress to appoint one chaplain to every two regiments. In July 1776, Washington ordered the commanding officers of each regiment to recommend as chaplains "persons of good character and exemplary lives." He reiterated to the army the necessity of moral discipline, stating that "The blessing and protection of Heaven on our Arms are at all times necessary but especially so in times of public distress and danger."

REVOLUTIONIZING CHAPLAINS 43

Thus, he implored "every officer, and man" to "endeavor so to live, and act, as becomes a Christian Soldier defending the dearest Rights and Liberties of his country."[10]

Based upon these public pronouncements alone, it would be easy to conclude that the Revolutionary leadership's insistence on appointing chaplains to minister to the troops and reform immoral behavior was solely an attempt to establish discipline and order in an army where rowdiness and disorder dominated. That was indeed a large part of it, but such conclusions are incomplete. Upon closer examination, the personal correspondence of several military and congressional leaders, as well as resolutions passed in Congress, reveal that top officials of the government expected much more of the army's chaplains than merely reforming soldiers' decorum.

By accompanying the army, chaplains reinforced the imagery of the Continental Army as a military force with a religious purpose. Washington and Congress used the image of American troops comprising a modern Army of Israel as a symbol aimed at encouraging Americans to take up the fight. In the Old Testament, the Children of Israel were delivered from slavery in Egypt and, following the successful military campaigns of their army, inherited their "Promised Land." In the common application of this story to the Revolution, the Continental Army acted as the Army of Israel, delivering Americans from the "slavery" of British tyranny to bring about America's "Promised Land," or the realization of America's future place as a bastion of political freedom and civil harmony. Once this promised state was realized, Americans anticipated that their country would enjoy economic prosperity as well as greatness in the arts and sciences. America's Revolutionary leadership used such imagery with the aim of strengthening the belief among Americans that their victory would be celebrated by their posterity for generations to come. Furthermore, as Americans threw off the familiar rule of their parent state and entered into new martial and political scenarios, the application of recognizable imagery—the Army of Israel—to the new Continental Army gave their efforts a biblical sanction and a sense of religious legitimacy.[11]

It became common in America during the 1760s and 1770s to relate the conflict with Great Britain to biblical events and stories. Many clergymen began to read the Bible through a lens of republican ideology. They depicted Israel as a republic and prophesied a millennial kingdom of both civil and religious liberty. Political leaders followed suit. For instance, when Patrick Henry insisted in 1778 that America's separation from Great Britain must be complete and permanent, he referenced the Israelites, who wanted to return to Egypt shortly after their departure into the wilderness. "The old leaven still works," Henry wrote to Richard Henry Lee; "the flesh pots of Egypt are still savoury to degenerate palates." But this republican reading of the Bible went beyond the mere application of scriptural lessons of morality to the present; it portrayed republicanism, albeit anachronistically, as the principle of governance endorsed by God from the beginning of human society. As historian Nathan O. Hatch has explained, "The clergy appropriated the means of traditional religion to accomplish the ends of civic humanism." Civic activity to resist tyranny and preserve republican freedom was thus equated with Christian activity. It is no surprise that such republican biblical interpretations were popular among patriot clergymen and statesmen alike, as they insinuated that to be a good citizen was to be a good Christian and vice versa.[12]

The frequent invocation of biblical verse and symbolism by American Revolutionary leaders also demonstrates the centrality of ancient texts in the American cultural imagination at this time; religious or not, many Americans—even deists such as Thomas Jefferson—considered the Bible a classical work of history. Accordingly, by alluding to or even quoting the Bible in their efforts to mobilize a religiously heterogeneous population, Revolutionary leaders hoped to simultaneously reach those people who considered the book scripture and those who viewed it as classical history, but nothing more.[13]

The Articles of War designed by Congress further cast the Continental Army as the Army of Israel. During the first years of the war, the maximum number of lashes a soldier could receive as punishment for misconduct was thirty-nine—an allusion to the Mosaic Law of "forty stripes, save one." This was far fewer than the one-thousand lashes permitted in the British army. Thus, like the providential purposes of the war chaplains preached to the soldiers at mandatory Sunday services, the symbolism in the army's initial method of administering corporal punishment was intended to reinforce in the minds of American soldiers the idea that the army they had joined was far more than a rebel force. If Revolutionary leaders could successfully conflate the Continental Army with the forces commanded by Moses and Joshua, the prospects of keeping Americans in the fight would increase dramatically.[14]

When the conduct of American troops fell short of such a lofty ideal of discipline and when their campaigns lacked the success of their Old Testament counterparts, officers expected chaplains to act as spokesmen for this ideal. Defeats on the battlefield were often followed by sermons on persisting in righteous causes. In such instances, the task of chaplains became keeping alive the notion of America's providential mission. Interestingly, when the army won a battle, it was readily acknowledged as the fulfillment of America's providential destiny and the result of the army's virtue. But when it lost, the outcome was explained in different terms. Losses did not cast doubt on the perception that Providence had assured an American victory, nor were they seen as evidence that the army was unworthy of victory. Rather, it brought into question the actions and strategies of the officers in command. For example, when the army lost the Battle of Brandywine and the Battle of Germantown, campaigns many in Congress thought should have been sure victories for the army, Washington, and not the army's "immorality," took the brunt of the blame. The army as a whole was praised for its successes, but only its leaders were criticized for its failures.[15]

Chaplains preached sermons to regiments prior to deployment and, once in the field, before engagements with the enemy, in order to inspire martial enthusiasm in the troops. The experience of Benedict Arnold and Aaron Burr before they embarked on their ill-fated invasion of Canada illustrates the effect such sermons could have on the way American soldiers viewed the war. Prior to deployment, Arnold, Burr, and their fellow soldiers attended religious services conducted by Reverend Samuel Springs in Newburyport, Massachusetts. Springs preached a moving sermon, after which the men paraded into the vestibule displaying their colors and arms as the clergyman passed through the company. Several officers then asked to visit the tomb of George Whitfield, the British evangelist who had been a prominent figure in the Great Awakening. The sexton removed the coffin's lid, and the officers cut the remnants of Whitfield's clothing into pieces, dividing them among themselves. By carrying relics from an American religious icon into battle, these officers "turned the expedition into a quasi-religious crusade."[16]

The activities of the army and the correspondence of its leaders display the clear symbolic role chaplains played in inspiring Americans to fight for their independence, but there are important pragmatic factors to be considered as well. For the duration of the war, the enlistment and retention of soldiers was a trying process. Congressional delegates and army officers alike looked to the religious instruction of chaplains as essential encouragement. In 1777, General Nathanael Greene reported to John Adams that there was a "great inattention and indifference that appears among the People in general about the recruiting the Army." In his reply, Adams listed several possible causes for this "unfavourable Temper in the People," not the least of which was "The Prevalence of Dissipation, Debauchery, Gaming, Prophaneness, and Blasphemy, [which] terrifies the best people upon the Continent from trusting their Sons and other Relations among so many dangerous snares and Temptations." Adams further explained that "Multitudes of People who would with chearfull Resignation Submit their Families to the Dangers of the sword shudder at the destructive Effects of Vice and Impiety." Adams was adamant that "Discipline alone . . . can stem the Torrent," and that to this end, "Chaplains are of great use." In his reply, Greene indicated his complete agreement with Adams on these matters.[17]

To Greene and Adams, chaplains were essential to their efforts in enlisting new men and to the army's overall success. Their concern for the army's moral condition was not necessarily religious; it was principally pragmatic. Nowhere in this particular lamentation of the immoral state of continental soldiers did they reference God or the blessings of heaven. In this instance, the necessity of chaplains generating moral reform throughout the army was explained strictly in terms of increased enlistments.

Desertion plagued the Continental Army throughout the war, and the Revolutionary leadership relied heavily upon chaplains to stem the tide of unplanned departures. American soldiers deserted for many reasons. Payment for military service during the Revolution was irregular at best, causing many to pack up and go home. Some deserted due to inadequate provisions such as food and clothing. Others left out of boredom during long periods of idleness. Still others left dispirited from defeat on the battlefield and even more did when the anticipated quick victory over the British never materialized. But the greatest causes of desertion among American soldiers were homesickness and the soldiers' need to provide economically for their families. Many young men who enlisted in the army were traveling far from home for the first time. Additionally, many had enlisted with the expectation of being posted locally. For example, the excuse eighteen deserters from a New Hampshire company gave in 1775 was "that they didn't intend when they enlisted to join the Army, but to be station'd at Hampton [New Hampshire]." While some Americans deserted to the British for money, the majority of deserters simply went home. When the army was encamped each winter, an estimated eight to ten men deserted every day. During the winter of 1777, Washington wrote to Congress that if they were unable to slow the rate of desertion in the army, he would "be obliged to detach one half of the Army to bring back the other." In the end, the average desertion rate in the Continental Army for the entire war was between 20 and 25 percent. Though in hindsight desertion does not appear to have significantly altered the outcome of any particular engagement, the fact remains that at the time, it was a source of real anxiety for American generals, who feared that it would harm morale and discourage recruiting in the future.[18]

Some of the methods the army used to stem the tide of desertion actually exacerbated the problem. For instance, officers frequently placed advertisements in newspapers offering rewards for the return of deserting men. These ads resembled those for runaway slaves in that the officers described both the soldiers' physical appearances and their personalities. Like furious slave owners, these frustrated officers often described deserters disdainfully. Thus the problem Adams and Greene were struggling to fix, low enlistment rates, was impacted by the army's handling of desertions. The army was losing men from both ends.[19]

The Revolutionary leadership enacted various measures to stop desertion and increase enlistments. Among these were declarations that deserters would be executed and the coercion of enlistments through drafts by individual states. However, a less dramatic attempt to solve these related problems was an increased dependence on chaplains. In 1777, when the rate of desertion was rising, Adams and Greene discussed the problem at length in a series of letters. One letter is particularly telling of what the two influential men believed the best solution to the problem was. In June 1777, Adams wrote, "There is one Principle of Religion which has contributed vastly to the Excellence of Armies, who had very little else of Religion or Morality." That principle, Adams explained, was

> the Sacred obligation of oaths, which among both Romans and Britons who seem to have placed the whole of Religion and Morality in the punctual observance of them, have done Wonders. It is this alone which prevents Desertions from your Enemies. I think our Chaplains ought to make the Solemn Nature and the sacred obligation of oaths the favourite Subject of their Sermons to the Soldiery. Odd as it may seem, I cannot help considering a Serious Sense of the solemnity of an oath as the Corner Stone of Discipline, and that it might be made to contribute more, to the order of the Army, than any or all of the Instruments of Punishment.

According to Adams, an honorable approach to the making and keeping of oaths was essential to the successes of both the ancient Roman and modern British armies. Conversely, the levity with which many Americans considered their oaths when enlisting contributed to the Continental Army's instability.

If this one principle could bring success to armies that, in Adams's opinion, had "little else of religion and morality," it would work wonders for America's army. If in their sermons the army's chaplains would depict oath-keeping as a sign of manliness and true Christianity, then Adams and Greene believed that soldiers would subsequently equate desertion with cowardice and sin. Such sermons would motivate American soldiers to stay in the army not just for the sake of their country but for the sake of their own souls.[20]

After occasions in which small groups of soldiers deserted their regiment, officers frequently turned to chaplains to limit the desertion's size and scope. For instance, in December 1775, Washington wrote to Jonathan Trumbull Sr. praising Reverend Abiel Leonard of Connecticut for his conduct as a chaplain and his ability "to animate the Soldiery and impress them with a knowledge of the important Rights we are contending for." Washington further noted that after several troops had deserted earlier that year while the army held British-occupied Boston under siege, Leonard "delivered a sensible and judicious discourse, holding forth the necessity of courage and bravery, and at the same time of perfect obedience and subordination to those in Command." In this instance, Washington credited Leonard entirely for preventing further desertions.[21]

Another event that illustrates the army's reliance on chaplains to maintain soldiers' enthusiasm for the war occurred in 1778. A group of officers petitioned Congress to appoint a chaplain fluent in German to minister to the many German American soldiers in the army's ranks. In their petition, the officers acknowledged both the martial and moral benefits chaplains brought to the army but were concerned that the language barrier denied many of the German-speaking soldiers these benefits when they attended mandatory Sunday services. But if the men could regularly hear a chaplain preach in their primary language, the officers argued, it would "not fail . . . to become the Soul of military Vigour in many of them." Clearly, chaplains were considered a vital source of this "military vigour," and these officers thought it was too great a risk to deny them this enthusiasm for the Revolutionary cause. Congress agreed and appointed a German-speaking minister, Henry Miller, to the post.[22]

But even the most persuasive chaplains were at times unable to prevent mass desertion. Brigadier General Alexander McDougall recalled such an occasion in a letter to Washington in 1776. McDougall's men threatened to desert when their pay was late, but McDougall pleaded with them to remain a while longer so that he could arrange for prompt payment from headquarters. "Encouraged by these hopes," McDougall wrote to Washington while his men deliberated, "the Troops were collected in the church, the proposal opened up to them, and warmly recommended to them by their chaplain. . . . There was reason at first to expect the Consent of the whole to Stay; but as they have delayed an answer So long, I fear not above two Thirds of them will Stay, owing to the Machinations of Some of the [junior] officers, who are bent on goeing." McDougall's experience exemplifies how commanding officers relied upon chaplains to inspire soldiers to persevere amid challenging circumstances. As McDougall saw it, if the chaplain's speech failed to inspire his men, the majority of his brigade would return home. He had placed nearly all of his hopes for stopping the mass desertion in the persuasive powers of a clergyman.[23]

The Revolutionary leadership's reliance upon sermons that applied biblical imagery to the Revolution as tools to reform and inspire American soldiers is further reflected in the anxiety of officers that they could not procure a sufficient number of competent chaplains. For this reason, Congress frequently revisited the policies and procedures regulating chaplain service. Initially, one chaplain was assigned to each brigade. This worked until the army was spread out following the campaigns of 1775, and Congress authorized the switch to regimental chaplains at Washington's behest.[24]

Washington was concerned not only with the number of chaplains in the army but with the quality of their preaching and the level of their commitment as well. Early in the war, Washington blamed the shortage of competent chaplains on the position's low rate of pay. He complained to John Hancock that a chaplain's pay was "too small to encourage men of Abilities—some of them who have Left their flocks, are obliged to pay the parson acting for them, more than they receive—I need not point out the great utility of Gentlemen whose Lives & Conversation are unexceptionable, being employed for that service, in this Army." Washington was not exaggerating when he stated that the army lacked competent chaplains. Congress frequently received petitions from clergymen purporting to be owed payment for their services. Each petition required an investigation, whereby Congress often discovered that the clergyman in question had either been absent the entire time or had largely neglected his duties. In response to Washington's appeal, Congress raised a chaplain's monthly pay to a level greater than that of a lieutenant.[25]

The distribution of one chaplain for every two regiments worked for nearly two years, but a shortage of funds in 1777 necessitated a change. Congress reverted to the policy of appointing one chaplain per brigade but increased chaplain pay to the level of a colonel. Washington was not amenable to this change, as he believed it would limit chaplains' ability to minister to the soldiers at a more personal level. When Hancock explained to Washington the reasoning behind these changes, he echoed the general's earlier remarks. Hancock wrote that "The Regulations respecting Chaplains in the Army are highly necessary. By increasing their Pay, and enlarging the Bounds of their Duty, the Congress are in Hopes of engaging Gentlemen of superior Learning & Virtue to fill these Stations." Congress thought that the pay increase necessitated an enlarged stewardship. Hancock was assuring Washington that even though the distribution of chaplains was not as the general desired, Congress agreed on the importance of procuring competent clergymen to fill such important positions.[26]

Soldiers in the Continental Army had expectations for their chaplains as well. American enlisted men expected chaplains to be eloquent, inspiring, and entertaining orators. When chaplains met these expectations, soldiers sang their praises. For instance, a physician enlisted to serve the men on the ill-fated 1776 expedition to Canada wrote that a chaplain, Reverend Ammi Robbins, delivered "animating and encouraging" sermons whereby "he gained the most strict attention of almost every hearer present, and was universally admired as an orator and divine." Similarly, on one occasion Reverend William Tennent preached a three-hour sermon to his regiments in an "animated and demonstrative" style that held his listeners' attention and left them "holding a profound silence for more than a minute after [he] was done." Yet when chaplains' performances disappointed, soldiers frequently complained and openly ridiculed the clergymen. The soldiers' patience wore especially thin with chaplains who simply read their sermons plainly, without emotion. One officer termed such clerical dullards "the old reading Trojans." There was boredom and discouragement enough in camp life. Like Congress, American soldiers expected chaplains to do more than fill a traditional post in the army; they expected to be entertained and inspired by them.[27]

Some clergymen worked tirelessly as chaplains, not necessarily to meet the lofty expectations of Congress and the army's generals, but rather to satisfy the heavy demands they placed upon themselves. One such clergyman was Timothy Dwight of Connecticut. In October 1777, Dwight left his position as a tutor at Yale College in order to serve as chaplain to the brigade of General Samuel Parsons. Dwight took his appointment seriously and went the extra mile to lift the soldiers' drooping spirits in the wake of unsuccessful campaigns at Brooklyn and White Plains. In addition to delivering lively sermons, Dwight composed patriotic songs and hymns, which were popular with the soldiers and commonly sung around camp. As a fellow chaplain described Dwight's service to the army, "Mr. Dwight . . . shines as one of the first characters in point of composition." Through these "shining" compositions, Dwight injected his brigade with renewed enthusiasm for the Revolutionary War.[28]

Dwight certainly garnered large amounts of respect for the way he ministered to American soldiers, but Washington and Congress regarded the aforementioned Reverend Abiel Leonard as the model Revolutionary chaplain. A thirty-four year old Congregationalist preacher from Woodstock, Connecticut, Leonard accepted an appointment as the chaplain to the brigade of Israel Putnam in 1774. We have already recounted his success in preventing a mass desertion during the siege of Boston. Washington was so pleased with Leonard's service that when the clergyman's home congregation petitioned for his return, Washington appealed directly to the congregation to spare their clergyman a while longer.[29]

Despite his success with Putnam's brigade and the esteem in which America's Revolutionary leadership held him, Leonard lamented the mixed effectiveness of military chaplaincies in general, as the army was still a far cry from the biblical standard established by Joshua and the Israelites. He blamed the low pay scale for the reluctance of competent clergymen to join the cause. When he returned to Woodstock on furlough in July 1777, his discouragement with the plight of the chaplaincy combined with the melancholy effects of an unidentified mental illness that had often affected his disposition in the years preceding the war, his distraught frame of mind led him to commit suicide on July 27. It is impossible to know the exact state of Leonard's mind when he took his own life that night, but in this instance the army's preeminent chaplain died discouraged in the limited progress he and his fellow chaplains had made in transforming American citizen-soldiers into a modern Army of Israel.[30]

The reality of America's Revolutionary chaplains' effectiveness in light of the lofty expectations Revolutionary leaders placed upon them was not as bleak as Leonard lamented in the despondency of his final days, but the overall results of chaplains' efforts were certainly mixed at best. There were other chaplains in addition to Dwight and Leonard who proved immensely successful at inspiring soldiers to bear their tribulations and deprivations—be it defeat in battle, late payment from Congress, or the lack of basic provisions in camp—with patience, and to remain hopeful for a providentially assured

American victory. Israel Evans, for instance, became extremely popular among the soldiers to whom he ministered. His sermon on loyalty in the aftermath of Benedict Arnold's defection to the British was so well received that soldiers requested copies of his text; he had it printed and distributed to soldiers at no cost to them. Benjamin Boardman proved so effective a preacher that the commander of the regiment to which he ministered, Colonel Samuel Wyllys, regularly suggested political topics for sermons, trusting the chaplain to speak more convincingly on such matters than the he could. Indeed, American chaplains were given responsibilities of military commanders in addition to their duties as spiritual leaders, a load far more burdensome than their counterparts in the British camps.[31]

Yet, just as American military officers were frequently found wanting, so too were many of the army's chaplains. We know that many chaplains abandoned their posts. Their dereliction of duty not only denied their regiments a minister but frequently resulted in chaplains losing the respect of the soldiery. A soldier from Connecticut, Jabez Fitch, described his regiment's chaplain, Reverend John Ellis, as a coward "who set off with us from Camp with great Zeal, but when we passed the Lines of General [Nathanael] Green's Encampment, he somehow seemed to Disappear." Fitch had no respect for men such as Reverend Ellis who sought after the glory of serving in the Continental Army but were unwilling to face the real peril of meeting the opposing British forces. Echoing the aforementioned frustration of Washington, one observer wrote that "the Regiments are generally Supplied with Chaplains, who are as destitute of employ in their way: as a person who is dismissed from his people for the most Scandalous of Crimes." The fact that the army attracted clergymen who could not maintain regular positions at the head of a congregation was a significant problem. Washington and company wanted the best of the best, but they were too frequently stuck with the country's least desirable churchmen. The chaplaincy as conceived by America's Revolutionary leadership, then, was not inherently ineffective. Its successes and failures largely stemmed from the behavior and varying levels of commitment of the men appointed to stand as moral exemplars to the army.[32]

Despite the limited effectiveness of the chaplaincy on the whole, the urgent need America's Revolutionary leaders felt to keep Americans in the war resulted in an elevated position for patriot clergymen among the country's Revolutionary forces. In hindsight, this recognition could not have come at a better time for American clergymen. The Revolutionary War commenced in a period of waning religious enthusiasm more than two decades removed from the Christian zeal of the Great Awakening. By formally inviting clergymen to participate in the creation and maintenance of an American army, Congress and the army's officers sanctioned a place for them on the new national political stage. Yet, in this prominent place, America's first national leaders valued clergymen for their pragmatic and symbolic role and not necessarily for the Christian theologies they espoused.

"We Never Were Guilty of a More Masterly Stroke of Policy"

Though the legislative assemblies of the individual American colonies traditionally opened with prayer, when the Continental Congress first met in 1774, it did not. Rather remarkably, the delegates made prayer the subject of one of their first debates. As John Adams recalled the occasion, "Mr. [Thomas] Cushing made a Motion, that [Congress] should be opened with Prayer. It was opposed by Mr. [John] Jay of New York and Mr. Rutledge of South Carolina, because we were so divided in religious Sentiments . . . so that We could not join in the same Act of Worship." Samuel Adams then spoke, asserting that he was "no Bigot, and could hear a Prayer from a Gentleman of Piety and Virtue, who was at the same Time a Friend to his Country." He suggested that Jacob Duché, the Anglican rector of Philadelphia's Christ Church, was such a man. The other delegates appear to have accepted this reasoning and invited Duché to pray in Congress the following day, granting the native Philadelphian the historical distinction of offering the first prayer in Congress. Owing to Samuel Adams's insistence, Congress set a precedent for the selection of its chaplains. It became a decision based upon more than just the clergyman's personal piety and virtue; it was also about his personal political views.[33]

During the Revolution, the Continental Congress turned daily prayer into a political ritual. All members of Congress participated in these prayers, but not all were religious. There were certainly some religiously devout men like Samuel Adams serving as delegates, but to depict them all as such and to explain any action by a *political* body as singularly *religious* in its nature is to paint the past with too broad a brush. There is more to the practice of Congressional prayer than a display of congressional "piety," and in order to fully understand the relationship of religion and politics during America's founding era, we must look more deeply at the complex motives behind such rituals.[34]

Like Samuel Adams's call for a chaplain who was simultaneously a pious

Christian and a proper patriot, congressional prayer during the Revolution was motivated equally by religious and political factors. This means that while some delegates saw these public prayers as a method of beseeching supernatural intervention, many also saw them as a practice beneficial to the formation and operation of government. In order to fully understand what congressional prayer meant to the leadership of the Revolution, we must do more than ask how and why Congress prayed. We must explore the types of responses prayer evoked from the delegates. Such an investigation reveals that there were multiple political motivations behind congressional prayer: the delegates used prayer as a way of promoting civil discourse in legislative sessions, and the chaplains speaking the prayers used the rite to reinforce the Revolution's religious symbolism and to urge greater unity among the colonists.

The prayers spoken in the Continental Congress can be organized into two categories: standardized prayers and individualized prayers. Standardized prayers were those read verbatim out of a denomination's standard prayer book. Individualized prayers were those a chaplain composed or offered extemporaneously. Of these two varieties, standardized prayers were the most common, but it was the individualized prayers that were most frequently remarked upon by the delegates in their personal correspondence.[35]

In Duché, Congress had a chaplain who was skilled at both types of prayer. Born in 1737, Duché studied at the College of Philadelphia (now the University of Pennsylvania) and was a member of its first graduating class. "He has distinguished himself as a scholar and orator, on many public occasions," the president of the college, Reverend William Smith, wrote of Duché, "and from the most disinterested motives has devoted himself to the church." After graduation and a brief period of study in Great Britain, where he was ordained a priest in the Church of England, Duché became an assistant minister at Christ Church in Philadelphia and eventually its rector. His extemporaneous preaching and masterful recitation of the liturgy attracted large congregations and earned him renown throughout the area. No detailed description of what specifically made Duché's prayers so eloquent has survived, but the fact that members of his congregation left worship services impressed with the way he had recited words that had been spoken by countless other clergymen over hundreds of years is meaningful. In matters of style and persuasion, Duché was to Pennsylvania ecclesiastical circles what Patrick Henry was to Virginia legal circles. When it came to public prayers, Duché came to Congress as a seasoned and expert clergyman.[36]

The first congressional prayer spoken by Duché was part standardized and part individualized and provides an excellent example of each. Duché commenced by reading the Anglican collect designated for September 7 in the *Book of Common Prayer,* which began with Psalm 35. The language of this particular psalm was coincidentally appropriate to the imperial crisis that brought about the formation of the Continental Congress in the first place. Its opening lines read: "Plead my cause, Oh, Lord, with them that strive with me, fight against them that fight against me. Take hold of buckler and shield, and rise up for my help. Draw also the spear and the battle-axe to meet those who pursue me; Say to my soul, 'I am your salvation.' Let those be ashamed and dishonored who seek my life; Let those be turned back and humiliated who devise evil against me." The collect continues in this same theme, calling upon God for deliverance from those who "devise deceitful matters against them that are quiet in the land."[37]

The collect's application to the colonies' struggles with Great Britain would not have been lost on the delegates, many of whom suspected a conspiracy in Parliament aimed at stripping white male colonists of their rights as free-born Englishmen. There is also every reason to think that it was expertly recited, given Duché's reputation as an orator. But the subject of the psalm and Duché's eloquent recital were just the beginning of the chaplain's performance.

To the surprise of all present, when Duché finished reading the collect, he began to pray extemporaneously. He beseeched God to "look down in mercy . . . on these our American States, who have fled to Thee from the rod of the oppressor . . . [and] to Thee have they appealed for the righteousness of their cause." He prayed God to "direct the councils of this honorable assembly [Congress]" and to "shower down on them and the millions they here represent, such temporal blessings as Thou seest expedient for them in this world and crown them with everlasting glory in the world to come." As for the British, he asked God to "defeat the malicious designs of our cruel adversaries" and to "convince them of the unrighteousness of their cause" that they may no longer "persist in their sanguinary purposes."[38]

Duché's prayer is a prime example of how Americans used providential language to frame the imperial crisis squarely in a good-evil dichotomy. While he depicted Congress as an "honourable assembly" appealing to God "for the righteousness of their cause," he described the British as "unrighteous," "malicious," and "sanguinary." Condemning British policy in such conspiratorial terms was by no means unheard of at this time, but Duché's language set him squarely against the pact he and several other prominent Anglican ministers had made earlier that year to remain loyal to the British government. By decrying in his prayer the actions and intents of George III and Parliament toward the colonies, Duché established himself as one of the most outspoken patriots within the Anglican clergy in America at that time. Many of the colonial elite who shared this extreme patriotic view of the conflict were present when he prayed. Thus, Duché's bold condemnation of Great Britain and liberal praise of Congress were certain to endear him to many of the delegates, effectively demonstrating that he fit the primary quali-fication for the job of congressional chaplain as described by Samuel Adams, an alignment of political opinion with American patriots.[39]

The delegates' response to Duché's prayer was, in fact, extremely posi-tive. John Adams wrote that the prayer "filled the Bosom of every Man pres-ent," that he had "never heard a better Prayer or one so well pronounced . . . with such fervour, such Ardor, such Earnestness and Pathos, and in Lan-guage so elegant and sublime—for America, for the Congress, for The Prov-ince of Massachusetts Bay, and especially the Town of Boston," and that it "had an excellent Effect upon every Body [there]." Samuel Adams agreed with his cousin's evaluation and wrote to Joseph Warren that Duché "made a most excellent extemporary prayer, by which he discovered himself to be a gentleman of sense and piety, and a warm advocate for the religious and civil rights of America."[40]

Duché's prayer was so well received that the president of Congress, Pey-ton Randolph, asked Duché to serve as the assembly's official chaplain. His primary duty as chaplain was the daily reading of prayers in Congress, though Randolph also asked him to preach before the delegates on special occasions. In time, Duché even officiated at Randolph's funeral. Several days after Duché began reading prayers in Congress, Joseph Reed, a delegate from Pennsylvania, commented that as a Congress, they "never were guilty of a more Masterly Stroke of Policy, than in moving that Mr. Duché might read Prayers, it has had a very good Effect, &c."[41]

Both John Adams and Reed spoke of the "effect" Duché's prayers had on Congress. But whereas Adams spoke in terms of the delegates' reactions to the first extemporaneous prayer, Reed spoke more of their general response to Duché's prayers over the period of several days. What Reed described as a "Masterly Stroke of Policy" was the appointment of Duché to act as chaplain and to commence each congressional meeting with prayer, as the ritual pro-moted civil discourse among the delegates. Thus, the "very good Effect" Reed said resulted from Duché's prayers pertained to the way Congress was functioning as a result. Abraham Clark similarly credited Duché with enabling Congress to work more effectively. Clark admitted two years later that he at first doubted whether many of his fellow delegates would tolerate being led in prayer by an Anglican chaplain but was both relieved and impressed at Duché's unique ability to compose "a form of Prayer Unexceptionable to all parties."[42]

Several delegates viewed the promotion of civil discourse in Congress as one of the chief benefits of congressional prayer. Civility in Congress was especially important as the colonies stood on the brink of revolution because the delegates disagreed on the form and scope their resistance to Parliament's imperial policies should take. For instance, the debate in Congress over prayer was only the second debate it had experienced. The first had concluded moments earlier and centered on the assembly's mode of voting: whether each colony would receive an equal number of votes or if voting was to be determined by a colony's "importance." Immediately following this heated debate, Thomas Cushing moved that Congress begin each day's session with prayer. The timing of Cushing's motion suggests that he intended it as a way of decreasing hostility and increasing cordiality among the delegates. Fifteen years later during the Constitutional Convention, a similar experience occurred. Benjamin Franklin attempted to restore civility to an acrimonious debate by motioning that the convention open each day with prayer, reminding the assembly that the practice had worked to this end in Congress during the Revolution. To some, increased civility among the delegates was reason enough to pray in Congress.[43]

But civil discourse was not the only consideration associated with the implementation of congressional prayer. Congress also appears to have relied on prayer to help legitimize its authority as a legislative body in the eyes of its constituents. Delegates to the First Continental Congress were selected in a variety of ways: in some colonies delegates were selected by the governor, in others they were chosen by the colonial assembly, and in still others they were designated by select committees in certain districts or counties. This variety, no less than its sometimes undemocratic nature, undermined any claim Congress might make that it had been created strictly by the voice of the people or by a collection of the colonial governments. Even among those colonies that chose their delegates through action of the democratically elected, their authority to do so was under attack by loyalists in the public sphere. Thus, appeals Duché made in prayers to the "King of kings, and Lord of lords who . . . reignest with power supreme and uncontrolled over all the Kingdoms, Empires and Governments," served both to request God's interposition on America's behalf and to portray Congress as a legislative body authorized to govern by divine authority.[44]

By portraying Congress as a divinely appointed assembly, Duché reinforced the religious symbolism America's Revolutionary leadership had ascribed to the struggle with Great Britain. Hence, through Duché, Congress portrayed itself as defending both the civil *and* Christian liberties of Americans and in doing so made the distinctions between the two more ambiguous. If Americans at that time viewed the Revolution as a war between good and evil and America represented the good, then Congress naturally appeared as a legislative body directed by God. In this sense, it is very possible that Congress used prayer as a way to bolster this image to the public.

For these reasons, prayer at nine o'clock each morning became routine for Congress. Duché would read the daily collect and the appointed scripture from the Church of England's *Book of Common Prayer*, after which Congress would proceed with the day's business. Additionally, delegates invited Duché to lead Congress in special religious worship services on other occasions, such as their appointed fast days and thanksgivings.

The individualized prayer Duché offered before his fast day sermon in 1775 is especially noteworthy and was consistent with both the spiritual and political purposes of fast days. As religious exercises, fast days were intended to bring people together in a concert of fasting and prayer and for them to ask forgiveness for their collective sins and the removal of divine displeasure. Accordingly, Duché pleaded for forgiveness on behalf of all Americans so that "the infliction of national punishments upon national guilt" would cease and that God would "put a stop to the unnatural effusion of Christian blood." Finally, he appealed to God for unity, not only among the colonists, but also with their "brethren" across the Atlantic.[45]

The language of Duché's prayer is significant for several reasons. By referring to a "national punishment" for "national sins," Duché portrayed the colonists as a united people. By bemoaning the loss of American soldiers on the field of battle as the loss of "Christian blood," he identified what he believed was the main source of American unity—Christianity. To Duché, the colonists shared not only a continent but a religion, at least the basic elements of one. Congress apparently did not object to the way the chaplain portrayed America. In fact, the message of the prayer and of the sermon that followed appear to have sat quite well with Congress, as only positive comments about the service and the observation of the fast in general were recorded. The text of the prayer was included in the sermon's publication later that year, offering the ideological ramifications of Duché's prayer for American unity to a much larger public audience.[46]

After the 1775 fast day, the delegates wrote little in their correspondence about the prayers offered in Congress. They occasionally mentioned Duché but said nothing about specific prayers. What exactly caused their reticence on the matter is hard to determine. Perhaps as a daily occurrence, prayer seemed to the delegates an unremarkable, mundane ritual. This is not to suggest that the importance of prayer to Congress as a religious, political, or pragmatic ritual had diminished but that its novelty may have worn off. Perhaps Duché's recitation from the *Book of Common Prayer* gave the delegates no reason to write home about prayers their correspondents could easily have read or heard on the same date. Both possibilities are reasonable, but there is no way of knowing for sure. Nevertheless, events in the latter half of 1776 brought significant changes to the way Congress prayed.

When Congress declared American independence in July 1776, several Anglican congregations throughout the newly sovereign states altered the prayers recorded in the *Book of Common Prayer*. In Philadelphia, Duché and vestry members at Christ Church in Philadelphia responded to the Declaration of Independence with a declaration of their own, resolving to "omit those petitions in the Liturgy wherein the King of Great Britain is prayed for." By doing so, Duché went expressly against the oath he made when ordained a priest in the Church of England. He had frequently warned in his sermons and prayers of the previous two years that George III and Parliament were in danger of losing the favor of Providence if they persisted in their "sanguinary" and "malicious designs." The deletion of George III from his copy of the *Book of Common Prayer* was Duché's way of signifying to Anglicans in America that England had indeed lost the favor of providence and that they should no longer pray for its government's success—or so it seemed, at least initially.[47]

In October 1776, Duché resigned as congressional chaplain, citing poor health and a need to focus on his parochial duties. He remained a patriot, or at least showed no outward signs of waning approval of the patriot cause, until September 1777 when the British occupied Philadelphia. While others fled the city, Duché remained. With British officers in his congregation on the first Sunday after occupation, Duché had an important decision to make. He could read the day's prayer as prescribed by the Church of England, or he could read the altered version. Duché chose the former; perhaps he hoped

that one penitent act of loyalty would be enough to compensate for the previous three years of patriotic preaching. He had no such luck. When he exited
the church after completing worship services, he was arrested and imprisoned by British officers.[48]

The British only held Duché captive for one night but left his patriotism
in his cell. A month later, he wrote to George Washington and urged him to
"represent to Congress the indispensable necessity of rescinding the hasty
and ill-advised declaration of independency" and to recommend "an immediate cessation of hostilities." Washington forwarded the letter to Congress, and
when its contents were leaked to the public, patriots deemed Duché a traitor,
an "apostate," and "the first of Villains." Henry Laurens went so far as to ridicule him as "the Ir-Revd. Jacob Duché." Duché's defection is a controversial
subject among historians, and his experience is instructive on the way historians force most Americans into a patriot-loyalist dichotomy. We will return
to that subject later in this chapter. For the moment, let it suffice to say that
few of Duché's countrymen were willing to vouch for him, and, believing that
the loss of his livelihood in America was almost certain, he fled to England.[49]

Duché's resignation left Congress without a chaplain for more than a
month. In December 1776, Congress passed a motion to appoint two chaplains instead of one. A week later, the delegates elected Reverend Patrick
Allison, a Presbyterian minister, and Reverend William White, an Anglican
minister, and eventually Duché's successor as rector of Christ Church. White
accepted the appointment, but Allison declined, and another Presbyterian
minister, Reverend George Duffield, was appointed in his stead. Both men fit
the two criteria for congressional chaplains as unofficially outlined by Samuel
Adams in 1774: piety and patriotism. However, because Duffield was serving
as a chaplain in the Continental Army at the time, he was unable to begin
praying in Congress until October 1777.[50]

Why did Congress decide to appoint two chaplains in the place of one?
By splitting the duties of the chaplaincy between two clergymen, Congress
provided itself an opportunity to employ chaplains from different denominations. This was a gesture directed more to the public than it was an expression
of preference on the part of the delegates. While it might appear that Congress appointed dual chaplains to better represent the denominational diver-
sity of its own membership, this was not likely a major consideration. After
all, until Duché's resignation in 1776, Congress had been content to hear an
Anglican minister read the daily prayers designated in the Anglican prayer
book. After the debate over congressional prayer in 1774, no delegate objected

to the fact that just one denomination was represented in the congressional chaplaincy. Rather, Duché remained so popular with Congress that when he resigned as chaplain, the delegates voted unanimously to reward him with a payment of $150 "for the devout and acceptable manner in which he discharged his duty during the time he officiated as chaplain." Hence, its own denominational composition was not the primary consideration when Congress appointed dual chaplains. The multidenominational composition of the chaplaincy was a symbol Congress projected outward toward the public.[51]

Congress intended this symbol to help preserve unity among its constituents. Between 1774 and 1776, the only occasions upon which a non-Anglican clergyman led congressional prayer were when Congress engaged in public worship. On its appointed fast days in 1775 and 1776, Congress met in the morning to be led in worship by Duché at Christ Church and again in the evening to worship with Reverend Allison at his Presbyterian church. The fact that congressional delegates were content to be led in prayer by only one chaplain when Congress was in session but insisted on diversifying its worship when in public suggests the delegates' concern over the way congressional religiosity was perceived by their constituents.[52]

Though the appointment of chaplains was ostensibly an internal decision, legislative chaplaincies were traditionally considered a great honor for American clergymen, even outside statehouse walls. In Virginia, for instance, the House of Burgesses and later the state's General Assembly frequently appointed the president of the College of William and Mary as chaplain despite the numerous other clergymen in the area with far less encumbered schedules. The public took notice of such signals of political respect for their spiritual leaders. After carefully tailoring the religious language in its fast day proclamations to transcend denominational differences, Congress took measures such as electing dual chaplains from different denominations to ensure that its public actions matched its rhetoric.[53]

Creating a multidenominational chaplaincy was as an act of political pragmatism, particularly where it concerned colonial unity. Religious leaders in Philadelphia were well aware that colonial unity rested in large part on friendly relations between members of different denominations. In May 1775, the Presbyterian synod of New York and Philadelphia advised the congregations under its governance that in order to preserve "the union which at present subsists through all the colonies . . . a spirit of candour, charity, and mutual esteem, [should] be preserved and promoted towards those of different religious denominations." Similarly, Thomas Paine urged Americans in his pamphlet *Common Sense* to focus on the commonalities among the denominations. "I look on the various denominations among us," Paine declared, "to be like children of the same family, differing only in what is called their Christian names." Congress was likewise aware of the delicacy with which the multiple denominations needed to be treated, as indicated by the form of the delegates' collective public worship.[54]

In order to avoid the perception of favoring one Christian denomination over all others, Congress worshipped with a variety of denominations on fast and thanksgiving days. On such occasions, the delegates frequently attended together the services of local Methodist, Baptist, and Catholic churches. In fact, for many delegates, this was the first time they had ever witnessed Catholic mass. The perception that Congress favored one sect over all others threatened all their efforts to unify the colonists. Because different denominations enjoyed popular support in different colonies and regions of the emerging nation, the appearance of denominational favoritism by Congress could be politically divisive. Furthermore, if the citizens of a dissenting Protestant denomination in a state with an Anglican establishment felt that the Church of England (or its post-Revolutionary institutional successor) would serve as the government's official religion after the Revolution, they would have been less likely to have supported that government. When Congress prayed behind closed doors, it was to promote civil discourse, and its chaplains used such moments to reaffirm the notion that congressional authority to govern and wage war against their parent state was God given. When Congress prayed in public, it took into consideration the way its religiosity would be perceived by its constituents. To Congress, public prayer was part of a public relations strategy.[55]

The appointment of a Presbyterian chaplain also affected the method in which Congress prayed. As an Anglican, White continued to read prayers out of the Church of England's *Book of Common Prayer.* As a Presbyterian, Duffield did not pray in accordance with any liturgical guide as Duché had. In fact, over the previous century the sect had displayed a strong aversion to standardized verbatim prayers altogether, considering them an uninspired remnant of Catholicism. Presbyterian ministers had the *Westminster Confession of Faith,* which provided a few guidelines for praying and directing other religious services but contained no prayers to be read verbatim. Thus the appointment of both a Presbyterian and Anglican chaplain by Congress meant fewer recited congressional prayers and more of the individualized variety. Unfortunately, no record of Duffield's prayers has been preserved.

But apparently, Congress approved of the way in which Duffield and White fulfilled their duties because both served as chaplains until the end of the war, and prayer remained a staple of congressional proceedings throughout the Revolution.[56]

Prayer mattered to members of Congress, but for an assortment of reasons. Historians asserting that incidents of congressional prayer merely attest to a high level of congressional piety neglect the practice's political elements and therefore arrive at one-dimensional and misleading conclusions. To call congressional prayer political is not to deem Congress impious or to accuse its delegates of insincerity. It means that there was more to the equation than just religious belief. Congressional prayer was religious, pragmatic, and political. Evidently, these three motives were not incompatible to the delegates. When Congress prayed for divine intervention in their Revolutionary cause, it was also praying as a means to preserve civility and unity among its own members, and in part to inspire the same among its constituents.

"The Ir-Revd. Jacob Duché"

Within the space of two years, Jacob Duché went from a celebrated patriot and ally of the Continental Congress to detested loyalist and pariah forced to flee the country. How can we explain this drastic transition in such a short period of time? There is no doubt that he defected from the patriot cause, but what is less clear is why he did it. There are two likely explanations. The first is that when the British army occupied Philadelphia, he betrayed the Revolution out of cowardice and for self-preservation. In this scenario, Duché appears as a clergyman of weak convictions who was prone to say whatever would please his audience. When he spoke to Congress or his patriot-filled congregation, he preached revolution. When British soldiers sat in his pews, he preached loyalty to the king. The second possible explanation is that Duché became conflicted over the Revolution as it turned from a war for the colonists' rights within the British Empire into outright rebellion. In this second scenario, Duché appears as a man overwhelmed by a set of once-complementary allegiances turned incongruous by the Declaration of Independence. When we consider the full context in which he chose to abandon the patriot cause, the second scenario is the most likely. Duché was conflicted well before the arrival of the British army in Philadelphia; the occupation of the city simply served as the catalyst that spurred the clergyman to abandon the Revolution once and for all.[57]

What was this set of incongruous allegiances? As an ordained minister of the Church of England, he had taken an oath of loyalty to the church and the king. As a Pennsylvania native, he personally related to the fate of his home colony and felt duty bound to protect the rights of his countrymen. Initially, Duché was able to justify his patriotic preaching and participation in Congress as a form of loyal resistance in which he opposed government policies without trying to overthrow the government itself. He justified the use of violence by his fellow colonists against the British army and spoke harshly against Parliament when he warned that its actions placed the empire's providential favor in jeopardy. Yet he intended such invective to highlight the seriousness of the crisis; he never rejected the king and Parliament altogether. But the Declaration of Independence brought about a political sea change, forcing colonists to choose sides and effectively entangling Duché's web of allegiances.[58]

The key to understanding Duché's defection is the letter the former chaplain wrote to Washington. Because he probably wrote this infamous letter under the duress of imprisonment or as a way to save his own skin, historians have not typically given the ideas he expressed therein the serious consideration they deserve. Duché never recanted his words after the British left Philadelphia, not even privately to his brother-in-law, who was then serving in Congress, Francis Hopkinson. Duché meant what he wrote; whether or not he composed the letter under the watchful eye of his British captors, his language was sincere.[59]

In his letter, Duché explained to Washington that he remained a supporter of American liberties but was apprehensive about American Independence. He confessed that this had contributed to his resignation in October 1776. "I wished to follow my countrymen as far only as virtue, and the righteousness of their cause, would permit me," the clergyman wrote, but conceded that "The current . . . was too strong for my feeble efforts to resist." Clearly he felt he had gotten in over his head. When he emerged as an advocate for American rights, he did not believe his fellow patriots would take the patriot movement to the extreme of declaring independence. Yet they had, and Duché had not immediately spoken up. Instead, he waited more than a year to break his silence, which he did when he urged Washington to "represent to Congress the indispensable necessity of rescinding the hasty and ill-advised declaration," so Congress could return to the consideration of "some well-digested constitutional plan," presumably something along the lines of that proposed by Joseph Galloway.[60]

There is more to this confession than a delayed reaction to independence, however. According to his letter, Duché resigned from the congressional chaplaincy not only because of the Declaration of Independence, but because he grew increasingly concerned in the months that followed that Congress was utterly incapable of making American independence a reality. By no means was he the only American expressing doubts over the competence of the men then serving in Congress, but he had a more personal connection to the delegates than most other critics. Chief among his misgivings was the inexperience and unsteady temperaments of newly arrived delegates. "The most respectable characters have withdrawn themselves, and are succeeded by a great majority of illiberal and violent men," Duché informed Washington. This was not to say that the ablest delegates had abandoned the Revolution, but that many had left Congress to draft new constitutions in their home states or to accept public office locally. "Your feelings must be greatly hurt by the representation of your natural province [Virginia]," Duché continued, "You have no longer a [Peyton] Randolph, a [Richard] Bland, or a [Carter] Braxton, men whose names will ever be revered . . . Your [Benjamin] Harrison alone remains, and he disgusted with the unworthy associates." The implication of Duché's speculation was that had many of the more capable and respectable delegates remained in Congress, independence could have been a realistic goal, but their replacements were not up to the task.[61]

As Duché saw it, the deficiencies of Congress were compounded further by the deficiencies of the army it created. "What have you to expect of [your soldiers]?" he asked Washington rhetorically. "Have they not frequently abandoned you yourself in the hour of extremity? Can you, have you the least confidence in a set of undisciplined men and officers?" Furthermore, the inability of Congress to adequately supply the army meant that in areas through which large numbers of soldiers passed, that "country must become impoverished." Then, as though Washington could have forgotten, Duché reminded him that "A British Army, after having passed unmolested thro a vast extent of country, [had] possessed themselves of the Capital of America [Philadelphia]." In Duché's estimation, continuing the war would only destroy Americans' property, further oppress their rights, and increase American casualties. "Humanity itself," Duché implored the general, "calls upon you to desist."[62]

The crux of Duché's confliction, then, lay less in the justness of American independence than it did in what he perceived as its futility and the counterproductive results failure would bring upon Americans. To him, the restoration of American rights remained a noble and essential pursuit, but he had no stomach for a prolonged war managed by an inept Congress and fought by utterly undisciplined soldiers. He made his private plea to Washington having convinced himself that he would "not enjoy one moment's peace till this letter was written." As we know, the letter and its subsequent publication brought Duché anything but peace.[63]

Yet this assessment of Duché as a patriot experiencing a conflict of conscience over independence raises a significant question: how could a man conflicted over the prospect of American independence so readily alter the liturgy on the very day independence was declared? Duché's alteration of the liturgy may alternatively be seen as an effort to preserve the Anglican Church in America, as an insistence on praying for the king could drive any and all patriots from Anglican congregations. Perhaps he feared that if he opposed the motion of the vestry to alter the prayer, he would be deemed a loyalist and persecuted as such. He had, after all, witnessed one of his clerical assistants, Thomas Coombe, brought to the brink of execution for his abandonment of the patriot cause earlier that year. Only the mediation of Duché and Reverend William White spared Coombe's life, after they convinced the incensed Philadelphians to deport him rather than kill him.[64]

It is also important to note that Duché was not the only American clergyman who changed the Anglican liturgy after the Declaration of Independence. In Virginia, once the state assembly sent instructions to its delegation in Philadelphia to move for independence, it appointed a committee of Virginia churchmen to alter the church's prayers in expectation of the Declaration of Independence. Adapting the worship of the state's established church to the altered character of Virginia's government was not simply a pragmatic act. It also served as a clear signal to Virginia's Anglican population that, where their relationship with Great Britain was concerned, they had figuratively crossed the Rubicon. In Boston, several Anglican churchmen acquiesced to patriot demands and stopped praying for the king. One of these clergymen, Reverend Edward Bass, explained that because he believed the Revolution was certain to fail, omitting the king from prayers was a short-term concession he made for a long-term benefit, namely the preservation of his church and ministry. Bass compromised, negotiating the ecclesiastical and political elements of his ministerial oath, but he believed he had chosen the better part.[65]

For members of the clergy, chaplain service was fraught with risks and rewards. In the case of Jacob Duché, his service as a congressional chaplain placed him in a series of circumstances he was unable to navigate. William

White, on the other hand, maneuvered the war masterfully as Duché's successor and was rewarded with a position of great respect and authority as one of the first bishops in the Protestant Episcopal Church. As the next chapter demonstrates, Thomas Paine's insistence that the American Revolution was a time "that tried men's souls" was as true, if not more so, for the American clergy as it was for the American laity. Yet, as trying as the Revolution was for many of these clergymen, it is clear that the Revolutionary leadership leaned heavily upon them to keep Americans in the war and to make its prosecution as smooth as possible.

THREE

Navigating Revolution

For many American colonists, choosing a side in the American Revolution was a difficult task. The process entailed far more than simply forming an opinion on the extent to which Parliament was violating the colonists' rights as Englishmen. Among numerous other considerations, individuals had to take into account their prospects for protecting their families, securing their property, and preserving their livelihoods on the basis of the choices they made. While some historical accounts depict zealous patriots and adamant loyalists throwing caution to the wind by allowing ideological principles alone to guide their decision making, in reality most took a far more measured approach to American protests and, eventually, to independence.[1]

Without a doubt, choosing between the competing identities of loyalist and patriot was a complex matter. Yet, while this tension between rebellion and loyalty could be severe, it is essential that we go beyond the point of decision and examine the dangers that arose after Americans declared allegiance to one side or the other. The politicization of Americans during the Revolution, particularly as it pertains to clergymen, is better understood as a pliable process than as the adoption of stringent sets of allegiances with predetermined consequences.[2]

The American Revolution was not a horse race. A person's fortunes were not always determined by betting on the winning horse. Supporting the Revolution did not always lead to financial prosperity and enhanced social status, just as proclaiming loyalty to the Crown did not necessarily lead to financial ruin and social isolation. The way in which a person navigated the rapid and often turbulent changes brought about by the American Revolution often had greater bearing on his or her fate in its aftermath than did the choice between rebellion and loyalty at its outset.[3]

A number of factors went into the decision to support the Revolution, but religious affiliation was rarely one of them. Though many Anglicans remained loyal to the king—who was not only their head of state, but also the head of their church—many others became significant contributors to the patriot cause. In some cases Protestant dissenters, many of whom looked to the Crown for protection against the hegemony exercised by local religious establishments, brokered deals in which they supported the Revolution in order to secure increased religious liberty and toleration. Even Quaker communities, which officially maintained their unequivocal pacifism, struggled internally to prevent young men from running away to join the Continental Army. Though historians have identified trends that label certain denominations as having been more prone than others to either loyalty or rebellion, there are far too many exceptions for such trends to become hard and fast rules. For the clergy and laity alike, religious affiliation did not always determine political disposition.[4]

This chapter focuses on the experiences of three clergymen during the Revolution: Samuel Seabury, James Madison (second cousin of the president of the same name), and John Joachim Zubly. It explains how and why each chose a side in the imperial conflict and the way in which each adjusted to the upheaval within his immediate community. There are countless others whose stories similarly reflect the anxieties surrounding the unknown ramifications for participating in the Revolution that were so pronounced within the ecclesiastical community when protests and war erupted. Yet the experiences of Seabury, Madison, and Zubly represent some of the most provocative accounts of clergymen making political decisions amid the social uncertainty of war.

Seabury, an Anglican and staunch loyalist from New York, not only remained in America after the war but rose to a position of ecclesiastical and social prominence despite his fierce opposition to American independence. Madison, an ardent patriot from Virginia, steadfastly stood against the loyalism of his colleagues at the College of William and Mary and rapidly rose to the rank of college president and Virginia's first Episcopal bishop. Zubly, an ambitious patriot and Lutheran minister in Georgia, retreated from his position as a member of the Continental Congress to a more neutral stance, only to be forced into an extreme defense of loyalists by the harsh treatment he received from his patriot neighbors. Each of these men has been examined individually by historians. But until now, they have not been viewed in the context of a broader ecclesiastical and political community in which

American clergymen were increasingly involved in national politics and more heavily reliant upon each other's support in adapting ecclesiastical structures for the newly independent country. Seabury, Madison, and Zubly provide a particularly apt set of profiles for this examination because they represent three different regions of the country and three different allegiances during the war: loyalist, patriot, and a patriot turned loyalist. Their profiles also juxtapose local idiosyncrasies of different parts of the country.

Taken separately, the plight of each of these clergymen is intriguing and provocative. But collectively, they present a broader perspective of what it meant to be a politicized clergyman during the Revolution and, by extension, the difficult decisions lay Americans had to make during the war as well. As the experiences of these three men demonstrate, navigating the Revolution typically meant surviving the domestic civil war created by the "international" dispute with Great Britain.

"Let Me Be Devoured by the Jaws of a Lion, and Not Gnawed to Death by Rats and Vermin"

Reverend Samuel Seabury was the archloyalist of the American clergy during the Revolution. The outspoken cleric sided with the British long before the imperial crisis turned from polite appeals to armed resistance, and he insisted upon the illegitimacy of patriot councils and congresses when the Declaration of Independence turned armed resistance into open rebellion. Whereas many Anglican clergymen exhibited conflicted consciences as their webs of allegiances became entangled over the course of a prolonged war, Seabury exhibited unflinching loyalty to the king, Parliament, and the Church of England. He published essays against the American position, engaged in a pamphlet debate with Alexander Hamilton, served as a chaplain to British troops in Connecticut and New York, and helped coordinate the massive evacuation of loyalists from New York City as the war came to an end. Seabury made his bed with the British in the conflict, and the British lost. Yet, curiously, Seabury did not suffer any harsh prolonged consequences for his activities.

After the British forces surrendered and the Treaty of Paris confirmed American independence, Seabury was the first churchman elected and ordained a bishop in the Protestant Episcopal Church. Without ever recanting or mitigating his anti-Revolutionary opinions, he remained in this prominent cultural and ecclesiastical position for the remaining thirteen years of his life. How could the archloyalist of the American clergy, whose politically charged pamphlets and sermons had enraged his patriotic countrymen, remain in America after the Revolution and play an important role in the Episcopal Church's ecclesiastical reconstruction?[5]

Seabury was able to survive the aftermath of the war and rise to religious and cultural prominence for two reasons. First, his success in securing ordination by a Scottish bishop before any of his American counterparts gave him a key point of leverage, making his inclusion essential to the formation of a national Episcopal church in the new United States. Second, and perhaps most important, he resided in a part of the country where loyalists and moderates exercised a great deal of influence during the war. Therefore, his neighbors were less resentful toward his outspoken loyalism than populations elsewhere would have been. More broadly, the curious case of Samuel Seabury demonstrates how British institutional, religious, and cultural elements lingered in the newly independent United States long after its political ties with Great Britain were officially severed in 1783.[6]

Samuel Seabury was born in Groton, Connecticut, in 1729 and raised in nearby New London. When he was fifteen, he enrolled at Yale, where he quickly demonstrated his commitment to a high church tradition. This tradition emphasized formality in ritual forms and church procedures as well as a resistance to ecclesiastical modernization. Seabury was especially resolute that a clear line of authority should exist in the ordination of men to the priesthood, which, in the case of this Anglican churchman, meant all priests must be ordained by a bishop of the Church of England. Seabury journeyed to the British Isles after graduation and studied medicine at the University of Edinburgh for a year before being ordained a priest in 1753. Returning to the American colonies, he accepted several ministerial appointments in a variety of locations, first in New Jersey and then at several churches in various New York towns before finally being appointed rector of Christ Church in Westchester. Here, Seabury built and maintained relationships with the clergy and parishioners of New London, Connecticut, where he often visited and preached. But it was in Westchester that Seabury first became politically active in the events that culminated in the American Revolution.[7]

When British imperial policy was appearing increasingly oppressive to Americans in the 1760s and 1770s, Seabury made his support for king and Parliament clear. Though he resisted the label "Tory" and the negative connotations it carried in the colonies, he insisted upon the authority of Parliament and the king over the American colonies, even if he disagreed with some of the specific policies and taxes they enacted. From the vantage point of both institutional and self-interests, he claimed that the church was better served by loyalty to the British government, observing that, east of the Hudson River, Anglican congregations were utterly dependent on that government for legal protection and financial assistance.[8]

Though he opposed the colonists' resistance to their mother country, Seabury understood the seriousness of the situation. Accordingly, he worked in concert with like-minded clergymen to help placate the building revolutionary fervor generally and hostility to the Church of England specifically. Seabury, Reverend Thomas Chandler, Reverend Myles Cooper, and Reverend Jonathan Boucher all believed that ecclesiastical restructuring of the Church of England was in the best interest of local colonists and the empire as a whole. They proposed the appointment of American bishops, insofar as attempts by English church officials to appoint an English churchman as the singular bishop of America had disastrously failed. Under their plan, American churchmen would serve as local bishops. To ease public concern over the political implications of American episcopacies, Seabury emphasized that these bishops would have no authority over non-Anglican lay people, except when called as witnesses in disciplinary hearings of Anglican clergymen—a rarity. Earlier, Seabury had vigorously supported the call for an English appointee as bishop of America, primarily because he believed it would protect New England Anglicans from persecution at the hands of the Congregationalist establishment in that region. For political reasons, there was relatively little hostility against the proposal for a single bishop of America in 1768 from Connecticut Congregationalists, when compared to the stance taken against the proposal by Congregationalists in other New England colonies. Seabury and his cohort believed this restructuring would have two important political results: by denying American bishops political authority, the government would relieve to some extent perceptions that British policy was being created by those in the metropolis to oppress those on the periphery, and it would ease much of the antagonism toward the church in America by those who saw it merely as an additional avenue by which the king and Parliament exerted control over the colonies.[9]

The plan met with a mixed reception in America. Before it was seriously considered by Anglicans throughout the different colonies, however, American resistance to Parliament intensified upon the implementation of the Coercive Acts of 1774, which closed the port of Boston and abrogated Massachusetts's charter as punishment for the Boston Tea Party. After a series of riotous protests, several of Seabury's closest friends and fellow advocates for

American episcopacies—including Cooper and Chandler—fled to England. They used their exile in London to lobby Anglican Church officials to support the plan to better regulate American episcopacies. They hoped that once the protesting colonists were defeated, the installation of American bishops would strengthen the Church of England's position in the colonies and afford American clergymen opportunities to rise in the church hierarchy.

Simultaneously dutiful and stubborn, Seabury remained in Westchester and New London, able to do so because his congregations agreed with, or at least tolerated, his political stance. Though not all of his congregants remained loyal to the king, many were loyal to their clergyman. Then in 1774, Samuel Seabury took up his pen in defense of the loyalist position, a decision that seriously threatened his ability to remain at his ecclesiastical post. Writing under the pseudonym "A. W. Farmer," Seabury authored three pamphlets: *Free Thoughts on the Proceedings of the Continental Congress, The Congress Canvassed*, and *A View of the Controversy Between Great Britain and Her Colonies*.[10]

In these pamphlets, he claimed that Congress was an illegal council filled with ambitious men guilty of exaggerating social distresses in order to assume political authority that was only the king's and Parliament's to give. He blasted the delegates for their talk of nonimportation and nonexportation pacts, pronounced under the guise of protecting rights, but secretly designed to "form a republican government independent of Great Britain." In this, he anticipated the Declaration of Independence that was still two years in the future. Then, playing off the traditional distrust rural farmers had for city merchants, Seabury argued that Congress was acting in the economic interests of its merchant delegates alone and that their proposed economic protests would be detrimental to rural farmers. "Will you be instrumental in bringing the most abject slavery?" Seabury asked his readers. "Will you choose such committees? . . . No, if I must be enslaved, let it be by a KING at least, and not by a parcel of upstart lawless committee-men. If I must be devoured, let me be devoured by the jaws of a lion, and not gnawed to death by rats and vermin."[11]

Seabury's message was clear: resistance to recent British imperial policies on the basis of "natural rights" was a façade erected by Congress to mask its members' insatiable lust for wealth and power. Though Congress promised to restore the colonists' rights as Englishmen, Seabury predicted that the result would be the direct opposite. He was not in favor of the new taxes and imperial policies imposed by Parliament. He merely believed the implications of such policies were being blown out of proportion. Seabury insisted that, with patience, Americans could see their grievances resolved.

All three pamphlets were polarizing. Loyalists, especially those in New York, praised "A. W. Farmer" for his well-constructed, forcefully stated arguments against the Continental Congress and local Revolutionary committees. Patriots, on the other hand, saw the pamphlets as the libelous work of an avowed Tory. Many Sons of Liberty meetings in New York featured burnings of Seabury's pamphlets. One young American even fired back with a pamphlet of his own. Only nineteen, Alexander Hamilton was a proud, outspoken student at King's College (now Columbia University). Despite the affirmed loyalism of the college president, Reverend Myles Cooper, Hamilton and many of his classmates responded eagerly to the tempestuous political atmosphere.[12]

Hamilton did his best to impress readers with the potency of his rhetoric in his rebuttal to "A. W. Farmer." In *A Full Vindication of the Measures of Congress,* he insisted that a reliance on the technique of weak remonstrance and polite petitions was foolish and doomed to fail. Restricting trade was, he said, the only effective method of resistance short of armed rebellion. Thus, Congress was not acting out of its delegates' self-interest alone but in the long-term economic and political interests of the whole continent. Hamilton sharply criticized the Tory clergyman, who would insist, as "A. W. Farmer" did, that it was the colonists' "Christian duty to submit to be plundered of all [they] have" or that "slavery" under the tyranny of a king was "a great blessing." In Hamilton's view, those making such claims were "fools" and "knaves." Enslavement by a king was still slavery.[13]

Hamilton's arguments were praised by the decidedly patriotic residents of the city. But if he thought he had shown "A. W. Farmer" the errors of his logic, he was mistaken. Seabury responded to the challenge with two more pamphlets. When Hamilton answered for a second time with *The Farmer Refuted,* he did little more than reiterate his first pamphlet. Historians have concluded that this pamphlet debate revealed Seabury's well-honed skills in written argument and Hamilton's relative youth and inexperience. Still, it mattered little to the area's Revolutionary leadership that Seabury had bested his challenger in print. On November 22, 1775, a militant band of the New York Sons of Liberty rode into Connecticut and raided Seabury's New London home. To their great satisfaction, they discovered the original drafts of the "A. W. Farmer" letters. Seabury was caught red-handed. At his trial, new charges were added to his authorship of the "A. W. Farmer" letters, including his refusal to open the doors of his church on the continental fast day declared by Congress four months earlier and his having signed the White Plains Protest against all unlawful congresses and committees. He was briefly imprisoned and subsequently allowed to continue his parochial duties while under house arrest.[14]

Seabury, a proud man, expressed humiliation at his condition. But his prospects soon changed as the British army approached New York City in August 1776, fresh from its evacuation of Boston. Seabury patiently waited for the right moment to make a move and finally acted at a time when his guards were preoccupied with reports that British spies were scouting the area. On August 27, Seabury took advantage of his guards' inattention and fled on horseback to British lines, where he was welcomed by the army. General William Howe was especially delighted to have Seabury among his soldiers and assigned him to serve as the army's chaplain in New York City. Seabury gladly accepted the assignment, knowing that until America's fate was determined, he had no cause to flee to England. At this point, a British victory still appeared the most likely outcome to observers.[15]

Yet, the surrender of British forces at Yorktown in 1781 dealt a severe blow to the optimism of loyalists, and the Treaty of Paris two years later made many of them increasingly uncertain about their future. The exodus of British troops from New York in 1783 meant that Seabury's services as chaplain were no longer needed. Instead, he assumed an important role in coordinating the mass exodus of American loyalists to other parts of the British realm. No specific records of Seabury's plans have survived, but his actions give every indication that he was planning to sail for England. In an undated letter to the British Treasury (likely written in 1783), Seabury spelled out his unfailing loyalty to Great Britain throughout the Revolutionary conflict. He also had prominent friends write letters verifying his loyalist "credentials." The former royal governor of New Jersey, William Franklin, wrote that Seabury "suffered greatly in person & property" during the war; Thomas Chandler attested to the fact that Seabury "was peculiarly obnoxious to those, who were disaffected to the British Government." These letters were probably meant to accompany Seabury's claim to the London-based Loyalist Claims Commission, which compensated American loyalists for lost property. While making such a claim did not necessarily mean that Seabury was planning to flee the newly independent states, he clearly saw that his future was uncertain and was keeping all his options open.[16]

No matter what Seabury's exact plans were, they changed in April 1783.

While helping other loyalists arrange to leave America, news from Connecticut reached Seabury that he had been nominated to the first episcopacy in that state. Now that the war was coming to a close, Anglican ministers set about restructuring the church in the newly independent state, a much easier task than it had previously been since the approval of the Church of England was no longer requisite. Because many of the Anglican clergymen who remained in that area were loyalists who had remained relatively unmolested by Revolutionaries, Seabury's political disposition did not obstruct his nomination. His selection was further aided by the fact that clergymen, not parishioners, chose their bishops. He also benefited from the effort Cooper and Chandler were making to advance his interests in England, making contacts with English bishops and making a case for Seabury's eventual ordination. The two exiled clergymen had even secured for Seabury an honorary doctor of divinity degree from Oxford University in 1777. Connecticut's Anglican clergymen respected Seabury and saw him as the most capable of obtaining ordination in an expedited fashion. If Seabury was considering leaving America for good, the news of his nomination appears to be all it took to convince him to stay. A bishopric, after all, was what he had been seeking for more than a decade. Seabury sailed to England, but not as a refugee. He planned to receive his new ordination and then return to Connecticut as soon as possible as the state's first bishop.[17]

Seeking ordination presented its own challenges, however. Bishops in England were hesitant to ordain an American bishop before the peace talks scheduled for Paris were concluded, as the status of the Church of England in America would remain uncertain until then. Yet Seabury, as stubborn and impatient as ever, persisted in appealing to any English bishop that would hear him. When he finally realized the futility of his efforts there, he chose an alternative to waiting: Scotland. Scottish bishops were reputed to be less rigid in their ecclesiastical procedures and less prejudiced against Americans, especially during the Revolution. Seabury quickly learned that this reputation was true on both accounts and was ordained in Aberdeen in November 1783. At long last a bishop, Seabury hastily returned to Connecticut.[18]

Once home, Seabury wasted no time addressing the needs of the church in his state. The most pressing need was the dearth of ordained priests created when the number of loyalist clergymen who fled America far exceeded the number of Anglican congregants who did the same. In some areas of the state, church membership had even increased during the war. This had been a principal reason for the expediency with which Connecticut clergymen elected a bishop, as having a bishop in the state would facilitate the ordination of new priests. In the first year of Seabury's service as bishop, he ordained dozens of new clergymen. At least seventeen of them assumed positions outside of Connecticut, demonstrating that a similar shortage of clergymen existed in other states and that Connecticut's neighbors intended to utilize the new bishop until they could procure one of their own.[19]

The Episcopalians in Connecticut proved to be ahead of the rest of the states in the newly independent country in this narrow respect, but not by much. Shortly after Seabury's return, other duly elected American Episcopalians traveled across the Atlantic and were ordained bishops of their respective states. This list included Reverend James Madison of Virginia, Reverend Robert Smith of South Carolina, and Reverend William White of Pennsylvania. These three men had supported the Revolution and strove to unify the former Anglican churches in the different states into one Protestant Episcopal Church. They worried that without this unification, the church would struggle to survive nationally, as its strength varied greatly from state to state. Their plan was widely supported by American church leaders and members alike. But Bishop Seabury's ordination presented a substantial obstacle. Would American Episcopalians agree to a national church that included a former loyalist in a position of honor and authority? If Seabury was excluded, would Connecticut and its neighboring states refuse to unite nationally with their coreligionists? In this struggle for ecclesiastical unification that foreshadowed the struggle to unite the states in the Constitutional Convention a few years later, compromise from all parties was essential for success.[20]

American Episcopalians had not forgotten the loyalist clergyman's pamphlets condemning the American Revolution. By 1786, there was no indication that the general opinion of Seabury had improved. Even prominent secular leaders closely watching the formation of the Protestant Episcopal Church were troubled by Seabury's continued presence. Rufus King, then part of the Massachusetts delegation to the Confederation Congress, saw Seabury's elevation in the church as an act undertaken by the high clergy that intentionally ignored the sentiments of church members. "I am very much dissatisfied with the appointment of this Bishop," King wrote to Elbridge Gerry. "I never liked the hierarchy of the Church—an equality in the teachers of Religion, and a dependence on the people, are Republican principles." When George Washington was asked by a former soldier for a letter of recommendation addressed to Seabury, the general was not happy about having to write the Tory clergyman, noting in his diary that he had no desire "to open a Corrispondence with the new ordained Bishop." These patriot leaders disapproved not only of Seabury's election as bishop but of his continued residence in America.[21]

Yet Seabury's fellow bishops could not take such a hard stance against him. To exclude Seabury from the hierarchy of the new church would doom the plan of a unified national church for two reasons. Not only would the other bishops' refusal to acknowledge the authority of a man duly elected by Connecticut's church leaders alienate the church membership in Connecticut and likely prevent that state from joining the proposed ecclesiastical union, but denying Seabury his place as an American bishop would also effectively negate the ordinations of the dozens of clergymen the bishop had already performed, not just those of priests who were already serving in Connecticut, but of those leading congregations in other states as well. If Bishops White, Madison, and Smith cut off Seabury, they would effectively cut off the church in Connecticut and the surrounding region, instantly defeating the plan for a national Episcopal church.

Seabury was not completely sold on the idea of a national church, anyway. He worried more about the effects inclusion in such an ecclesiastical alliance would have on the parishes and parishioners of Connecticut than he did about his potential exclusion. He objected to many of the ecclesiastical positions of the clergymen in the southern states, especially their decision to allow the laity to participate and have a voice in conventions called to form the new church. James Rivington, one of Seabury's friends who shared this disdain of southern church procedures, warned the bishop to stay aloof from those he termed "Southern Bastards." Eventually, compromises were made and Seabury joined the Protestant Episcopal Church of America, along with Connecticut. His continued residence in America was secured because he possessed a key point of leverage at a pivotal juncture. The survival of the Episcopal Church in America depended on a national union. Without Seabury, the union—and the church—was doomed.[22]

The case of Samuel Seabury demonstrates that the fate of a loyalist clergyman was not set in stone when the war began, or even after the British surrendered. While hundreds of loyalist ministers fled America for other parts of the British Empire, many others continued to make a go of it in the United States. Contingency and local idiosyncrasies mattered, as Seabury's experience shows, because a distinct set of circumstances enhanced Seabury's ability to negotiate continued residence and prominence in America. If a loyalist clergyman resided where patriotic sentiment was weak—or checked by a strong loyalist presence—he could likely maintain his clerical post during and after the war. A clergyman's fortunes were dramatically boosted once British forces occupied his home base, as New York City was in Seabury's case.

But even in areas where patriotic sentiment ran high, officials found room for avowed loyalists in the Revolution's aftermath. In Virginia late in the war, four Anglican clergymen fled to British lines: Reverends John Bruce, William Andrews, Thomas Price, and William Harrison. After the surrender at Yorktown, American forces took these men prisoner. All four were charged with treason, but none was convicted. Two of the four experienced a loss of prestige. Bruce returned to Princess Anne County, where he was never again considered for clerical or political stations and quietly lived out the rest of his life. Andrews fled to England in recognition of the bleakness of his prospects in America. The other two clergymen, Price and Harrison, immediately resumed their parochial duties, almost as if nothing had happened.[23]

How do we explain the double standard? Price and Harrison were members of the gentry, and Bruce and Andrews were not. In fact, the Prices and the Harrisons were among the so-called first families of Virginia, whose wealth and extensive landholdings afforded them significant power and influence in the state. Price's and Harrison's familial ties trumped their loyalist positions during the war, demonstrating that even in the most patriotic regions of the country, a loyalist could return to a prominent social and cultural place if he was related to the right people.[24]

Loyalist attorneys' experiences mirrored those of loyalist clergy. Alexander Hamilton, for instance, expressed a strong desire that many of New York's brightest loyalist attorneys—along with many wealthy merchants—be permitted to remain in the state, as their minds and professional expertise were essential in the formative years of the newly independent state. He speculated that New York would "feel for twenty years at least, the effects of the popular phrenzy" against loyalists. In Virginia, the Revolution created seismic shifts in the legal profession. Many loyalist attorneys fled the state, while many of the patriotic attorneys were rewarded for their roles in the Revolution with prestigious positions on judicial benches. This created an urgent need for skilled attorneys to try cases at a time when court dockets swelled with post-Revolutionary legal disputes over land and prewar debt.[25]

Seabury's rise to ecclesiastical power also speaks to the persistence of British institutions and culture after the war. Though American victory effectively severed the country's political ties to Britain, institutional and cultural breaks with the mother country developed much more slowly. The Protestant Episcopal Church and its hierarchy are perfect examples of this. Though religious leaders were working to transform it into a truly "American" church, immediately after the war Americans who had previously held sway in the Church of England still exercised control in the newly restructured church. The fact that the church hierarchy elected bishops regardless of the people's sentiments meant that a former loyalist could rise within a church in a way he never could in other areas of American life. Rufus King was right when he wrote that the method of selecting American bishops, and Seabury's selection in particular, flew in the face of republican ideals, the very ideals many Revolutionaries believed they had fought to instill in their country.

Seabury served as a bishop until his death in 1796. The contempt many Americans held for him never vanished, but it was checked by his position of prominence in the new Protestant Episcopal Church. Seabury's loyalism during the Revolution, however, came with at least one enduring consequence: the loss of his political voice. Before the war, his sermons teemed with politically charged passages. In his post-Revolutionary sermons, such passages were noticeably absent. To speak out on political matters would have severely tested the patience of his harshest critics and confirmed enemies. Seabury had played his cards well during and after the Revolution. To persist in politics would have been pushing his luck.[26]

"That Great Republic Where . . . All Men Are Free and Equal"

Until now, few historians have understood the significance of Reverend James Madison in the American Revolution. Perhaps more than any other clergyman of his time and place, Madison formed his political opinions from a combination of both Enlightenment philosophy and religious doctrine. At the onset of the Revolutionary War, Madison was ordained to the priesthood of the Church of England and employed as a new faculty member at the royally chartered College of William and Mary. Madison unequivocally aligned with the patriot cause and, like many other clergymen who supported the Revolution, frequently used the pulpit to preach to large congregations on the providential destiny of the newly independent states. Yet, Madison stands out among these other clergymen for two reasons: the circumstances in which he chose to support the Revolution and the rapid rise in social and political status he experienced as a result of his patriotic activity during the war. He was a lone patriot on an otherwise Tory faculty and an Anglican leader supporting the disestablishment of the church, and he became a college president only five years after graduation and an Episcopal bishop only eleven years after ordination.[27]

Madison was born into a wealthy Virginia family in 1749, the fifth son of John and Agatha Madison. Residing in frontier-facing Augusta County, he lived far from the economic, social, and political centers of colonial Virginia. In order to achieve prominence beyond Augusta County, he had to travel to Williamsburg. This was a common practice for the children of wealthy Virginia landowners. Thomas Jefferson and James Madison Jr. (fourth president of the United States and Reverend Madison's second cousin—the "Jr." included throughout this chapter in order to distinguish between the two men) were each born in counties that neighbored Augusta. Jefferson's ambition took him to Williamsburg and George Wythe, while James Madison Jr. ventured to Princeton and John Witherspoon. For ambitious young men and their ambitious fathers, wealth and prestige in a rural county was not enough. Important connections in elite social and political circles were needed to attain positions of power and influence in colonial Virginia. John Madison was ambitious for his son and set the young James upon the path to colonial prominence.[28]

While Madison was still very young, his father sent him to a private academy in Maryland run by the well-respected Anglican clergyman Jonathan Boucher. Madison excelled there, though Boucher later recalled Madison as a "pert and petulant" student. At the age of nineteen he enrolled at the College of William and Mary and then studied law under the tutelage of George Wythe, a prominent attorney and long-standing burgess in Virginia's colonial assembly who had earned the reputation as a radical patriot by his intense opposition to the Stamp Act. In spite of—or perhaps because of—his "pert and petulant" personality, Madison graduated at the top of his class in 1772 and was selected to address faculty and students at the annual founder's day ceremonies. His speech on this occasion stands as one of the earliest expressions of Madison's political opinions. *An Oration, in Commemoration of the Founders of William and Mary College* is a benign title for a text containing radical claims with regard to American civil and religious freedom.[29]

Relying heavily on Locke's *Second Treatise on Government,* and in several instances quoting it at length, Madison sounded a clear call to action for his fellow students in the escalating imperial crisis. "The Extent, as well as the Duration of legislative Power, ultimately terminates in the Will of the People," Madison declared. "They are the original Springs of Government,

they are the first and only Principles, by which the whole must be regulated."
Madison urged his fellow students not to be idle observers of the imperial
conflict, asserting that "the Feelings of a People are the surest Indicatives of
their growing Oppressions. To this End, they should ever keep in View their
own Importance, the Sight of which once lost, Slavery . . . unarmed, unas-
sayled, tramples under Foot the most valuable Rights of Freedom. A People,
struggling with their Fate . . . must kindle into Life the Patriot's Fire." The
references to the will of the people as the origin of government was common
rhetoric among Americans at this time, but by his plea for his fellow students
to "kindle into Life the Patriot's Fire," Madison was advocating aggressive
and potent protest of British imperial policy instead of the passive and weak
petitions proposed by milder patriots. In the defense of American liberties,
Madison declared himself a firebrand.[30]

To Madison, the oppressive policies imposed upon the colonies by Parliament represented an emergency that threatened not only American civil liberties, but the prosperity of society as a whole. "Civil Liberty becomes the Parent
[state] of every social Blessing," Madison declared, adding that it "invigorates
the Mind, gives it a bold and noble Turn, unrestrained by the most distant
Idea of Controul." With civil liberty unfettered by oppressive "Social Institutions" prone to exceed the jurisdiction of their governing authority, Madison
argued that American arts and sciences would flourish. Furthermore, Madison asserted that the preservation of civil liberty would benefit a country on
the battlefield, insisting that a culture in which civil liberty is celebrated naturally produces military valor. Here, Madison was arguing that Great Britain's
imperial might depended on a liberal American policy, and he may have also
been hinting that if peaceful negotiations between the colonies and their parent state failed, the American's celebration of civil liberties would give them
a wartime advantage.[31]

Madison next evoked the historical memory of the reign of James II (1685–
88) to paint a dire picture of what could transpire if colonists left the recent
acts of Parliament unchecked. Madison described English society at that time
as one in which the government acted solely in the king's interest, unrespon-
sive to "the Voice of Law" and the voice of the people; "Vice rioted with Impu-
nity, Perjury received its Sanction from regal Authority" and "the Abolition of
Justice triumphed." This was a dire prediction of the path down which Great
Britain was once again heading. But then Madison struck a more hopeful
chord, reminding his audience that "Britain awoke, as from a Dream," and
that its people "waved the Standard of Freedom," by welcoming William of

Orange, whose "influence dispelled each Fear . . . burst each mental Fetter, and set Reason free." This was a formulaic but significant recounting of a pivotal event in English history. Madison's audience could not have missed the intended message. It was up to Madison and his "Fellow Students" to take their cue from their ancestors and the Glorious Revolution. Madison explained to his peers that their education put them in a position of social leadership and warned them that it was no "less criminal to sleep upon the Watch, than to desert the station."[32]

Madison's political stance was bold. His references to John Locke and Jean-Jacques Rousseau aptly demonstrated that Parliament and the king's ministers were repeatedly violating the social contract and were grossly overstepping the bounds of their jurisdictions and oppressing the colonists. Such a stance placed him in ideological company with other fervent Virginia patriots such as Patrick Henry and Richard Henry Lee. Some of his suggestions were dangerous, particularly the implications of his allusions to the Glorious Revolution. By recounting William of Orange's triumphant entry into England and James II's flight to France, Madison was suggesting that if the king allowed the government in London to continue passing laws aimed at restricting American rights, they would be forced to oust the monarch in favor of new leadership. Though he made it clear that he sincerely hoped the situation would never warrant such an extreme act, by directly declaring this in 1772, Madison effectively flirted with treason. It was not until the eve of independence that patriots began to directly decry the actions of the king. What Madison presented to his audience was a warning that the conflict with the parent state was not going away on its own. Their attention and action were required, if they were to arrive at a just and honorable solution.[33]

Madison also broached the subject of religious liberty in his speech and offered a fresh and surprising perspective for a devout Anglican at an institution affiliated with the church. "I am well aware that even the Idea of a free Toleration, in Matters of Religion, has been a Source of endless Apprehensions," Madison began, "But should we revert to the original Principles of Society, we shall find that [government] was constituted only for the Preservation of civil Interests: That the Duty of the Magistrate respects these Things alone . . . And that all civil Power, Right and Dominion is bounded and confined to the only Care of promoting these Things." On the establishment of state-sanctioned and state-supported religions, Madison made the compelling argument that it caused more harm than good to all involved parties. "Though worn as Armour by the strong," he explained, religious establishment "destroys even their Activity, while upon the weak, it turns into a Load, and cripples the body it was designed to protect."[34]

Madison was protesting the practice of religious establishment within the state, not the inclusion of religion in ordering and governing society. In fact, he insisted throughout the course of his life that religion was absolutely vital to a well-governed and virtuous society. He suggested that a government may make "a Profession of Faith," but that it should be "purely social" and not to be considered "as Articles of Religion, but, as Sentiments which the good Order of Society requires." He did not clearly define what he meant by "purely social," or where the category's boundaries were drawn, but he explained why state-decreed articles of religion were counterproductive to religion's aim of creating a truly moral society. The teachings of Jesus, as Madison understood them, opposed the coercive imposition of a specific religious creed upon a people via inquisition, or its more common manifestation, requiring religious tests for public office holding. Such practices hindered order and advancements in society. Under such principles, Madison argued, many Christians in periods of other country's histories had been made "Pagan, Jew, or Mahometan." The legal establishment of the Church of England swelled the ranks of the church with disingenuous converts and heightened resentment of the church among dissenters. Religious establishment was good for no one.[35]

Madison's remarks on religious toleration in 1772 proved to have lasting significance, as they informed the way Madison responded to attempts by the Virginia Assembly in 1785 to establish religious liberty in the state. As one of the state's most prominent Anglican churchmen after the Revolution, Madison was widely viewed at the time of this debate as a leading candidate for Virginia's first bishop. Many looked to him to lead the fight against the proposed statute on religious freedom and to protect the church's tax revenue. Though at this moment Madison did not openly speak out in favor of the statute championed by his close friend Thomas Jefferson and his cousin James Madison Jr., he did not actively oppose it either. Madison apparently believed that occupying a neutral position was necessary in reconciling his ideological support of religious liberty and the institutional interest inherent in his prominent position within the church hierarchy. He must have known the passing of the statute would present huge obstacles for the church in the immediate future. The exception to his reticence on the matter was his attempt to save the church's glebe lands by employing attorneys and advising vestries throughout the state on how to act, efforts that eventually proved futile. But this all occurred after the statute was passed. In the debate over religious establishment, he stood by his conviction that religious toleration was in the best interest of all parties in a society that championed liberty. Perhaps more remarkably, he did so without jeopardizing his place in the church hierarchy, as he was elected Virginia's first Episcopal bishop in 1786.[36]

But in 1772, when no serious threats to the religious establishment were being made, the political and religious sentiments of Madison's speech were very well received. After studying the law for several months with George Wythe he was admitted to the Virginia bar. Remaining in Williamsburg, he only tried one case before deciding against a legal career, accepting instead an offer in 1773 to join the faculty at William and Mary as a professor of natural philosophy and chemistry and to seek ordination as an Anglican priest. Despite Madison's radical politics, there is no evidence of any contentious relationships with his colleagues.

In 1775, when Madison finally traveled to England for his ordination, colonial protests of British imperial policy were rapidly spreading throughout Virginia. Despite widespread patriotic sentiment in Williamsburg and the surrounding region, the faculty at the College of William and Mary remained, with the exception of Madison, staunchly loyal to the king and Parliament. Versed in the philosophy of Rousseau's *Social Contract* and Locke's *Second Treatise on Government,* as well as the writings of English "country Whigs" such as John Trenchard and Thomas Gordon, who argued against monarchical tyranny and for the supremacy of the people's voice in government through elected assemblies, Madison adamantly opposed the policies of the British government aimed at taxing the colonies. He believed without reservation that such acts infringed upon the colonists' rights as freeborn Englishmen and that Americans were justified in taking up arms against the British army. Inasmuch as his later writings reveal Madison was strongly opposed to war and violence in general, his justification of its use in the Revolution suggests that he viewed America's plight as an exceptional case.[37]

While in England for his ordination, Madison took it upon himself to spy for the Continental Congress and the newly formed Continental Army. Madison used his position as an ordained priest of the Church of England to escape being searched when boarding a ship destined for America. Had he been searched, port officials would have found classified government documents pertaining to the American rebellion in his baggage and sewn into secret compartments in his clothing. He admired George Washington and must have taken great pleasure in assisting the general and other Revolutionary leaders with information obtained behind enemy lines. What information these documents contained and from whom he obtained them is not known. But Madison willingly smuggled them to America, risking the punishment prescribed for treason: execution.[38]

Madison also reported to friends and fellow Revolutionaries on the mood of the British people and the unlikelihood that the government would accept the appeals for redress from the Continental Congress. In a letter from London to a fellow patriot in Williamsburg, Madison lamented, "I am now in this celebrated Metropolis, chagrined and vexed probably ten Times a Day to hear Men [in America] who undoubtedly are making a Struggle for Liberty unparalleled in antient Story, abused, reviled, condemned. The Spirit of this Nation [Great Britain] I am convinced is altogether Anti-American." He noted that while he met a few Britons sympathetic to their cause, nearly all who were associated with the government were decidedly unsympathetic to the colonists' protests. With this inside information, Madison continued his attempts to dissuade mild patriots from pursuing redress through more polite petitions and to persuade them to instead support the newly formed Continental Army.[39]

Like so many other Revolutionaries, Madison risked a great deal by supporting the split with Britain. Had the Americans lost, his property and life would certainly have been in danger, as would his faculty position at William and Mary. On the other hand, he had much to gain should the Revolution prove successful. As the lone patriot on the college's faculty, American victory would have virtually ensured the dismissal of his loyalist colleagues and his promotion within that institution. Surely Madison could not have been blind to such prospects, considering his astute attention to social position and ambition for opportunities to rise in rank and stature. But the fact that as the most junior faculty member Madison insisted on patriotism when his colleagues relentlessly remained loyal to the Crown suggests that Madison was acting in large part out of a principled conviction to the patriot cause and not from personal convenience based on circumstances. After all, Madison's perilous efforts to obtain and smuggle British war plans to America did not derive from any outward pressure. He initiated and carried out such acts entirely of his own free will.[40]

Even though Madison did not assume his strong Revolutionary posture for personal gain, it came nevertheless in 1777 when several of the college's professors fled to England. Soon after, many Virginians grew weary of William and Mary's president, John Camm, and his unceasing loyalty to the Crown.

That June, Camm was dismissed by the Visitors (the college trustees and governing board). They appointed in his stead the newly ordained Reverend Madison. Madison's appointment only four years removed from assuming a professorship must still stand as one of the most rapid rises within academic ranks in American history. Madison was only twenty-eight. Though his scholarship certainly qualified him, it was his political convictions—and connections—that served him best. The Visitors had received an infusion of fresh patriotism with the election of Madison's supporters Thomas Jefferson, Edmund Pendleton, Benjamin Harrison, and Thomas Nelson to its board. The timing of the loyalist exodus from the faculty fortuitously aligned with this shift in the Visitors' political disposition, and Madison's support of the Revolution paid huge dividends very quickly.[41]

Madison was further honored by Virginia's Revolutionary leadership at this time with an appointment as chaplain in the Virginia Assembly. In this role, he led the Assembly in prayer each morning, a duty he was quick to politicize. In a popular but unverified anecdote, Madison is remembered for never referring to heaven as a "kingdom" in his prayers. Instead, he called it "that great Republic where there was no distinction of rank, and where all men are free and equal." Whether or not apocryphal, this sentiment suggests Madison's personality as well as his radical political, religious, and social principles.[42]

By no stretch of the imagination did Madison's appointment as college president mean Madison and his fellow Williamsburg patriots were out of the metaphorical woods. A sense of contingency still loomed large over these Revolutionaries. By assuming the presidency of William and Mary as most of its professors were fleeing Virginia, Madison's lot was to lead the college through the most trying and uncertain period of its history. With the departure of so many faculty members, the college was grossly understaffed. It fell on Madison to begin filling the vacancies. He engaged Reverend Robert Andrews as professor of moral philosophy, James McClurg as professor of anatomy and medicine, and George Wythe as professor of law. Each of these men was an ardent patriot, clearly an unspoken job requirement added to expectations of scholastic ability. A relatively blank slate also enabled Madison to overhaul the way William and Mary approached higher education. In time, Madison would fully subscribe to Jefferson's plans for pedagogical reform that aimed at educating future generations for citizenship in the new American republic. But this would, in large part, have to wait until after the war.[43]

Despite the staunch loyalty of the college's former faculty, the majority of the student body was drawn to the Revolutionary side of the conflict. As what was initially hoped to be a short conflict turned into a prolonged and bloody war, enrollment at the college dropped drastically. Students departed in droves to enlist in the Continental Army, leading Madison to describe the campus as a "desert." The students too young to join the Continental Army were formed into a local militia unit, and Madison accepted appointment as its captain. The college's prospects for survival were bleak. The decrease in enrollment created a severe drop in revenue from tuition and placed the college, Madison, and its few faculty members in financial straits. In January 1781, Reverend Madison even began to contemplate returning to the practice of law at the war's end because "Divinity & Philosophy" would "starve a Man."[44]

Just five months later, however, Madison hastily announced the temporary closure of the college, but not for financial reasons. The disruption was a result of the approaching British army led by Lord Cornwallis. When British troops entered Williamsburg, Madison was forced to leave his home and the college while the British occupied the school's buildings. Even after Cornwallis was driven out of Williamsburg toward Yorktown, the American and French troops replaced the British in the college's buildings. The college did not reopen until the war was over.[45]

When William and Mary finally resumed classes, it reopened as a college transformed by Revolution. Under Reverend Madison's leadership, the college became a bastion of Enlightenment thought and during the 1790s functioned as a dependable ally of the emerging Republican Party as Madison and his colleagues promoted the party's vision of an agrarian nation with power resting primarily with the people in the individual states and not with the federal government. Madison frequently used his oratorical skills to pronounce that God intended the newly independent states to form a "Republic of Virtue," destined to spread westward across the continent and as a refuge from the corruption of Europe. Closely mirroring the ideas of Thomas Jefferson, he described the empires centered in Europe as aged, weighed down by the corruption that had persistently built up over the years. The United States, by contrast, was an "infant empire," benefiting from its geographical separation from the corruption of the "Old World" and destined by God to serve as the world's center of civil and religious freedom. The young country must eradicate any remaining vestiges of European-style aristocracy, Madison maintained, and promote land ownership in order to establish yeomanry among a greater proportion of the population and avoid being drawn into European wars. Madison envisioned the United States as a powerful nation, but it is unlikely that he would have called it a "Christian" nation. Though Madison valued Christianity and frequently spoke of its effectiveness in providing civil order and stability, he did not see it as the central feature around which the nation was forming. The universal and empirical implementation of Enlightenment philosophy, not a general subscription to the theology of Christianity, would make America a distinct nation among the powers of the earth.[46]

Even after he was ordained Virginia's first Episcopal bishop in 1786, Madison's unceasing embrace of Enlightenment philosophy at times drew the ire of his fellow clergymen. "Bishop Madison became an unbeliever in the latter part of his life," wrote William Meade—Madison's successor as presiding bishop—years after Madison's death, explaining that "Secular studies . . . led him to philosophize too much on the subject of religion." Some even accused him of being a deist. One student admired Madison's teaching style but described him as a "priest buried in the philosopher." Many of Madison's close friends were quick to jump to his defense. They believed, as Madison did, that the "spirit of skepticism" central to the Enlightenment did not necessarily preclude genuine religious belief.[47]

Madison believed the American Revolution occurred in accordance with God's will, but it was his rational and philosophical observation of the crisis in the early 1770s, and not his religious beliefs, that convinced him to support the patriot cause. The rational empiricism through which he viewed the world turned the imperial conflict into far more than a religious crusade or a political dispute over imperial policy. To Madison, the American Revolution was the only way to ensure that he and subsequent generations inhabiting the American continent could be ensured civil and religious liberty. With both religious doctrine and enlightened reason in his ideological and oratorical toolbox, Madison was able to successfully navigate the War for Independence and lead many others to do the same.

"Mixing the Sacred Character with That of the Statesman"

Seabury and Madison each chose a side in the Revolution and remained undeterred despite the tumult of war. This was not the case for Reverend John Joachim Zubly. At the beginning of the conflict, the Swiss immigrant was a devoted patriot, Georgia's sole patriotic pamphleteer, and a member of the colony's delegation to the Second Continental Congress. Yet when Zubly became ill and died in 1781, two years before the war officially ended, he was memorialized by a Georgia newspaper as one of the state's most ardent loyalists, with several anti-Revolutionary publications to his credit. How one of Georgia's most notable patriots died a stalwart loyalist is a fascinating story. It turns out he grew frustrated and alienated by the unprincipled wartime behavior of his countrymen. Zubly's rise and fall highlights the tension that many clergymen felt between broad intellectual principles and local interests. It also sheds light on the civil war that consumed Georgia.[48]

John J. Zubly was born in 1724 in St. Gall, Switzerland. His parents and siblings immigrated to South Carolina in 1736 when that colony was avidly promoting Swiss immigration. Though only twelve years old, Zubly remained in Switzerland to complete his theological training in the German Reformed Church. Once ordained in 1744, a German-speaking congregation in Vernonburg, Georgia, wrote to the trustees of that colonial settlement (then residing in London) requesting that they appoint Zubly as their minister. Accordingly, Zubly moved to America and was reunited with his family. When local church politics prevented Zubly from securing the position for which he was requested, he took to traveling throughout Georgia and South Carolina, preaching to any congregation that would hear him—though he was most popular among German-speaking immigrants. For a while he joined his father's ministry in Purrysburg, South Carolina, and ministered in the neighboring settlement of Wando Neck. But in 1760, he accepted the leadership of the Independent Presbyterian Church of Savannah, Georgia. It was a small congregation of Protestant dissenters, but one to which several of the city's most influential men belonged.[49]

Zubly was a short and spirited man. German was his native tongue, but he was fluent in French and English as well. His German accent was so thick that his peers often described his speech as "broken English." He was easily drawn into debates and often sought them out. Even John Adams, who carried a similar reputation for relishing a good argument, described Zubly as "a warm and zealous spirit." In 1746, Zubly married Anne Tobler, a fellow immigrant from St. Gall. As they commenced building a life together in Georgia, Zubly's fiery spirit and ambition served his family well, as he proved exceptionally opportunistic in becoming a wealthy planter and respected community leader.[50]

Zubly quickly joined the ranks of Savannah's elite, but not through his ecclesiastical activity alone. In the late 1740s and early 1750s, Georgia's economy was flourishing. After the colony's prohibition of slaveholding was lifted in 1749, the demand for land skyrocketed, as did its value. Zubly got in on the ground floor of this economic boom. He purchased a brick home in Savannah, a rice plantation near the city, and dozens of slaves. But his appetite for land was voracious. By 1764, Zubly had accumulated nearly 820 acres of land and 26 slaves and had begun operating a ferry across the Savannah River. His lavish home in the heart of Savannah housed not only his family, which consisted of three children, but also an extensive library described by the Pennsylvania clergymen Henry Muhlenberg as "a fine collection of old and new books, the likes of which I have seldom seen in America." To his fellow colonists, Zubly was more than a passionate clergyman; he was a respectable planter and a shrewd investor. Propertied men in Savannah held Zubly in such high esteem that they selected him to serve as a justice of the peace.[51]

Zubly relished in his economic successes, but he longed for intellectual stimulation and recognition beyond what colonial Georgia could offer. In 1746, he was befriended by the famed itinerant preacher George Whitfield, and he caught a firsthand glimpse of the continental renown a preacher could attain. A few years later, Zubly embarked on a tour of the northern colonies and acquainted himself with many of New Jersey's and Pennsylvania's political and religious leaders. The experience had a profound and lasting impact on him. In the 1740s, Philadelphia was the most cosmopolitan city in British North America. It provided its residents easy access to books and many of the colonies' brightest philosophical and theological minds. After enjoying the intellectual vigor of this city, Georgia must have appeared all the more rural and peripheral to the ever-ambitious Zubly. He returned home eager to participate in this broader intellectual environment and began to regularly correspond with northern theologians including Muhlenberg and Ezra Stiles, frequently sending them copies of his sermons. The sharpness of his mind and the quality of his writing did not go unnoticed. In recognition of his work, the College of New Jersey (now Princeton University) awarded Zubly honorary AM and DD degrees in 1770 and 1774, respectively. On the eve of the American Revolution, Zubly was a rising star.[52]

When changes in British imperial policy precipitated riotous protests in American streets, Zubly wasted no time in using the crisis to shore up his newfound position of influence. In 1766, he published his first political pamphlet, a sermon simply titled *The Stamp Act Repealed*. Like other clergymen celebrating the repeal of the Stamp Act in their sermons, Zubly lamented the fact that the law had been enacted in the first place. But what separated Zubly from most of his ecclesiastical counterparts is that he tempered his condemnation of the policy with a warning against an even worse potential fate than taxation without representation: war. While he could not condone the policy Parliament enacted, he observed that "internecine war" would bring more severe travails than could any tax. "Oppression and rebellion are both wicked," he declared, seemingly warning Parliament and the colonists alike to tread carefully in the future. Repeated acts of Parliament akin to the Stamp Act and the escalation of protests by colonists would surely end in war. Zubly used the adjective "internecine" to emphasize the divisiveness and destruction war with the parent state would bring upon the colonists. Perhaps it also previewed his own internal confusion about the crisis. War would force Zubly to sort through his conflicted thoughts and emotions, a chore with potentially devastating consequences. It was best for the colonies, and Zubly, to avoid such scenarios altogether. Though *The Stamp Act Repealed* was a relatively conservative celebration of the colonists' "victory," it still established Zubly as Georgia's premier, and only, Revolutionary pamphleteer.[53]

Zubly's second political pamphlet continued on the same ideological thread as his first, but it represented an increasingly harder stance against Parliament. In 1769, Zubly published *An Humble Enquiry Into the Nature of the Dependency of the American Colonies Upon the Parliament of Great-Britain.* In this pamphlet, Zubly grappled with the constitutionality of the Declaratory Act, which Parliament coupled with the repeal of the Stamp Act to maintain its claimed authority to levy taxes upon the colonies. *An Humble Inquiry* was by no means Zubly's finest display of prose style. He rambles throughout the pamphlet and frequently gets carried away on tangential topics. Perhaps he was merely struggling to incorporate several arguments and pieces of evidence in a cogent and fluid argument. Or perhaps these many detours in his cluttered prose reflected Zubly's internal confusion on the imperial crisis. Either way, the gist of the pamphlet resonated with its readers: by insisting upon its right to tax the colonies, Parliament was treating the colonists as conquered peoples, not as fellow Englishmen. "The Parliament has a right to tax," Zubly wrote, but not indiscriminately upon the whole empire, for "Every representative in Parliament is not a representative for the whole nation." Zubly was neither the first nor the last colonist to make this argument. This pamphlet is more significant for what it reveals about Zubly's evolving political position than any contribution Zubly was making to the development of an American Revolutionary ideology. Though he continued to urge moderation in the colonists' response to the acts of Parliament, Zubly was clearly drifting toward a more radical position.[54]

The next time Zubly weighed in on politics in the press was in his 1772 pamphlet, *Calm and Respectful Thoughts*, which was published in the midst of a heated contest between Georgia's Commons House and the royal governor, James Wright. The political crisis arose when Governor Wright tried to block the legislature's choice of Noble Wimberly Jones to continue as the house's speaker. Wright suspected Jones was the leader of the colony's opposition to Parliament's authority and believed that by removing Jones from the speakership he would deal a serious blow to protesting Georgians. But the Commons House refused to budge, and Zubly chimed in on its side. He argued that "the very design of a House of Commons was to prevent too extensive or undue influence of the Crown; if any proceedings of the House become matters of favour of the Crown, what becomes of the intrinsick right and authority of the Commons?" Though Zubly penned *Calm and Respectful Thoughts* with Georgia's legislative crisis in mind, it had clear implications for the broader imperial crisis of representation in government as well. By using the same constitutional arguments that Parliament employed to prevent royal meddling in parliamentary proceedings, Zubly was insinuating that colonial assemblies were on par with Parliament both in their relationship with the Crown and in their sovereignty over the colonists.[55]

With each successive pamphlet, Zubly presented an increasingly patriotic stance against the mother country. He never ceased cautioning against action that would lead to an internal war, but he had clearly grown impatient and frustrated with Parliament and convinced that the colonists' liberties, present and future, were at risk. It is no surprise, then, that when the Georgia Provincial Congress met in a Savannah tavern in July 1775 to elect a delegation to the Second Continental Congress (Georgia was the only colony not to send a delegation to the first Congress in 1774), the delegates invited Zubly to open their meeting with a sermon.

The sermon he preached and later published as *The Law of Liberty* had a profound effect upon his audience. In the style he had perfected over the previous decade, Zubly was radical in one moment and cautious in the next. He claimed that Britain had reacted rashly and violently to colonial protests and that for the purpose of enforcing "some Acts for laying on a duty to raise a perpetual revenue in America . . . A fleet and army has been sent to New-England . . . blood has been shed, and many lives have been taken away." The colonists should not stand for such violent force and destruction "so wantonly kindled" by their parent country. Yet Zubly added a warning by echoing the words of several other moderates in urging his audience to never lose "out of sight that our interest lies in a perpetual connection with our mother country," to "convince our enemies . . . that we esteem the name Britons, as being the same with freemen," and that their "duty to the King [was] supreme." In the version of the sermon Zubly published, he prefaced his speech with a letter addressed to the Earl of Dartmouth, who then served as the royal secretary of the American Department. He claimed that if Parliament would just make a firm and public commitment to preserve Americans' rights as Englishmen, the crisis would end "instantly." If not, further bloodshed could result in political separation. "The Americans have been called 'a rope of sand,'" Zubly warned, "but blood and sand will make a firm cementation, and enough American blood has already been shed to cement them together into a thirteenfold cord, not easily to be broken." This was a pivotal moment in Zubly's move toward a well-defined Revolutionary position. Instead of relying on constitutional arguments alone, he invoked colorful and anger-filled imagery of his countrymen's spilt blood to advocate the firm and lasting unification of the colonies in opposition to their parent state at all costs.[56]

Inspired by the sermon, the Provincial Congress tapped Zubly to travel to Philadelphia as part of Georgia's delegation. The delegates surely heard Zubly's repeated insistence on loyalty to the king. Perhaps they were attracted to his impassioned but cautious approach, thinking it would provide a needed check on overly zealous members of their delegation. After all, formal separation from Great Britain was a subject that was not yet spoken of openly. Perhaps they thought that when push came to shove, Zubly's Whig principles would win the day and he would make good on his implied threats of political separation. If this was the case, they were dead wrong. Indeed, whatever motivated the Provincial Congress to send Zubly to Congress, it was a decision its members quickly regretted.

Traveling by sea, Zubly and the rest of the Georgia delegation arrived in Philadelphia on August 10, 1775. Congress was then in recess and would not resume until early September, so Zubly used the free time to travel throughout the area introducing himself to prominent clergymen. Nearly all of his clerical acquaintances expressed approval of his membership in Congress. After lodging at John Witherspoon's home and visiting with the Reverends George Duffield and Samuel Stillman, Zubly wrote in his diary that he was "Surprizd at the genl pleasure it gives my friends that I come as a Delegate." One clergyman with whom Zubly was already acquainted, Reverend William Tennent of South Carolina, even expressed jealousy of Zubly's inclusion in Congress. But the most detailed expression of approbation regarding Zubly's position as a delegate came from Robert Livingston, who was then serving as president of the New York Provincial Congress. Livingston suggested that Zubly's inclusion in Georgia's delegation was "the design of Providence" and that Zubly must "be attentive to the religious Liberty of America." Livingston's remarks offer a partial answer to the question of what interested clergymen to participate collectively in the politics of revolution making. Clerical involvement in Revolutionary politics gave the clergy an inside track in preserving and expanding the influence of churches during and after the Revolution. In addition to genuine Revolutionary convictions prompting their actions, this suggests that many clergymen saw the Revolution through a lens of religious interest.[57]

Not everyone was as excited as Livingston to have an ordained priest numbered among the delegates to Congress. John Adams, though a firm advocate for the alliance between the colonies' political and spiritual leadership that he had helped build, was wary of clergymen acting as statesmen. "As [Zubly] is the first gentlemen of the cloth who has appeared in Congress, I cannot but wish he may be the last," Adams wrote to Abigail. "Mixing the sacred character with that of the statesman . . . is not attended with any good effects. The clergy are universally too little acquainted with the world . . . to engage in civil affairs with any advantage. Besides, those of them who are really men of learning," Adams concluded, "have conversed with books so much more than men as to be too much loaded with vanity to be good politicians." Adams clearly possessed a low estimation of the clergy's potential to act as effective statesmen, but he was not alone in this view. Several years earlier, when Ezra Stiles learned that Zubly and other Georgia clergymen were serving as justices of the peace, the New Englander wrote in his diary that he "greatly disapprove[d]." Stiles, like Adams, was a strong advocate for clergymen using the press and their pulpits to express opinions on political matters. But both men believed the clergy's proper place in the political sphere was to make critical observations and calls to action from without statehouses, not from within. Adams's and Stiles's disapproval of Zubly's participation in Congress demonstrates that though they each appreciated the alliance between political and clerical figures, it was a partnership filled with tension.[58]

Zubly was miserable in Congress, and he quickly made many of the other delegates around him miserable as well. As the delegates moved from talk of reconciliation to talk of separation, Zubly grew concerned that they were moving too rashly and "made a point of it in every Company to contradict &

oppose every hint of a desire of Independency or of breaking our Conexion with Great Britain." Zubly did not necessarily demonize his opponents in Congress, but he certainly looked down upon many of them as his intellectual inferiors, writing with an air of conceit that "Some good men may desire [independence] but good men do not always know what they are about." Drawing upon his early years in Switzerland, Zubly attempted to warn his fellow delegates of the perils and disadvantages of living in a loose alliance of republics. In terms of eighteenth-century Swiss political discourse, Zubly acted in the spirit of *kantonligeist*, embracing a narrow, provincial view, favoring the autonomy of Swiss cantons over the wider interests of the Swiss alliance. In a debate over foreign trade regulations, Zubly declared, "A republican government is little better than government of Devils. I have been acquainted with it from six years old." The entire dynamic of a federation of republican governments was reason enough for Zubly to oppose many of the motions made in Congress, even those that did not hint at separation from Great Britain.[59]

Zubly made one particularly strong enemy in Congress, Samuel Chase of Maryland. Chase was an attorney and a radical patriot from the earliest stages of the imperial crisis. He came to Philadelphia with a history of making vicious personal attacks against his political opponents, and his behavior in Congress only cemented this reputation. The main point of contention between Zubly and Chase was the former's objection to strict nonimportation and nonexportation pacts against England. Zubly did not initially oppose the measures outright but asked that Georgia be excused from such policies, as he believed it would place a greater burden upon the economy in his colony than on any other. Furthermore, he insisted that such actions would be interpreted by Great Britain as a clear indication that the colonies intended to declare their independence. Chase adamantly disagreed, arguing that making such exceptions for individual colonies would "produce a disunion of the Colonies." As the debate continued over several days in late October and early November of 1775, Chase's language became more vituperating. "If [Zubly] speaks the opinion of Georgia, I sincerely lament that they ever appeared in Congress," Chase declared on the legislative floor. "The gentleman's advice will bring destruction upon all North America." Zubly fired back, stating he would rather "bear the character of a madman" than deem the plan Chase was advocating wise and prudent. "A glove has been offered by the Gentleman from Georgia," Chase retorted in language suggesting an offense to his honor; "that gentleman's system would end in the total destruction of American liberty. I never shall dispute self-evident propositions."[60]

Chase was certainly one of the more radical patriots in Congress and Zubly one of the more conservative, but this heated exchange speaks to more than mere difference in political opinion. It demonstrates the persistence of intercolony strife and prejudice. In one breath, Chase championed colonial unity as paramount in effectively protesting Parliament. In the next, he readily dismissed Georgia as unnecessary to Congress if its delegates opposed the majority. From Chase's perspective, Georgia was both geographically and politically on the American periphery. That is certainly how Zubly interpreted Chase's slight. The majority of delegations supporting an economic protest that disproportionately burdened Georgia signified to Zubly that the appearance of universality of opinion among the colonies was more important to Congress than the universal welfare of the colonists. All colonies were not created equal.

Chase was certainly Zubly's most outspoken critic, but he was not the only one. During this debate Zubly read the writing on the wall: the trajectory on which Congress was moving was shifting sharply toward independence and against him. Despite his attraction to contentious debates, the opposition he faced in Congress was too much. In early November 1775, Zubly made preparations for his return to Savannah, this time by an overland route. Some historians have suggested that Zubly left Congress in disgrace after Chase revealed evidence that the Georgian had been carrying on a secret correspondence with former governor Wright. But this story is apocryphal, as there is no evidence in the congressional record or elsewhere to support such accounts. Regardless of the precise conditions under which Zubly left Congress, it was with feelings of dismay and a sense of failure that Zubly set off from Philadelphia before dawn on November 10, 1775.[61]

Zubly returned to Savannah frustrated with the congressional proceedings in Philadelphia but seemingly content to be out of the political fray. There is no evidence that Zubly intended to make trouble for patriots in Georgia. In fact, his political reticence and inactivity in the weeks immediately following his return home suggest that he planned to remain neutral. But two months after his return, the Council on Safety issued a summons for Zubly to appear before its members and explain his conduct while in Congress. The distressed clergyman did not oblige. Instead, he took up his pen and wrote a detailed letter explaining his disagreements with the other delegates in Philadelphia and published it in the *Georgia Gazette*. He maintained that the colonies should not be taxed without representation in Parliament but insisted that political separation was a much too drastic measure and a particularly ill-advised one for Georgia. The southernmost American colony was not ready to stand alone, and Zubly feared that in an alliance with the twelve colonies to the north it would be neglected and therefore doomed. Clearly Zubly thought he would fare better explaining himself publicly in the press than privately behind council doors; this more public option afforded him more control over his reputation, or so he hoped.[62]

Shortly thereafter Congress declared the thirteen colonies independent states, effectively ramping up hostilities among local populaces throughout the country. The Georgia Council on Safety, like many of its counterparts in other states, insisted that citizens take an oath of loyalty to the United States of America. Such oaths are a key reason the war against what had become a "foreign" country (Great Britain) quickly transformed into a civil war among local populaces. Loyalty oaths destroyed the political middle ground. They forced conflicted individuals, those without opinions of the war and those consciously seeking neutrality, to choose a side. When a person refused to take such an oath, his or her reticence was frequently interpreted as a declaration in favor of Britain. Many of these people were born and raised in the colonies. Yet, for declining to take the oath, the council instantly branded them "disloyal" and "enemies" of the state.[63]

Zubly tried to navigate this critical moment, informing the council that he would swear loyalty to Georgia but he could not and would not pledge allegiance to the United States. As Zubly later recounted, "I offered to swear, that while I enjoyed the Protections of the State, I would in all Things do my Duty as a good and faithful Freeman. [I] Would give no Intelligence to, nor take up Arms in Aid to the Troops of the King of Great Britain. . . . I have hesitated to take an Oath of Allegiance to other States, who are bound by no Oath to us." However, his attempt to split the difference was futile, as the Council on Safety refused to accept Zubly's "halfway" oath. It confiscated his property and banished him from Georgia. Zubly fled to his property in the Black Swamp of the South Carolina backcountry and from there pled publicly in a published letter for the council to rethink its treatment of loyalists and to afford them the same constitutional respect the Revolutionaries had been demanding from Parliament. The council and general public alike ignored Zubly's appeal. An outright British victory was now the only likely avenue by which Zubly could have his property and former life restored.[64]

Forced exile is fertile soil for feelings of bitterness, as Zubly experienced firsthand. His belief that he had been unjustly dealt with was amplified when news reached him that his home, including his precious library, was destroyed in a fire. This was a devastating loss. Any hope that a British victory in the war would restore him to all his property and possessions vanished. A few months after the British finally captured Savannah in December 1778, Zubly returned to the city a changed man.[65]

After Georgia's royal government was restored, its reinstated officials advertised the colony as a haven for persecuted loyalists, and the tables were turned on the patriots remaining in those parts. Indeed, returning loyalists were just as harsh to patriot leaders as the patriots had been to loyalists. The reinstated royal officials reclaimed lands the rebels had confiscated from the loyalists and returned the deed in kind. Zubly spent a good deal of time sifting through what remained of his home. He especially lamented the destruction of his library, a loss that "wounded" him "in the tenderest parts." In his journal he insisted that he would "watch against every Notion of Revenge . . . tho I do not mean to deny myself Justice, I would guard against Passion[,] Revenge & Hatred." Yet he did not return to speaking terms with most of his former friends who had been party to that "Act of Villainy & Injustice." This sustained estrangement was not entirely Zubly's fault, as many of those men shunned his worship services. As Zubly saw it, "they love Rebellion more than the Gospel." Zubly was attempting to practice the Christian doctrine of forgiveness, but his journal reveals that it was a constant struggle. Though his patriot neighbors reveled in the Lockean principles of life, liberty, and property, he believed that they had treated him in an entirely unprincipled way.[66]

It was precisely this treatment that pushed Zubly from a tentative perch of neutrality into full-fledged loyalism. And it was the loss of so much that was dear to him that prompted him to publish a series of essays in a local newspaper in 1780, all of which aimed to convince Revolutionaries to once again become loyal subjects of the king. Though these essays were published under the pseudonym Helvetius, readers could readily identify Zubly as the author. After all, Helvetius is a Latin term referring to the Swiss people, and the writing style was distinctly Zubly's.[67]

There was little written in the Helvetius essays that had not already been voiced by loyalists elsewhere, but the essays signified a stark change in Zubly. Whereas the pamphlets he published before joining the Continental Congress were written with an air of objectivity and were based heavily on constitutional reasoning, in the Helvetius essays Zubly laced his legal theory with harsh invective. He blamed the prolonged war on the "thoughtless wretches" in Congress and alleged that the entire Revolution was a conspiratorial plot laid by "a few designing and desperate men" who then "set up a popular pretence the most distant from their real designs." Because Congress met the terms of Britain's offers for reconciliation with "haughtiness and inflexibility," Zubly deemed the Revolution an unjust and therefore "unlawful" war. He further asserted that the Revolution's conspiratorial origins and the rashness of America's patriot leadership qualified the American side of the fighting as "a crime against humanity" and that the blood of the conflict's countless victims "hangs over [their] heads."[68]

Zubly also used the essays to publicly decry his enemies, further demonstrating his lingering bitterness and animosity. He blamed Thomas Paine and particularly bombastic passages in *Common Sense* for inciting violence against those wishing to remain loyal to the Crown or neutral in the affair. Then he spoke directly to his plight as a result of his refusal to swear allegiance to the United States. "Men who under pretence of publick war commit private robberies, and form themselves into bodies that they may the better effect their villainous purpose," Zubly fumed, "are no better than highwaymen, and deserve no better treatment." If Zubly believed the Helvetius essays would convince Revolutionaries to switch sides so late in the war, he was gravely disappointed. There is no evidence that his final publications had any such effect. In fact, because he published his essays in a decidedly loyalist newspaper, it is unlikely that his essays were read by a patriot audience of any significant size. The main accomplishment of the Helvetius essays was providing a frustrated and bitter clergyman a forum in which he could air his grievances.[69]

In 1781, Zubly became ill with a respiratory ailment. In his dying days, he remained optimistic that the British army would subdue the American rebellion and set the world back in its proper order. Zubly's prognostications were wrong on both accounts. He died on July, 23, 1781 at the age of fifty-six. Unlike Madison and Seabury, Zubly was unable to navigate the consequences of his political choices. At one point a wealthy and prominent patriot, he died a destitute and despised loyalist.

The experiences of Seabury, Madison, and Zubly provide key insights into the difficulties inherent in navigating the consequences of the American Revolution. Seabury and Madison were successful, in part, because they chose a side and never wavered. Whereas Madison was fortunate that his side won, Seabury demonstrated a high level of resourcefulness in the way he leveraged his ordination as a bishop to not only remain in the United

States but retain ecclesiastical prominence therein. But Zubly was not as fortunate as Madison and was less resourceful than Seabury. When the fate of the British army in the conflict began to turn toward defeat, he continued to alienate American patriots with his harsh invective. Had he lived to see the war's end, it is very likely that he would have joined his family in its exile to the Bahamas.

FOUR

Clergymen and the Constitution

Clergymen were noticeably absent when the Constitutional Convention convened in Philadelphia on May 15, 1787. Coming nearly four years after the official end to the Revolutionary War, this convention was the next major moment in which religion and politics became a significant issue on the national political stage. Unlike the Continental Congress that successfully guided the country through the Revolutionary War, there were no clergymen doubling as statesmen and no chaplains opening sessions with politicized prayers. And unlike the public pronouncements Congress made during the war, the framers of the Constitution made no mention of God or Providence in the final document they presented to the American people. In forming the country's new government, the convention omitted references to the sacred and focused solely on the secular.[1]

Outside the stuffy confines of the Pennsylvania State House, however, Protestant clergymen had a significant impact on the Constitution. In the ratification debates that embroiled the country between 1787 and 1788, religious ministers voiced both praise and disdain for the new Constitution from their pulpits, in newspapers, and as delegates to state ratifying conventions. The rapidly expanding print media of late-eighteenth-century America disseminated their arguments to an anxious national audience that believed the fate of the nascent republic and the legacy of the Revolution were at stake. In this all-important national conversation, religion became a conspicuous subject and clergymen prominent spokesmen.

Yet, until now, historians have paid little attention to the influence politicized clergymen wielded in the ratification debates. When they have, they have usually limited their analyses to the effect the Constitution had on

church-state relations. Such approaches do not capture the significant contribution politicized clergymen made to the processes of state and national
formation. Politicized clergymen on both sides of the contest used the ratification debates to negotiate the impact of the Constitution on American religious life as well as the continuing impact of religion on government.[2]

This chapter illustrates the three principal themes around which these
negotiations occurred. First, as clergymen spoke publicly for or against the
Constitution, Americans argued over the appropriateness of religious leaders engaging in the political arena. Both Federalists and Anti-Federalists
acknowledged the clergy as an increasingly powerful special interest group.
Federalists cited instances of clerical support for the Constitution as a sign of
God's approbation for the new government while deriding those clergymen
who campaigned against ratification as preachers exercising too much sway
on the "ignorant" portion of the population. Anti-Federalists, on the other
hand, criticized clergymen who publicly supported the new Constitution for
acting out of ecclesiastical self-interest, chastening them for mixing the gospel of Christ with the politics of men. Though the Revolution had established
religious ministers as significant political players in the emerging nation, in
the late 1780s their participation remained controversial.[3]

Second, Federalist and Anti-Federalist clergymen, along with their lay
allies, clashed on the implications of the proposed government to the oft-
spoken-of providential mission of America. Anti-Federalists insisted that the
country's return to "tyranny" in the form of a strong national government
was comparable to the desire of many Israelites during the Exodus who clam-
ored to return to the "fleshpots of Egypt." They equated the adoption of the
Constitution to abandoning the idea of America as God's chosen nation. On
the other hand, Federalists argued that the Constitution was a necessary step
in regaining social order, an essential element in maintaining the favor of
Providence moving forward. American providentialism was clearly a malleable idea. The notion used by lay and clerical patriots alike a decade earlier as
a clarion call to Revolution was thus appropriated in the late 1780s by competing factions as they pursued their respective political and economic interests.

The third theme centered on a question more contentious and with
broader implications than the mere size and role of the federal government.
For many Americans, no issue was more important or more divisive than the
question of whether or not religion could be separated from public morality. Where the debates over the Constitution are concerned, public morality

refers to people dealing with each other honestly and virtuously in the public sphere as well as the honest and virtuous dealings of elected officials with the public. Did any Christian sect have a monopoly on morality? Could Christianity, broadly defined, claim to be morality's sole proprietor? Arguments about oaths of office, religious establishments, and religious tests for office holding were not merely issues of power and pragmatism. They reflected Americans' struggle to incorporate the Enlightenment's secular approach to government with the traditional role of religion in politics.

Historians such as Gordon S. Wood have long maintained that "the Constitution represented both the climax and the finale of the American Enlightenment," that it signaled "an end of the classical conception of politics and the beginning of what might be called the romantic view of politics." According to Wood, Americans believed that in creating and ratifying the federal Constitution, they had reduced "the variety and perplexity of society" to "a simple and harmonious system." Such claims assume a political consensus among Americans that simply did not exist. Wood imposes artificial boundaries upon the American Enlightenment, oversimplifying the varied political implications of Enlightenment philosophy on American politics and neglecting its continued impact on American culture and society. As one scholar explained, classicalism and romanticism are "the systolic and diastolic of the human heart in history." In late-eighteenth- and early-nineteenth-century America, the need for enlightened order and for a more romantic spirituality worked alternately as motives for the country's founding generation. The Constitution was hardly a signpost marking the end of the Enlightenment and the start of Romanticism; it was but one of several arenas in which Americans attempted to negotiate the idealism of Enlightenment philosophy with the reality of everyday life.[4]

Assertions that the Constitution was the climax of the American Enlightenment are particularly challenged further by the debate over the necessity of religion to public morality during the ratification process and its continuation thereafter. Like the political leadership of the country, American clergymen and their parishioners acted from multifarious influences. By analyzing the contribution of politicized clergymen to the ratification debates and the meaning of religious topics considered therein, we are forced to rethink the conclusions made by previous generations of historians on the interplay of religion and Enlightenment philosophy within the American republican experiment.

"When Ministers Undertake to Meddle with Politics"

To many eighteenth-century Americans, the clergy comprised a powerful special interest group. Despite this perception, the reality is that America's religious landscape was too diverse and the political views of individual clergymen too disparate to treat the clergy as a unified group on the issue of ratification. While the majority of American clergymen active in the ratification process supported the Constitution, some prominent clergymen, such as William Bentley of Massachusetts, were sympathetic to Anti-Federalist arguments. Other church leaders, such as Bishop Madison of Virginia, were only mild supporters of the Constitution and saw it as a temporary fix to the country's political and financial problems that would last twenty years at best. Yet Federalists ran with the tenuous perception of a Christian consensus to further validate the new Constitution to the American public. They either dismissed the criticism of the Constitution by Anti-Federalist clergymen as somehow illegitimate or ignored it altogether in order to make it appear as though the nation's spiritual leaders had placed their stamp of approval on the handiwork of the nation's political elite. The Federalists' ratification campaign stands as one of the earliest examples of American political leaders overemphasizing the opinions of a few prominent Christians in order to draw support from the rest of their coreligionists.[5]

Anti-Federalists deemed the clergy a special interest group for an advantageous reason as well: to portray Federalist clergymen as a political cabal, conspirators in league with the dubious delegates to the Philadelphia convention seeking to satisfy their economic and political ambitions. Through this portrayal, Anti-Federalists sought to capitalize on the general fear of conspiracies already deeply woven into the fabric of American political culture. Furthermore, it was an attempt to heighten extant anxiety among proponents of religious liberty that many of their recent victories over religious establishments would be short lived if they allowed the clergy to act in concert with the country's national political leadership. Clergymen were firmly installed on the national political stage by 1787, and the fact that both Federalists and Anti-Federalists exploited their presence demonstrates that at this moment religion remained an effective tool for manipulating public opinion.

James Madison watched the ratification debates unfold in each state as closely as any Federalist. Though Madison was frustrated that the convention in Philadelphia had dismissed much of what he intended the Constitution to include and much of what he hoped it would be, he remained fully invested in its adoption. He frequently corresponded with friends and political allies throughout the country, anxious for updates on the prospects for ratification in those places. In Madison's political calculus, he included clergymen in the category of "learned professions" that were "with but few exceptions in favor of the [Constitution] as it stands." Though such exceptions were relatively few, Madison tracked them fastidiously. In a letter to Edmund Pendleton, he compared the Virginia ratification debate to that occurring in Massachusetts, writing that "the Clergy of all Sects" supported the Constitution "as unanimously in [Massachusetts] as the same description of characters are divided and opposed to one another in Virginia." To Madison, the clergy represented an important special interest group within each state but not a predictable block vote nationally.[6]

When Madison discussed the politicization of clergymen, he did so in a measured, dispassionate way. Other observers, however, were far less emotionally reserved in sharing their opinions on the way clergymen attempted to influence the political opinion of the American public. Some Anti-Federalists claimed that clerical support for the Constitution was based upon their professional interest and nothing more. Ratification was in "the Interest of Clergy," a New York Anti-Federalist wrote, "as civil tumults excite every bad passion—the soul is neglected, and the Clergy starve." Based upon such reasoning, "civil tumults" such as Shays's Rebellion were bad for ecclesiastical business. The civil order promised by the loudest advocates for the Constitution would return unruly Americans to church pews, where they would once again defer to their spiritual leaders and continue to pay their salaries. Furthermore, because those salaries were typically paid with currency, other Anti-Federalists lumped the clergy with lawyers and speculators as men "depending on money payments" for whom the adoption of the Constitution would "afford security."[7]

Expectedly, Federalist clergymen were quick to disavow any "unnatural" interest influencing their calls for ratification. During the Massachusetts ratification convention, Baptist minister Samuel Stillman rose as a delegate and declared, "I have no interest to influence me to accept this Constitution of government, distinct from the interest of my countrymen, at large. We are all embarked in one bottom, and must sink or swim together." Stillman reminded his audience, "I too have personal liberties to secure, as dear to me as any gentlemen in the Convention." Federalists and Anti-Federalists were at an impasse where the "interest" of the clergy was concerned. Federalists refused to see clerical support for the Constitution as anything more than fellow citizens speaking out for their "personal liberties," while Anti-Federalists refused to see clerical support for the Constitution as anything more than the despicable, interested actions of ministers willfully neglecting their oaths to place God and the needs of their congregations first.[8]

Yet public debate over the clergy's participation in the ratification process went far beyond questions of interest and disinterestedness and focused on the legitimacy of clergymen's political participation in the first place. One New York writer claimed that the clergy had become an integral part of the young country's "political classes." Edmund Randolph of Virginia lamented that this classification was all too fitting. "Religion, the dearest of all interests, has too often sought proselytes by fire, rather than by reason," Randolph argued on the floor of the Virginia ratifying convention, "and politics, the next in rank, are too often nourished by passion, at the expence of the understanding." Reason, not passion, was paramount in deliberations over the proposed Constitution. Randolph worried that the inclusion of religion in the debates would push the precarious balance of the two heavily toward passion.[9]

To modern observers, there was no shortage of hypocrisy and blatant political bias in debates over the participation of clergymen in the ratification process. Though many Virginia Federalists made public appeals for clergymen to prepare sermons that praised "Almighty God, for inspiring the members of the late [Constitutional] Convention with wisdom, amity and unanimity," they in turn rebuked Anti-Federalists for "polluting . . . the Temples of the Lord" by using Sunday church services as a forum in which to deal out "their vile Declamations against the Constitution." Other Federalists readily urged Americans to trust the judgment of the clergy and "a majority of good men" in favor of "giving [the Constitution] a chance," but decried clergymen who publicly opposed the Constitution as operating "beyond the limits of their office." In this moment we see the emergence of a peculiar and enduring pattern in American political culture. When secular factions believe that clergymen are on their side, they champion their participation in political processes as legitimate and even essential. But when the tables are turned, the same factions declare clerical participation in politics an "unholy" alliance between church and state.[10]

The highest-profile altercation over the participation of clergymen in the ratification debates surrounded the public endorsement of the Constitution by a convention of Baptist clergymen. In October 1787, the association of Baptist churches in Pennsylvania and New York met in conference to draft and publish a circular letter heartily endorsing the Constitution. This letter was clearly a coup for Federalists and quickly drew a firestorm of criticism from Anti-Federalists. "The clergy, I find, are, generally, very busy in proving by their present (as well as by some past) conduct, that *politics* and *theology* are by no means incompatible," an anonymous Philadelphian wrote in a local newspaper. "I had hitherto imagined, this order of men paid and maintained by the people to keep them in mind of their duty to GOD and their neighbours. But, it seems, they have a sufficiency of leisure upon their hands to fix, at least, *one eye* pretty steadily upon the political affairs of the world we are in." A New York Anti-Federalist writing as "A Baptist" reminded clergymen that they "are bound to concern themselves only with those things which appertain to the kingdom of heaven." He expressed utter bewilderment and frustration "that the association should have recommended this new constitution, not only because it was a subject that they had nothing to do with—but also because . . . it was never read in the association, and many of the members had never heard or understood the contents." The hasty action of the clerical association, he claimed, justified the "observation which has often been made that when ministers of religion undertake to meddle with politics, they generally conduct weakly or wickedly." Concluding his essay, "A Baptist" urged clergymen to abstain from debating the policies of the United States government, and instead confine themselves to studying "the policy of the kingdom of our Lord Jesus Christ."[11]

These were old arguments made fresh in the context of severe public division. In many ways, Americans in the late 1780s were adhering to Revolutionary precedents in which patriots chided loyalist clergymen for engaging in politics just as loyalists returned such criticisms at patriot clerics. A faction welcomed and even encouraged ministers to speak publicly on secular matters such as the Constitution, so long as their political opinions agreed with its own. But when a faction discovered that a clergyman opposed its politics, heaven help that man of the cloth. According to the prevailing political rationale of the ratification debates, he must have abandoned the Kingdom of God for the governments of men.

"This New Species of Divine Right"

Under the Articles of Confederation, the United States was akin to the biblical city of Babel. At least that is how one anonymous Federalist writer from Georgia portrayed the country's post-Revolutionary social and political discord. During the 1780s, the national government was riddled with ineffectiveness and inefficiency. Chief among these problems was the inability of the Confederation Congress to raise enough revenue to pay its wartime debts and the difficulty it had in passing even the most inconsequential pieces of legislation, owing to the nine-of-thirteen majority required by the Articles. Compounding his frustration with the inefficiency of the new government, this anonymous Federalist pointed to Shays's Rebellion in Massachusetts as a dire warning that the union's collapse from within was nigh. "It is high time that we understand one another," he declared. It was time that Americans were "reduced to one [political] faith and one government, otherwise there will be as great a confusion of constitutions amongst us as there was of tongues at the subversion of Babel." To this political writer, the proposed federal Constitution was the solution to all that ailed the young country, a panacea by which America could retain its providential favor and avoid the social tumult associated with God's displeasure.[12]

Other Americans agreed with this interpretation, or at least valued the persuasive power of imagining the loss of America's "chosen" status so soon after it was presumably confirmed by success in the Revolutionary War. In New York, a Federalist lamented what he viewed as the anarchic tendencies exhibited by Americans in the 1780s. "How little the bulk of mankind reason . . . [and] what an easy matter it is to alarm and inflame the multitude," he bemoaned, "but how very difficult to reason them into the propriety of wise laws, and a wise government." This New Yorker promoted the Constitution as the country's only hope against the unbridled passions and disorder of the masses, insisting that ratification would quickly reveal to Americans everywhere "that Providence has still many blessings in store for this western world. That we have reason to believe the same powerful and gracious hand which hath hitherto so marvelously nourished and brought us up, will not leave us to fall into anarchy and division; but will still make us one great, united, free and happy people." For many Federalists, American providentialism remained a potent language by which to sell their fellow Americans on the new Constitution.[13]

But Federalists did more than tap into the extant vocabulary and ideology of American providentialism. Through their biblical allusions, they made substantial contributions to the American providential tradition as well. This occurred most notably through comparisons of the United States to the ancient nation of Israel. Beginning with the Articles of Confederation, several clergymen directed Americans' attention to the similarities of the country's new national government and the "Hebrew constitution" the Israelites established following their Exodus from Egypt. In a 1781 sermon, Reverend Joseph Huntington compared Israel's thirteen tribes (creatively increased from the conventional twelve by including the tribe of Levi and dividing the tribe of Joseph into the tribes of Ephraim and Manasseh) to America's "thirteen united, *free and independent states.*" Like each autonomous tribe, each state "managed their internal police within themselves; had each of them their legislative body, for their own state or tribe; also their judges, and courts of justice." Just as the disparate tribes of Israel were united with a governing "national" council of seventy elders called the Sanhedrin, the disparate states of America were united by the Confederation Congress. As historian Eran Shalev explains, ancient Israel provided "a historical example and divine sanction to the novelties of the American federal experiment." The republican interpretation of the Bible evolved along with the Revolution. With independence, Americans expanded their views of the ancient Israelites, from "republicans" who displayed their righteousness by their resistance to Pharaoh's tyranny to the creators of the first *federal* republic. As much as Americans may have believed they were beginning "the world over again," they constantly looked to the past for models and vindication.[14]

As the American experiment with federalism advanced, Federalists adapted and tweaked their anachronistic biblical model to fit the new Constitution. This trend was exemplified by Reverend Samuel Langdon of Massachusetts, who in a 1788 sermon urged his audience to consider the way the ancient Israelites adapted their government to their post-Exodus circumstances. While fleeing Egypt and journeying to Canaan, the power to govern primarily lay with each tribe, and the collective tribes were only loosely coordinated by the Sanhedrin. This was largely owing to the pragmatic difficulties of governing a large mobile population and coordinating its military efforts to expel the Canaanites from the "Promised Land." But once the Israelites were permanently settled in Canaan, they created a more powerful national federation of tribes. As it was with Israel, Langdon argued, so it should be with the United States. For Americans, the Revolutionary War was their "Exodus," and independence was their "Promised Land." The Articles of Confederation were sufficient for a time when Americans were fleeing British tyranny, but Langdon insisted that the country should continue to mirror Israel's progression, moving "from abject slavery, ignorance, and a total want of order" to "a national establishment." Thus, Langdon claimed that ratification of the

Constitution was essential if the nation was to maintain its "providentially appointed" symmetry with ancient Israel.[15]

As much as Huntington, Langdon, and other clergymen promoted the similarities between constitutional developments in ancient Israel and the United States, their claims were less valuable in promoting the Hebrew constitution as a viable political model than they were in selling religious Americans on a secular Constitution. When Madison prepared for the Constitutional Convention with a nearly exhaustive study of Western governments, ranging from the ancient to the contemporary, he did not include the "Mosaic constitution." When the Convention framed the new government in the Philadelphia State House, they did not reference the Old Testament as a guide. American statesmen did not claim that the new Constitution matched a biblical archetype in order to influence the technical aspects of state formation; these claims were Federalist propaganda in the contested process of ratification. Clergymen analyzed the Hebrew "republic" in a political context as a way of ascribing divine approbation and religious significance to secular government. With the advent of a Constitution that omitted any reference to God, the Federalist clergy adapted the language of American providentialism to make the political religious and the religious political. They wanted Americans to believe that in building a stronger federal government, they were actually building up the Kingdom of God on earth.[16]

Some Federalists went even further in their use of providentialism and Old Testament biblicism to promote the Constitution by assigning the document an almost canonical status. Benjamin Rush provides an illuminating example of this strategy. Rush was a Philadelphia physician, devout Christian, and eager student of the Enlightenment. He had signed the Declaration of Independence as a member of the Continental Congress, but he left public office in 1778 to pay full attention to his medical practice. His election to the Pennsylvania ratifying convention marked his reentry into the political arena. Convention minutes recorded Rush asserting that he "as much believed the hand of God was employed in this work [of drafting the Constitution], as that God had divided the Red Sea to give passage to the children of Israel or had fulminated the Ten Commandments from Mount Sinai!" To Rush, "the unanimity of the [Constitutional] Convention, the general approbation of the Constitution by all classes of people, and the zeal which appeared everywhere . . . from New Hampshire to Georgia" were "reasons to believe that the adoption of the government was agreeable to the will of Heaven." He argued that "the

Vox Populi" was the *"Vox Dei,"* that in a republican government, God manifested his will through the people. As the convention's secretary summarized the speech, Rush was expounding upon a "new species of divine right."[17]

What are we to make of Rush's hagiographic endorsement of the controversial Constitution? Did he really believe the proposed government was the product of divine intervention, or was he relying on religious hyperbole in order to court political support for ratification? His language is best understood if we examine both the pragmatic and ideological context in which he spoke. Pragmatically, Rush declared that the Constitution bore a divine stamp of approval as a way of facilitating its quick ratification by the Pennsylvania convention. If the convention delegates went through the Constitution line by line dismissing the language and clauses with which it found fault and amending the text throughout, Rush feared ratification would never occur. Furthermore, if this same process was mirrored in the other twelve states, the Constitution was sure to drown in a sea of irreconcilable amendments. To prevent this fate, Rush adopted what one of his biographers terms a "block-amendments strategy" whereby he endeavored to keep the attention of the Pennsylvania convention—and those outside the state who read his published speeches—on the merits of the Constitution as a whole.[18]

Rush used this strategy early in the Pennsylvania ratifying convention. Ardent Anti-Federalist William Findley compared the Constitution to a new house, declaring that the purpose of the state convention was to examine its parts, accepting those which were "fitting . . . and rejecting everything that is useless and rotten." "That is not our situation," Rush retorted, "We are not, at this time called to raise the structure. The house is already built for us, and we are only asked, whether we choose to occupy it. If we find its apartments commodious, and upon the whole that it is well calculated to shelter us from the inclemencies of the storm that threatens, we shall act prudently in entering." But if the state conventions found the "structure" otherwise, Rush concluded, "all that is required of us is to return the key to those who have built and offered it for our use." Pragmatically speaking, Rush used his religious praise for the Constitution as a way of counteracting the Anti-Federalist strategy of death by amendment.[19]

As for the ideological context of Rush's metaphysical language, we have seen that biblical references were prevalent in American political culture at this time. But because of Rush's religious devoutness, it is possible to view his rhetorical style as possessing a greater level of biblical literalism than we would assume in the writings of men such as Thomas Jefferson, who used biblical allusions in a far more conventional way. When Rush used religious language in his letters and speeches, it was often as a way for him to mesh his religious beliefs with his scientific and philosophical studies. He recorded many of his meditations on this subject in his commonplace book. In one such instance, he wrote that "The affairs of men are governed alternately by and contrary to their wills, to teach us both to use our Reason and to rely upon Providence in all our undertakings." On another occasion, he wrote that "God reveals some truths to our senses and to our first perceptions," but "many errors are [also] conveyed into the mind through both, which are to be corrected only by reason." As an example of such a multifarious path to knowledge, Rush explained that without astronomical inquiry and investigation, mankind might still believe that the sun revolved around the earth. For Rush, men and women did not need to choose between enlightened reason and revealed religion. As paths to knowledge, they were complementary and interdependent. Accordingly, Rush sought to make sense of the Revolutionary events shaping his life by Christianizing the Enlightenment and enlightening Christianity.[20]

It was likely in this vein of thought that Rush professed his strong approval for the Constitution. Though his use of biblical language aligned with earlier American precedents for appropriating religion for ostensibly political ends, the ideological implications of Rush's claims went beyond mere political propaganda. It had been over a century since the divine right of kings had been a viable political theory in the British Atlantic. Constitutional thought in England, and subsequently America, had been largely shaped by the liberalism of Thomas Hobbes, John Locke, and others who maintained that civil society originated by social compact and not by divine appointment. By 1788, these ideas were prevalent, even commonplace, in American society. But the idea that some form of divine intervention influenced state formation had not yet vanished entirely. Rush had not been in the Constitutional Convention, but owing to his experience as a former member of Congress, he found it incredible that the framers had agreed on a system of government despite the many competing interests of the states they represented. When Rush ascribed the near unanimity of the delegates to divine intervention, he was suggesting that God still intervened in the formation of civil governments but that he did so in more enlightened, republican ways. It was, in a sense, the divine right of republics.[21]

Several other Federalists, however, were less philosophical and more fanatical in the way they appropriated and abridged Rush's theme of a "new species of divine right," using it instead to promote the Constitution as a test of Americans' Christianity. A Virginian writing as "Americanus" declared that the Constitution was "like the *Christian religion*, the more minutely it is discussed, the more perfect it will appear." He foretold that one day, "the *Bible* and the *Federal Government* will be read and reverenced [together]." "A Pennsylvania Minister" asked the public "whether men can be serious in regard to the Christian religion, who object to a government that is calculated to promote the glory of GOD, by establishing peace, order and justice in our Country?" Extending his rhetorical query to criticize Anti-Federalists, he asked "whether it would not be better for such men to renounce the Christian name, and to enter into society with the Shawnese or Mohawk Indians, than to attempt to retain the blessings of religion and civilization, with their licentious ideas of government?" In these oversimplified versions of Rush's theme, the Constitution was not merely a divinely inspired document but on the same theological level as scripture. To oppose ratification was to oppose the Christian canon.[22]

When viewed collectively, distinct patterns emerge from the Federalists' religious vocabulary. Besides the clear biblicism in their comparisons of the United States and ancient Hebrew constitutions, they placed a strong emphasis on terms such as "social order." They classified "chaos" and "disorder" as societal sins so as to depict the Constitution as a godsend, at once a tool of both God and government to "close the floodgates of immorality." To deny the civil and religious virtue of the Constitution was "licentious" and a view befitting "savage" Native American tribes but not "civilized" Christian societies. This was extreme language that hearkened back to the providential vocabulary of the American Revolution. Just as Revolutionaries declared "resistance to tyrants is obedience to God," Federalists conflated support of the Constitution with devotion to the Christian faith. The religious angle of promoting the Constitution was just one of many Federalist approaches, but it stands out because it added a simplistic trial of Christian belief to the more nuanced explanations of the political and ideological merits of the Constitution that men such as James Madison and Alexander Hamilton presented to the public. By canonizing the Constitution as a text and by Christianizing its spirit, religiously concerned Americans attempted to infuse the inherently secular document with spiritual meaning.[23]

The Federalists' sacrilization of the Constitution also reflected a high degree of self-consciousness about governments as man-made institutions. In discussing the relationship of the human body to the body politic,

Jean-Jacques Rousseau wrote that "the constitution of man is the work of nature; that of the state is the work of art." Yet, even as an artificial construct, American statesmen, like their European counterparts, saw some governments as more natural than others. The proposed constitution, Federalists argued, preserved the people's rights to life, liberty, and the pursuit of happiness—rights that the Declaration of Independence declared to have been "endowed" upon "all men" by "their Creator"—better than the Articles of Confederation or any other form of government could. Thus, by invoking religious language and symbolism in their campaign for ratification, Federalists showcased the way in which man-made government and the philosophy of natural rights ambiguously depended on God as a foundation.[24]

But Anti-Federalists did not cede to their opponents an exclusive claim to the language of providentialism in the ratification debates. In fact, they turned the tables on the Federalists by depicting ratification as a patently antiprovidential act. In examining the religious language and themes of Anti-Federalists, however, it is important to remember that this was not a cohesive group with a clear-cut ideology. What made many Americans "anti-Federalist" was the mere fact that they opposed Federalist calls for ratification, and not any uniform set of objections. Reconstructing the critiques of the Constitution made by Anti-Federalists, then, is inherently a challenging task. It involves piecing together speeches, pamphlets, articles, and letters that individual Anti-Federalists wrote with a variety of motives and in disparate contexts. Instead of a lucid, coherent Anti-Federalist ideology, what emerges from an examination of these opponents of the Constitution can be nothing more than thematic patterns. Yet these patterns are significant because they provide historians insights into the reasons so many Americans fought so vigorously to block ratification.[25]

Where the use of religious language and symbolism is concerned, the expressions of Anti-Federalists throughout the country display widespread uncertainty and anxiety about the future of the young country. These expressions revealed hesitancy among many Americans to accept vague assurances from Federalists that adopting the new federal Constitution was the only way they could secure the fruits of their recent Revolution. For instance, an Anti-Federalist from Virginia writing as "Denatus" wrote off claims that the Constitution was "a gift from heaven" as the ravings of "enthusiasts" who actually "know very little of gifts from heaven." An anonymous Massachusetts Anti-Federalist criticized the absence of any reference to God and his providence in the Constitution. "If civil rulers won't acknowledge God," he warned, God "won't acknowledge them; and they must perish from the way." Another opponent of the Constitution insisted that the proposed government was "deistical in principle, and in all probability the composers had no thought of God in all their consultations." To these men, there was no textual evidence that the Constitution was in line with America's providential destiny. In fact, they insisted that inasmuch as the text was the document's providential measure, the Constitution was wholly inadequate.[26]

Some of the harshest critics of the Constitution warned that the proposed government would quickly be overrun by "enemies" of Christianity. James Winthrop of Massachusetts, writing as "Agrippa," was almost persuaded to be a Federalist, but instead expressed his frustration that "the framers of this new Constitution did not think it necessary that the president should believe, that there is a God." This sentiment was echoed by several other Americans, including "Samuel," who rejected the Constitution because it allowed "a Pagan, a Mahometan, [or] a Bankrupt" to "fill the highest seat and every seat." We will turn our focus to the debate over the president's religious beliefs later in this chapter, but where the inclusion of providentialism in the ratification debates is concerned, the frequent invocation of the legal extension of tolerance to non-Christians in the Constitution is significant. While Federalists emphasized the way the Constitution was drafted in convention and the societal order it promised to restore as religious reasons to vote for ratification, Anti-Federalists called attention to the failure of the Constitution to favor and protect Christianity as religious reasons to vote against ratification.[27]

Other Anti-Federalists criticized those who depicted ratification as a test of an individual's Christianity. "Has it come to this, that no person of any denomination is a *Christian*, except those who pray for the adoption of the proposed Federal Constitution?" lamented "Lycurgus," a Pennsylvania Anti-Federalist. "If that constitution is as good as its most zealous devotees can imagine, I can by no means suppose that it will be considered at the *last day* (or ought to be at any other time) as a test of *Christianity*." The authors of "all such *scurrilous* reflections" who seek "publickly to *unchristianize* all such as do not pray for their particular system," he concluded, were merely trying to "prevent an *open, free, candid*, and *impartial* examination of such a momentous question" as the implementation of a new government. In many ways, claims and disclaimers about the Constitution as a measuring stick for the Christian devotion of an individual or a nation foreshadowed the tumultuous election of 1800. In 1787–88, as in 1800, political partisans deemed a proposed change in government essential to maintaining a person's religion, and their opponents were quick to call them out for manipulating personal spirituality for political gain. The Constitution hardly represented a moment of consensus among Americans on the role of religion in politics. More accurately, it set the tone for the debates on the matter that have flared up ever since. Historians will never find the framers' "original intent" where the relationship of religion to the political processes of the country is concerned because consensus on the matter never existed. Examining religion's role in the process of Constitution-making and ratification reveals more about the origins and development of American political culture than it does about the character of the country's governmental institutions.[28]

Some northern Anti-Federalists invoked the issue of slavery in order to counter Federalist claims of divine approbation for the Constitution. Their logic held that God could not possibly approve of a document that protected and perpetuated one race of men holding another in bondage as property. Hugh Hughes became one of the most outspoken Anti-Federalists on this issue. A political ally of George and DeWitt Clinton of New York, Hughes published essays that were simultaneously antislavery and Anti-Federalist. Hughes asked the public: "Is this the Way by which we are to demonstrate our gratitude to Providence, for his divine Interposition in our Favor, when oppressed by Great Britain? Who could have even imagined, that Men lately professing the highest Sense of Justice and the Liberties of Mankind, could so soon and easily be brought to give a Sanction to the greatest Injustice and Violation of those very Liberties?" Hughes concluded that the Constitution's endorsement of slavery would hardly qualify the country for the continued protection of Providence; rather it was "a Disgrace to the very Name of Christianity itself" that would "tarnish the Lustre of the American Revolution."[29]

Hughes and the Clintons were opposed to the Constitution in part because it threatened the sovereignty of their state, New York, as well as their faction's power therein. Yet this does not automatically discount their criticisms of the Constitution and its endorsement of slavery as disingenuous. As historian David Waldstreicher persuasively argues, the Constitution's "silences" on the issue of slavery are meaningful. The mere omission of the word slavery does not excuse the document from a proslavery label. Instead, "the debates and compromises over slavery played a central role in the creation of the U.S. Constitution, shaping the character and nature of the government it framed." The Constitution is decidedly proslavery, Waldstreicher concludes, because it "enacted mechanisms that empowered slaveholders politically, which would prevent the national government from becoming an immediate or likely impediment to the institution." Eighteenth-century Americans such as Hughes and the Clintons recognized this at the moment the Constitution was proposed and used its protection of slavery as a potent weapon in the political arsenal of the Anti-Federalists.[30]

But antislavery could never have become a successful Anti-Federalist rallying point nationwide. Though the Clintonians and other northern opponents of the Constitution attempted to coordinate their efforts with their southern counterparts, the Constitution's protection of slavery was actually one of the most attractive features of the new government in the South. For instance, when Charles Cotesworth Pinckney returned to South Carolina from the Philadelphia Convention, he happily reported to the state ratifying convention that "considering all circumstances, we have made the best terms for the security of this species of property [slavery] it was in our power to make. We would have made better [provisions] if we could, but on the whole I do not think them bad." For Pinckney and other southern Federalists, the proslavery provisions of the Constitution made ratification easier to sell. When southern Anti-Federalists took up the slavery issue, however, it was hardly to warn the public of the dangerous ground upon which the Constitution would place the nation. Instead, Anti-Federalists such as George Mason criticized the Constitution for not protecting slavery enough. "There is no clause in the Constitution that will prevent the Northern and Eastern states from meddling with our whole property of that kind [slavery]," Mason declared on the floor of the Virginia ratifying convention, adding that "There ought to be a clause in the Constitution to secure us that property, which we have acquired under former laws, and the loss of which would bring ruin on a great many people." Though Hughes and Mason both fought against ratification, where slavery was concerned, they could not have been further apart ideologically. Thus it was only in the northern states, where an abolitionist spirit was slowly kindling, that Anti-Federalists could declare the Constitution detrimental to America's providential mission on account of slavery.[31]

In small numbers during the eighteenth century, and in growing numbers during the nineteenth century, clergymen became prominent leaders in the antislavery movement. But the documentary history of the ratification debates suggests that in 1787–88 secular Anti-Federalists such as Hughes carried the antislavery banner in opposition to the proslavery Constitution more often than their clerical counterparts did. This observation does not serve as a retroactive indictment of Federalist clergymen for putting ecclesiastical and political interests over their humanitarian charges as Christian ministers. After all, many clergymen had actively condemned slavery during the Revolution, and the preaching of the Federalist clergy in the 1790s provided a fundamental ideological base and rhetorical tradition from which leaders of the nineteenth-century antislavery movement would consistently draw. But in this pivotal moment of American national formation, the cross of Christian humanitarianism was borne by politically motivated laymen instead of spiritually driven clergymen.[32]

Similarly, it was a layman, and not a clergyman, who provided what is perhaps the most telling example of why many Anti-Federalists took so much exception to Federalist claims that the Constitution's ratification was essential for maintaining national providential favor. Richard Henry Lee of Virginia was neither a scoffer of religion nor a religious zealot. An attorney from Westmoreland County, he belonged to the Church of England and its post-Revolutionary ecclesiastical descendant, the Protestant Episcopal Church. Yet Lee typically restricted his public writings to legal and constitutional reasoning. Thus he was deeply troubled by the ease with which Federalists were willing to overlook obvious flaws in the proposed government and enthusiastically ascribe divine sanction to the Constitution as a whole. Lee believed Federalists did this in order to mute debate and inhibit attempts to amend the document in the various state conventions. In terms of political strategies, he was the antithesis of Benjamin Rush. "It is neither prudent or easy to make frequent changes in government," Lee wrote to Edmund Pendleton, adding that "bad governments have been generally found the most fixed." Constitution-making was no trivial matter and it was incumbent upon Americans to approach the proposed government with close attention to potential flaws. Blatant defects, such as the absence of a bill of rights, should be addressed during the ratification process. Correcting them later could prove extremely difficult, if not impossible. "From *Moses* to *Montesquieu* the greatest geniuses have been employed on this difficult subject" of Constitution writing, Lee wrote in the same letter to Pendleton, "and yet experience has shown capital defects in the system produced for the government of mankind." Lee's message was clear: even the "Mosaic constitution" had defects; Americans should not view the proposed Constitution as somehow exceptional in this regard. To Lee, depicting the Constitution as an inspired, nearly canonical text was more than a cunning political maneuver employed by his opponents. It was a great and dangerous disservice to Americans.[33]

Some Federalists fired back at Lee, claiming that constitutional perfection was unattainable and that Americans should be pleased that the proposed government was the best mankind had yet devised. One writer even criticized Lee's focus on the Constitution's defects as an obsession with "the doctrine of infallibility" so common "in the *papal* dominions." By using language associated with American anti-Catholicism, Lee's critic was not necessarily calling him a Catholic but was assigning the label to his version of political theology. In this writer's view, American political theology was not to be fixed in perpetuity by an "infallible" document. Future Americans would be free to alter their government according to the needs of their respective generations; the spirit of American political theology was to be "protestant," not "papal." Yet Lee maintained his position that without a bill of rights, the Constitution would remain inadequate. No amount of Federalist insistence or providential rhetoric could persuade him otherwise.[34]

"It Has Been Much Oftener a Motive to Oppression Than a Restraint from It"

The Constitution did not establish the United States as a land of religious liberty. Though it freed the federal government from religious restrictions and the first amendment "guaranteed" Americans the right to worship according to the dictates of their own consciences, the realization of total religious liberty has proven elusive. American history is littered with examples of religious persecution, often at the hands of local, state, and national governments. The history of Jews, Muslims, Catholics, Mormons, and other religious groups outside "mainstream" Christianity exposes American religious freedom as one of the country's most egregious founding myths. Arguing that the United States *became* a land of religious liberty at the moment of the Constitution's adoption is akin to arguing that America became a land of racial equality with the passage of the Thirteenth, Fourteenth, and Fifteenth Amendments in the 1860s. It is simply not the case. Federal laws on the books do not always reflect or create reality on American streets.[35]

What, then, are we to make of the arguments over religious tests during the ratification debates? Historians commonly examine the exclusion of such tests dictated by Article VI, Section 3, of the Constitution as a moment in which religious liberty became enshrined as a central feature of the founding era. There were certainly Americans eager to make religious liberty an immediate reality, yet many individual states continued to implement and enforce religiously restrictive laws within their own borders that a fledgling federal government was unable to overrule. It was not until the mid-twentieth

century that the U.S. Supreme Court began to consistently enforce the provisions in the Constitution for religious freedom upon the functions of state
government. At most, the framers of the Constitution and the first Congress
can be credited with laying the legal foundation for a government that began
to regularly use its power to protect the rights of conscience more than 150
years later. There is much more to the debate over religious tests as a prerequisite for federal office holding than the pragmatic and legal operations of
government. It was about more than whether or not the country would support an established church or officially adopt a national religion. The broader
implication of this debate was what early Americans thought about the connection between religion and public morality.[36]

Madison touched on this very subject when writing to Jefferson in the fall
of 1787. He conceded that in a republic as large as the United States, natural
and artificial majorities united by a "common interest" or a "common passion" would arise. Restraints were necessary to prevent such a majority from
oppressing minorities. Many Americans claimed that religion would serve
as an effective check on such corruption and oppression. Madison, however,
was unconvinced, writing that "The inefficacy of this restraint on individuals
is well known. The conduct of every popular Assembly, acting on oath, the
strongest of religious ties, shews that individuals join without remorse in acts
against which their consciences would revolt, if proposed to them separately
in their closets." Madison's comments were philosophical reflections based
upon historical empiricism. Still, as Americans set about organizing a republic much larger than their classical predecessors would have thought possible or prudent, participants in the ratification debates frequently invoked
religion as the surest safeguard against corruption and immorality among
public office holders. Accordingly, they called for the Constitution to institute religious tests, or at least religious oaths, as a prerequisite for office
holding in the federal government. Madison concluded that such tests and
oaths would do more harm than good because, historically, religion "has been
much oftener a motive to oppression than a restraint from it."[37]

By banning religious tests as prerequisites for federal office holding in
Article VI, Section 3, Madison hoped to reconstruct on a national scale the
religious liberty he and Jefferson had recently helped to achieve in Virginia,
and many other Federalists rallied around this effort. Isaac Backus, a Baptist
minister from Massachusetts and fierce opponent of the Congregationalist
establishment in that state, believed that the prohibition of religious tests was
one of the best features of the Constitution. In fact, it is the primary reason

Backus agreed to attend the Massachusetts ratifying convention at all. According to his diary, when his townsmen informed him of his selection as a delegate to the convention, his initial thought was, "I should not go." But upon further reflection, he changed his mind. "As religious liberty is concerned in the affair," he wrote, "and many were earnest for my going, I consented." Once in Boston, a contingent of delegates cited the prohibition of religious tests as a significant reason for opposing ratification because it opened the government to "Papists and Pagans," so that "the Inquisition may be established in America." Backus vigorously defended the Constitution against such overly dramatic and hypocritical charges. "Nothing is more evident, both in reason, and in the holy scriptures," Backus argued on the Convention floor, "than that religion is ever a matter between God and individuals; and therefore no man or men can impose any religious test, without invading the essential prerogatives of our Lord Jesus Christ. . . . [If] the history of all nations be searched . . . it will appear that the imposing of religious tests hath been the greatest engine of tyranny in the world." Concluding his remarks, Backus demonstrated the illogic of Anti-Federalist claims that Article VI, Section 3, would lead to Catholic-imposed inquisitions in the United States, as such events could only come about through the implementation of religious tests. Backus did not believe the Constitution would destroy religious establishments in one fell swoop, but he clearly saw the question of its ratification as a major battle in the prolonged war to liberate American consciences.[38]

Another Massachusetts Federalist echoed Backus's sentiments but took his zeal for the Constitution even further. Under the title "Truth," this anonymous writer trumpeted the fact that in the Constitution, "Religion [is] left to its guardian God—all *tests, oaths,* and *hamperings of the conscience* of our fellow men [are] entirely done away." This and "millions" of other reasons, he concluded, "evince the *perfection* of the proposed Constitution, and ensure its cordial adoption, if common sense and common honesty have not forsaken the majority of the people." It is unlikely that this political activist used the term "common sense" incidentally. With such language, he invoked the influential rhetoric of Thomas Paine that had successfully encouraged millions of Americans to break their social and political ties with the king of England. In this rhetorical vein, he insinuated that by adopting a Constitution with an explicit prohibition of religious tests, Americans were continuing their ongoing Revolution to put off the tyranny of monarchy and to clothe themselves in the robes of republican liberty.[39]

Other Federalists who cited the prohibition of religious tests as reason enough to support ratification did so for reasons less grandiose than Madison's vision of the United States as a land of religious liberty. Instead, they appealed to Article VI, Section 3, solely as a way of defending the Constitution against Anti-Federalist charges that the proposed government was "godless." A telling example of this appeared in Connecticut newspapers in which "A Landholder" wrote at length about the history of religious tests. "The pretense for making these severe laws . . . was to exclude the Papists," he explained, "but the real design was to exclude the Protestant dissenters." Owing to the disingenuous implementation of such laws in individual colonies and states, he declared that "the nature of [religious tests] and the effects which they are calculated to produce make them useless, tyrannical, and peculiarly unfit for the people of this country." These were practical arguments about the proper place of religion in the new nation. According to this writer's logic, the Constitution was neither abandoning nor assaulting religion by excluding religious tests. Instead, it was opening the government to white, landholding men of all faiths. If these provisions were an assault on anything, it was the hegemony that specific denominations had traditionally exercised on American governments. If such a religious test was implemented on a national level, it would doom the new nation to failure from the outset by incapacitating "three-fourths of the American citizens for any public office; and thus degrade them from the ranks of freemen."[40]

It is important to observe, however, that not all Federalists toed the line with Madison and company when it came to the Constitution's prohibition against religious tests. Federalists in several states called for the inclusion of religious requirements by amendment. They were not trying to block ratification but merely saw the need to tweak the Constitution. Samuel Adams was initially reluctant to give his full support to the Constitution because it prohibited religious tests. Another Federalist, Edmund Pendleton of Virginia, expressed a similar concern in a letter to Madison. "My last Criticism you will probably laugh at, tho' it is really a Serious one with me," Pendleton wrote. "Why require an Oath From Public Officers, and yet interdict all Religious Tests, their only Sanction?" Pendleton argued that "a belief of a Future State of Rewards & Punishments, can alone give conscientious Obligation to Observe an Oath" and that a "Test should be required or Oaths Abolished." To Pendleton, religious tests and oaths of office were an all-or-nothing proposition, and he was convinced that the inclusion of both would be beneficial to ensure the virtue of federal office holders. Ultimately, his appeal did not convince Madison. Instead, Pendleton put aside his reservations about the

Constitution and assured Madison of his "unequivocal acceptance of it, with all its imperfections." These examples demonstrate that arguments for and against the inclusion of religious tests were not entirely bound by faction lines. Even within the Federalist camp there was not consensus on the issue.[41]

Anti-Federalists extracted an entirely different meaning from the exclusion of religious tests in the proposed Constitution. Many of them saw the provision as part of an elaborate conspiracy concocted by irreligious men to completely destroy religious life in the United States. The Constitution "was a plot to take away our religious and civil liberties, and make slaves of us," claimed one Anti-Federalist, adding that with ratification, "our religion [would be] taken away from us, and that popery, or no religion at all, would be established in its stead." Others claimed that religious tests were not impediments to religious liberty but in fact necessities for maintaining such a freedom. For example, John Leland of Virginia complained that "No religious test is required as a Qualification to fill any office under the United States, but if a Majority of Congress with the [President] favour one System more than another, they may oblige all others to pay to the Support of their System." To Leland, a "Constitutional defense" was needed for the protection of religion in the long term, as "it is Very Dangerous leaving religious Liberty at [the government's] mercy." Like their Federalist opponents, these Anti-Federalists declared that they acted in the name of religious liberty. Yet the Anti-Federalist approach to such liberty was far more conservative than that of their counterparts who believed that the consciences of Americans would only be set free when the government ceased to meddle with religion entirely.[42]

Certainly the most extreme language Anti-Federalists employed where religious tests were concerned depicted the United States under the presidential leadership of a non-Christian. In a list of the Constitution's deficiencies, "A Watchman" emphasized that "There is a door opened for the Jews, Turks [Muslims], and Heathen to enter into publick office and be seated at the head of the government of the United States." A New York Anti-Federalist writing as "Curtiopolis" explained the dangerous possibilities the proposed Constitution created because in addition to Protestant dissenters such as Quakers and Baptists, "it admits to legislation . . . Mahometans, who ridicule the doctrine of the trinity . . . Deists, abominable wretches . . . [and] Jews." Since the Constitution gave "the command of the whole militia to the President—should he hereafter be a Jew, our dear posterity may be ordered to rebuild Jerusalem." Amos Singletary, a delegate to the Massachusetts ratifying convention, similarly trumpeted a warning to his fellow religiously minded delegates:

"I think we are giving up all our privileges, as there is no provision in *this here* self same Constitution, that men in power should have any religion—and though I hope to see *Christian* Creatures, yet by *this here* constitution a *Papish* or an *Infidelist* are as eligible as they." Lest modern readers assume that such fanatical—if not bigoted—claims were simply expressions of genuine concern for the spiritual well-being of Americans, we must consider the political calculations behind such rhetoric.[43]

By invoking the image of a Catholic, Jewish, or Muslim president, Anti-Federalists forced Americans to consider a future religious landscape in which Protestant Christianity was not the dominant faith. The idea of a Catholic, Jewish, or Muslim ascending to the presidency in the 1790s was inconceivable. At this time, there were approximately twenty-five thousand Catholics in the United States, comprising less than 2 percent of the white population. American Jews numbered just over a thousand, and most of them lived in one of six coastal cities. American Muslims were so rare that historians estimate their total population could have been counted on one hand. Yet the fact that most eighteenth-century Americans had never met a Muslim did not stop Anti-Federalists from utilizing inherited prejudices against Muslims in their campaign to reject the Constitution. As historian Denise A. Spellberg writes, "The image of Muslims as citizens remained at the foreign perimeter of possibility, but their role in domestic debate about religious identity and citizenship demonstrated new strategic possibilities for opponents of the Constitution." By arguing the possibility of a Muslim president, Spellberg explains, the ratification debates "moved imagined Muslims from the margins to the heart of the debate about religious rights and political equality." Anti-Federalists hoped that their charges would severely damage the position of the Federalists by forcing them to publicly defend Catholics, Jews, and Muslims and thereby lose popular support.[44]

Yet, the calculations of these Anti-Federalists went beyond the ratification question. What if the religious demographics of the country did in fact change at some point in the future and these populations of religious "others" grew to the point that a non-Protestant could occupy the presidency? In such a future state, Protestant Christianity would no longer dominate American religious life. This was the scenario Anti-Federalists were asking Americans to consider; this was the fear they were trying to instill in their audiences. In this sense, imposing religious tests nationally was less about maintaining a citizenry that believed in God than it was about political strategy and maintaining a hierarchical system of religious-political hegemony.

While many historians continue to insist that religion was inherently connected to eighteenth-century American conceptions of republican virtue, the ratification debates challenge this myth. A "Christian Sparta" in which classical republicanism rested upon Christian conceptions of morality and virtue was a vision of many eighteenth-century Americans, but not all. The fact that religion became such a volatile issue in the press and on the floors of state ratifying conventions demonstrates that Americans did not *automatically* assume religion was *necessary* to maintain public virtue and that even American clergymen were unconvinced of the viability of a secular government that depended alone on a particular brand of religious morality. Religion as a foolproof guard against public corruption was not an agreed-upon tenet of American political thought. While religion was a significant issue that carried real influence in the creation of the American republic, the founding generation did not agree upon it as a fundamental and stabilizing principle upon which the republic was founded.[45]

FIVE

Preaching Party

"Ring the Bells backward! The Temple, the Temple is on Fire! The High Priests look aghast . . . and all cry out, The Craft, the Craft is in Danger!" With these expressive lines, Englishman John Trenchard sarcastically opened the third installment of his popular 1720 work, *The Independent Whig.* Trenchard went on to observe "that no Order or Society of Men is so apprehensive of Disrespect, or can so little bear the Examination into their Pretensions, as the greatest Part of the Ecclesiasticks. . . . If you ridicule or laugh at the Professions of Law and Physick, the Lawyers and Physicians will laugh with you." But if you "touch the Pretenses and Vices of the Meanest of the Ecclesiasticks, so many of their Body are in an Uproar: They roar loud . . . [that] Religion itself is in Danger of being subverted." Trenchard directed his remarks to members of the English clergy who abused the power and trust of their office to fatten themselves and fill their pockets. But the implications of this indictment extended beyond the contemptible character of corrupt clergymen. Clergymen were a sensitive, defensive lot in eighteenth-century England. When threatened, they sought to silence their critics by declaring that religion was in danger.[1]

The Independent Whig, written for an early-eighteenth-century English audience, was popular in Revolutionary America for its expressions of Whig political philosophy. Though Trenchard's critique of corrupt clergymen was aimed at his English contemporaries, his criticism serves as an apt description of the way American clergymen responded to the erosion of their social and cultural authority in the decades following independence. In the wake of the Revolution, long-standing efforts to disestablish churches gained momentum and began to succeed in several states. While many ministers rejoiced in what they viewed as the liberation of Americans' consciences, others despaired at what they suspected was a death knell for their once prominent position in American society. Like their English counterparts in the 1720s, when post-Revolutionary American clerics felt threatened, they fought back and roared loudly.[2]

In the 1790s, clergymen actively participated in the formation of America's first political parties, and their participation was directly tied to post-Revolutionary shifts in American religious and political culture. Some of these politicized clergymen were eager to destroy the hegemony of established churches. Others were anxious to shore up their cultural authority. Still others seemed to follow the political disposition of their respective congregations in order to remain popular and socially relevant. At first glance, it is tempting to conclude that ministers from established churches—and those recently disestablished—became Federalists because of the party's message of hierarchy and social order, believing the party's success would help them to regain and retain their traditional voice in American society. Similarly, it is tempting to conclude that ministers from dissenting Protestant denominations became Republicans because of the party's opposition to elite, monarchical-like control over society and government, believing that the party's success would further the influences of their respective denominations in the new national religious landscape. While there were numerous examples of these two trends throughout the country, they do not adequately explain the early political partisanship of American clergymen on a national level. Local power dynamics and cultural idiosyncrasies created too many exceptions to make such assertions hard and fast rules.

Because there were no public opinion polls or voter registration by party in the 1790s, it is not possible to quantify the partisanship of the American clergy with any degree of precision. Yet the politicized sermons and newspaper essays of Federalist and Republican ministers help us to compare the nature of clerical activism in different states and regions. Indeed, to understand how and why American clergymen preached party from their pulpits, it is essential that we understand the challenges they were facing in different localities. Doing so reveals more than the voting habits of a few dozen ministers. It grants new insights into the formation of political parties in general. National issues and federal policy often dominate historical narratives of the power struggles between Federalists and Republicans. But in many instances, local issues mattered as much as national issues, if not more. In the case of late-eighteenth-century clergymen, they helped build political parties nationally in order to maintain their cultural authority locally.

"The People Must Be Taught to Confide in and Reverence Their Rulers"

The Federalist Party certainly benefited from the partisan activity of ministers in state-established churches, as well as those from denominations that had recently been disestablished. This was particularly the case in Massachusetts. But in other states, such as Virginia, many in this same clerical demographic supported the Republican party. Why did the Federalist message of deference to elites and the preservation of established hierarchies appeal so much to some of these ministers but not to others? In the case of Virginia, the appeal of Federalism to such clergymen was mitigated by more pressing social and religious concerns.

The ministers of the state-established Congregationalist Church in Massachusetts made up a group commonly called the Standing Order. Though state law prohibited clergymen from holding public office, the ministers of the Standing Order wielded substantial cultural authority and dominated their society through the seventeenth and eighteenth centuries. Massachusetts ministers were rarely wealthy, yet the laity respected and commonly deferred to them because they were among the most educated men in the colony and were charged with using biblical exegesis to explain and justify the colony's unique culture. To be a Congregationalist minister in mid-eighteenth-century Massachusetts was to be at or near the top of the social ladder.[3]

But as the turn of the nineteenth century approached, the Standing Order slowly drifted into crisis. Several political and social developments assaulted the power of Congregationalist ministers, but the most threatening of such in the 1790s and early 1800s were cries throughout the country for the disestablishment of state-sponsored churches. These cries were loudest south of Massachusetts, where, in the aftermath of the Revolution, many of the new state governments embraced religious liberty as a basic human right. But there was also a growing movement for disestablishment within Massachusetts led by Baptist ministers such as Isaac Backus. The state's Baptist population had steadily increased since the Great Awakening and was growing increasingly impatient with the stranglehold the Congregationalist Church held on power.[4]

Many Congregationalist ministers in Massachusetts joined their counterparts in neighboring Connecticut in publicly rejecting the language of religious liberty and freedom of conscience that Republicans championed. They claimed that such language was merely a façade masking a sinister Republican plot to destroy religious life in the United States. In this sense, religious liberty and all that the phrase implied was a contagion that would eventually infect their state if the philosophies of men such as Thomas Jefferson and James Madison were allowed to dictate government policy. Reverend Ludovicus Weld, for instance, called Republicans "destroyers" who sought to dismantle the country by pretending to be "The Friends of the People" who desired to "break the shackles of tyranny." Reverend Asahel Hooker similarly argued that the Republicans sought "great things for themselves . . . under the profusion of smooth words, and fair professions of regard to 'the rights and liberties of the people.'" But once they obtained positions of power, Hooker warned, they would "wage war against religion, under the pretence of saving it from a destructive alliance with the political interest of their country." Calls for religious freedom, Reverend Zebulon Ely concluded, were nothing more than "the lullaby of liberty and equality" Republicans used to "cover sinister designs" and to acquire power. In this context, the emphasis the Federalist Party placed upon deference to traditional elites became an attractive idea by which Congregationalist ministers could inoculate their congregations from the contagion of religious liberty and, by doing so, protect their own cultural authority and livelihood.[5]

Massachusetts ministers strongly in favor of protecting the state's religious establishment were not the only clergymen drawn to the message of the Federalist Party. In fact, the rise of Federalism in Massachusetts created a temporary bridge over the ever-widening gap between liberal and orthodox ministers within Congregationalism. This theological schism originated in Boston, where wealthy merchants flocked to liberal ministers whose latitudinarian preaching justified their pursuit of wealth, as opposed to the austerity traditionally valued in the Calvinism of the Puritans. Eventually, these merchants and liberal preachers took control of the city's Congregationalist churches as well as the theological faculty at Harvard. This symbiotic union allowed wealthy merchants to bypass the stringent requirements for full church membership of more orthodox congregations and thereby gain social legitimation. In turn, liberal ministers built financial stability based upon support from their wealthy patrons as opposed to the support of the state alone. While many of these liberal ministers supported the continuance of the state established religion, it was less of a priority for them than it was for the more orthodox Congregationalist clergy. The latitudinarian doctrine and the relaxed standards for church membership infuriated many of these orthodox Congregationalist ministers who made up the vast majority of churchmen outside Boston, but there was no easy institutional solution to these doctrinal disputes, because the church had no central governing body. Instead, the schism was left to grow wider until total separation between the two factions eventually occurred in the early nineteenth century.[6]

In the 1790s and the early 1800s, however, orthodox and liberal ministers united temporarily under the umbrella of the Federalist Party. This political unity had less to do with safeguarding the religious establishment than it did with protecting the clergy's authoritative voice on religious and political matters in light of the spreading effects of the Reign of Terror in France. The Massachusetts clergy initially reveled in the events of the French Revolution, particularly the major blow it dealt to the Catholic Church in that country. In fact, they joined many of their countrymen in declaring the French Revolution an extension of the American Revolutionary spirit. But they changed their tune when the principles of "liberté, egalité, and fraternité" trumpeted by French revolutionaries rapidly shifted into near anarchy as the Jacobins extended their hostility toward Catholic priests to all Christian ministers. They also became alarmed at the extreme violence Jacobins perpetrated, as that Revolutionary group executed more than forty thousand of their countrymen as "enemies" of the Revolution. Those "enemies" whom they did not kill, they imprisoned in wretched conditions. Based on their own experiences a decade earlier, Americans understood all too well that some violence and deprivations were necessary aspects of a struggle to overthrow a tyrannical political order. But the nature and extent of violence under the Jacobins seemed entirely unnatural and appalling to many Americans. As news of the Reign of Terror flowed across the Atlantic, many Americans became convinced that the French Revolution was nothing like their own. Those Americans who remained devoted supporters of the French Revolution—the majority of whom aligned themselves politically with the emerging Republican Party—earnestly hoped that the Jacobins' reign would be a brief anarchic moment in what would otherwise be a virtuous and thoroughly republican revolution. The benefit of hindsight tells us that this was wishful thinking. But to these American Francophiles, it was hope born out of a belief that republicanism would spring forth from the infant American nation to renew the corrupt, aging polities of Europe.[7]

Members of the Standing Order certainly did not share this optimism. They worried that French sympathizers in the United States would similarly try to overthrow all forms of authority, both secular and religious. "Who are the open and avowed opposers of Christianity?" Reverend John Prince of

Salem asked in a 1798 sermon. "Are they not those men who are endeavour-
ing to put down all rule and all authority in every nation, that *their* will and
power alone may govern the world?" According to Prince, American Francophiles were not only deluded; they were dangerous. As the divide between
Federalists and Republicans on foreign policy grew, the Congregationalist
clergy expanded their application of the "dangerous" label from American
Francophiles to the entire Republican Party. The partisanship of Congregationalist clergymen on issues beyond the French Revolution generally
matched that of Federalist clergymen elsewhere. Those key political issues
are examined later in this chapter, but none of them mobilized the Standing
Order of Massachusetts in the same way that the Federalists' opposition to
the French Revolution did. Congregationalist ministers firmly aligned themselves with the foreign policy of the emerging Federalist Party, insisting that
the preservation of the party's influence nationally was essential to maintaining clerical authority locally.[8]

The fundamental distrust of "the people" at the heart of the Federalist platform was especially attractive to Congregationalist ministers watching their
place in the social hierarchy of Massachusetts grow increasingly tenuous. The
comments they made in their politicized sermons echoed the sentiments of
lay Federalists such as Boston merchant Stephen Higginson, who wrote that
in order prevent the American experiment with republicanism from degen-
erating into utter anarchy, "the people must be *taught* to confide in and reverence their rulers." While Congregationalist clergymen never referred to themselves explicitly as "rulers," they certainly saw themselves as leaders the people
must treat with respect and deference. It makes sense, then, that so many of
these clergymen became active Federalists. The party appeared as a lifeline of
sorts, a way to slow or altogether halt democratizing forces that threatened the
privileged place of clergymen in Massachusetts society. The Federalist Party
was the Standing Order's last best hope. In hindsight, the prognostications
of Federalist clergymen were right. Although the fall of the Standing Order
was the result of numerous social, religious, and political forces at play, it was
only after the demise of the Federalist Party in the 1810s, and the continued
democratization of American society in the 1820s, that the shell of this once-
powerful Congregationalist establishment finally shattered in 1833.[9]

Virginia was a significantly different situation than Massachusetts where
the partisanship of clergymen who favored religious establishments was concerned. More than any other state, the partisanship of Virginia's Episcopal
ministers demonstrates how the appeal of Federalism to proestablishment

clergymen was mitigated by other factors. When the Revolution broke out, ministers of the Church of England in Virginia were much more evenly split between patriotism and loyalism than Anglican ministers in other colonies. This had a lot to do with the way the Anglican clergy had become so intertwined with the colonial government, as well as the increasingly local origins of these ministers. In the eighteenth century, it became common for Virginia parishes to fill ministerial vacancies with clergymen who had been born and educated in the colony instead of "importing" ministers from England. Historian George Brydon argues that, as a result, Anglican clergymen in Virginia "more commonly voiced the ideals and attitudes of the people of the church into which they had been born rather than those of the people of England which was three thousand miles away." The colony's homegrown clergy felt greater personal connections to Virginia and more easily related to the political grievances of their neighbors than their religious counterparts in other states. Accordingly, more Anglican clergymen chose to remain in post-Revolutionary Virginia than chose to flee the country.[10]

The church reorganized after the Revolution and became the Protestant Episcopal Church, but its religious dominance had an expiration date. In order to persuade religious dissenters to support the Revolution, the Anglican establishment had negotiated increased religious liberty for dissenting sects and denominations. In 1786, religious freedom became the law of the land. Virginia's Episcopal clergymen continued to wield considerable political influence but were left without the benefit of state support.[11]

The fact that a majority of Episcopal ministers had opposed Jefferson and Madison's campaign for religious liberty in the 1780s did not prevent many of them from supporting the Republican Party in the 1790s. There are no concrete statistics of party affiliation among the Virginia clergy, as there was no party-based voter registration at this time. Typically, the political disposition of a clergyman during this era is only identifiable if he made it known in the sermons he preached or the letters he wrote. So it is significant that many Episcopal ministers who had once been highly vocal on political issues either fell silent or preached fervently in opposition to Federalist policies and candidates. This suggests that the Episcopal clergy in Virginia did not flock to the Federalist Party as had ministers accustomed to state-supported religion in other states. Religious affiliation was less indicative of political disposition in Virginia than it was in Massachusetts.

There are several possible explanations for this inconsistency. The first goes back to the fact that most of these Episcopal clergymen were Virginia born and raised. They likely felt a fierce loyalty to the state and its interests within the new union, and in many ways Jefferson and Madison had based their opposition to the Washington and Adams administrations on what they thought was in Virginia's best interest. The Virginia economy was agrarian based and Hamilton's economic plan for the country threatened to marginalize the Old Dominion. It is reasonable, then, to speculate that in choosing sides, many Episcopal ministers set aside their contention with Madison and Jefferson over matters of church and state in order to protect Virginia from the ill effects of Federalist policies. After all, the few decidedly Federalist areas in this otherwise Republican bastion of a state were in Richmond (Federalist John Marshall's hometown) and surrounding the upper Chesapeake, where commerce was a major sector of local economies. In these places, clergy and laity alike united in an uphill battle against the Republican majority. The Episcopal clergymen who actively promoted the Republican Party in Virginia were not surrendering their religious stance so much as they were prioritizing their ideological positions in order to protect what they believed was best for their home state.[12]

But Episcopal clergymen in Virginia may also have been drawn to the Republican Party because they were more democratic to begin with than their religious counterparts elsewhere, particularly where ecclesiastical organization was concerned. The creation of a national union of Protestant Episcopal churches almost failed before it started when northern ministers rejected the practice of southern Episcopalians allowing laymen to vote in their conventions. Northern Episcopal leaders such as Bishop Samuel Seabury thought southern Episcopalians were already too democratic in the years immediately following the Revolution. Southern Episcopalians in turn thought Seabury and other northern churchmen were too hierarchical and intransigent in preserving the Anglican high church tradition. These tendencies in ecclesiastical government cannot fully explain the partisanship of the disestablished Virginia clergy nearly a decade later, but they suggest that many of Virginia's Episcopalian ministers approached the political divisions of the 1790s already embracing a democratic spirit.[13]

"The Selfish Enlargement of Mind"

Alexander Hamilton's plan for the development of American manufacturing and commerce never mobilized Federalist clergymen in quite the same way it did the secular base of the party. The common ground on which secular and religious leaders in the party met was the shared desire to maintain a culture of deference to elites. This was by design. When Hamilton and his political collaborators developed Federalist talking points, they accounted for the ambition of clergymen to retain their traditional authority. The most popular fodder among the Federalist clergy was the Republican Party's embrace of democratic principles set forth in the radical Enlightenment and its support for the French Revolution. During these early moments in the formation of American civil religion, Federalist ministers did not separate religious and political concerns. Instead, they tied the fate of the federal government to the fate of American religion in general.[14]

While Hamilton and his secular followers largely focused on the way Enlightenment philosophy made men such as Jefferson too "soft" and "effeminate" to effectively lead the country, the clerical wing of the party based its political attacks on more spiritual implications of elevating Republican "philosophes" to positions of power. They were especially critical of the rise of deism in America as a result of the Enlightenment. Deists accepted the existence of God and his role as the creator of man and nature but rejected the notion of divine intervention in human affairs ever since. They were particularly skeptical of miracles, believing them to be the fabrications of superstitious men unwilling to accept rational explanations for events based upon the natural laws of the world. As several states eliminated religious tests for office holding during the last quarter of the eighteenth century, Americans throughout the country warned that the blessing of religious liberty carried with it the risk of a government run by deists and other "infidels." Some Federalist clergymen were even more cynical in their outlook. Prominent ministers such as Ezra Stiles claimed that the public was increasingly under the false impression that "deists, and men of indifferentism to all religion are the most suitable for civil office." There were, in fact, deists claiming that their beliefs made them superior public servants, and nearly all such men supported the Republican Party. Still, deists were a minority within the party. Framing the deist-Republican connection as a secret conspiracy allowed Stiles and other like-minded clergymen to publicly portray Republican calls for religious liberty as a façade for plans to destroy religion altogether. They argued that philosopher-politicians lacked the ability to effectively lead the young country in this world and endangered Americans' salvation in the next.[15]

Though these Federalist ministers claimed that their warnings against deism were fueled entirely by a genuine concern for Americans' spiritual well-being, their prejudice appears to have been born out of a keen ecclesiastical self-interest as well. Deism was a private religion. There was no deist church. Most men and women explored the rational religion in private homes and salons. Thus the spread of deism threatened to decrease the number of bodies in church pews each Sunday. In fact, without any empirical data, many clergymen blamed deism for the post-Revolutionary drop in church attendance. Boston minister Jeremy Belknap wrote of deism as if it were a plague ravaging Christian congregations everywhere. "A Species of vulgar infidelity . . . is insinuating itself into the minds of the thoughtless," Belknap wrote, "and the most sacred truths are rejected and ridiculed, without an examination of their evidence, or a consideration of their importance." American clergymen at this time frequently drew a correlation between communal spirituality and church attendance, and at times they gauged the level of society's spirituality by the full and timely payment of their salaries. For example, in 1801 a pair of Episcopal ministers leading St. Michael's Church in Charleston remarked that "it [was] hurtful to their feelings, as regular bred clergymen, who wish to support themselves with Dignity, as well as comfort, that their faithful service should any longer be undervalued, especially at a time when blessings of an unexampled Influx of Wealth hath happily superseded the Plea of inability to pay the demands of the Church." The economy was thriving in Charleston, yet the city's clergymen were not. In this case, ministers interpreted their pecuniary condition as the result of a decreasing religious commitment among their congregation. Late-eighteenth-century clergymen's worries for American spirituality, and the effects of deism thereupon, did not preclude their concern for the income that maintained their lives and lifestyles.[16]

But the spread of deism threatened more than the size of Christian congregations or the value of ministers' pocketbooks. There was also much at stake in the very way deists chose to describe their ideology. By referring to their religion as "rational," deists effectively implied that traditional Protestants and enthusiastic evangelicals were "irrational." Since colonial days, ministers had maintained their place among the educated elite of American society. It was from this prestige that the clergy drew much of its cultural and social authority. The inference that Protestant Christianity was "irrational" cut at the source of clerical prominence. Deism represented a personal assault.[17]

Just how real was the threat of deism? There is no accurate way of knowing precisely how many deists existed in America during the 1780s and 1790s. Furthermore, eighteenth-century deists existed along a spectrum. As historian Eric Schlereth explains, some deists used the "rejection of supernatural revelation in favor of reason as the only source of religious knowledge . . . to offer moderate calls for the reformation of Christianity," while others "hoped that deism would destroy all religious systems that included supernatural or metaphysical teachings." While some deists attacked organized religion, others faithfully maintained their pew rentals. Though deist newspapers and volunteer associations became common in the 1800s, at no point in the early republic was there a central organization to which all deists belonged. It is likely that eighteenth-century clergymen were just as incapable of accurately gauging the number of American deists as are present day historians. Dismissing the clergy's warnings of the spiritual danger that deism presented to Americans would be imprudent, but it is important to understand that such warnings created a straw man that was convenient to attack publicly for ecclesiastical and political gain. In the ill-defined and unorganized body of American deists, Protestant ministers discovered a convenient scapegoat on which to lay the blame for decline in American religiosity, as well as a powerful foil for Federalist candidates at all levels of government.[18]

Despite the extreme nature of these antideist claims, the Federalists were not as anti-Enlightenment as their political rhetoric led so many to believe. Over the last three decades, historians have steadily shifted away from the idea of a singular, monolithic Enlightenment toward the notion of myriad overlapping enlightenments that occurred around the globe. Though these different enlightenments informed and inspired one another, each developed amid unique intellectual, cultural, and political circumstances. Americans, then, could embrace one strand of Enlightenment reasoning while rejecting others. For Federalists, the musings of radical French philosophers were a serious threat to the hierarchical order of American society. Yet this did not prevent Federalist policy makers from embracing more conservative brands of Enlightenment reason.[19]

Hamilton, for instance, drew a great deal of Revolutionary inspiration from the Scottish Enlightenment, particularly the writings of David Hume. Hume was skeptical of rationalists who insisted that reason was the basic driving force of human behavior. Hume argued that desire, not reason, governed behavior, famously writing that "Reason is, and ought only to be the slave of passions." During the Revolution, Hamilton condemned British oppression of American rights and interests—their "desires"—without concluding that monarchy was inherently corrupt, as had many of his fellow Revolutionaries. Hume's realism strongly informed Hamilton's controversial economic program as well. He based his plan upon the premise that the desires of the country's wealthy elite to remain both wealthy and elite would keep the Revolutionary experiment in republican government afloat. For Hamilton, the enlightenments of the seventeenth and eighteenth centuries were a philosophical menu to be ordered from à la carte as one's political and intellectual dispositions required.[20]

In many instances, the Federalist clergy followed Hamilton's intellectual habits. During the Revolution, many clergymen who eventually became stalwart Federalists relied on select Enlightenment philosophies in their advocacy for the patriot cause. They filled their sermons with references to liberal thinkers such as John Locke and Whigs such as John Trenchard. When loyalist clergymen condemned the Revolution by citing Romans 13:1–4 ("Let every soul be subject unto the higher powers . . ."), patriot clergymen could not counter such attacks by scripture alone. They had to apply republican ideology to explain the American exception to this apostolic decree, chiefly that by acting tyrannically, the king had broken the "social contract" and was no longer under the protection of these scriptural verses. The patriot clergy may not have admitted it, but in such instances Christian theology and ancient scripture by themselves proved inadequate tools to fully justify and inspire revolution. American clergymen—including future Federalists—turned to Enlightenment philosophy to fill in the gaps of their spiritual politics.

Lay and clerical Federalists, then, were not necessarily hypocritical in their condemnation of Enlightenment reason and the Republicans that continued to embrace it. As historian Jeffrey Pasley explains, "The Federalist backlash against enlightened culture and philosophy was perhaps more a theme or a talking point than a fully formed intellectual position. All of the Founders were children of the Enlightenment in the broadest sense, and there would have been no American republic without the political science of John Locke." The Federalists' strategy was "to bring popular anti-intellectualism . . . into play against Jefferson." In their view, moderate enlightened philosophy had facilitated the successful transfer of power from the ruling elite in England to the aggrieved elite in America. It was the more progressive and democratic Enlightenment espoused by Democratic-Republican clubs that threatened to take the Revolution too far. Americans who embraced such radical thought provided Federalist leaders with yet another convenient foil in the partisan newspapers. In their political writings, Federalists echoed the warnings of the conservative Irish theorist Edmund Burke, who insisted that the radical philosophers of France had become so obsessed "with their theories about the rights of man, that they [had] totally forgotten [man's] nature." Stable, prosperous government necessitated skilled and practical men to maintain order, but in France "the selfish enlargement of mind and narrow liberality of sentiment of insidious men . . . [had] ended in open violence and rapine." Federalists maintained that if the United States allowed this egalitarian and democratic philosophy to infiltrate government policy, it would disrupt America's long-standing deferential culture, throwing society into the same type of violent chaos experienced in Revolutionary France. In such a spirit, the Federalist printer John Fenno published a 1795 sermon by the chaplain of the U.S. House of Representatives, Reverend Ashbel Green, in which Green praised God for the Federalist government "which unites and establishes liberty with order.[21]

A similar logic informed the way Federalist clergymen collaborated with their secular counterparts to attack Republicans for supporting the French Revolution. As previously mentioned, Americans throughout the country initially celebrated the French Revolution as the spread of their own "Spirit of 1776." But the Revolution spun out of control in 1793 when a group of radical Parisians called Jacobins pushed for the adoption of more extreme democratic principles and resorted to violence to get their way. The French Reign of Terror became a politically divisive subject in America and went a long way in crystallizing the emerging political factions into full-fledged parties. Federalist clergymen readily joined their secular counterparts in using "Jacobin" as a derogatory term for their political opponents. But these partisan clerics expanded the implications of Jacobinism beyond the political conditions of France and the United States. They argued that Jacobinism was a threat not only to the precarious balance of liberty and order but to American religious life as well.

For instance, the Reverend Timothy Dwight of Connecticut preached in 1798 that if the Jacobin influence in America continued to grow, "we may change our holy worship into a dance of Jacobin frenzy." Dwight's close friend and political ally the Reverend Jedediah Morse made no mystery of what he believed was the source of such insidious and rampant Jacobinism in America. Morse argued that the Democratic-Republican clubs and the Republican Party they backed were bastions of dangerous ideas and that it was incumbent upon all God-fearing Americans to vote Federalist in order to save American religious life. "We have in truth secret enemies. Not a few, scattered through the country," Morse warned in 1799, "whose professed design is to subvert and destroy our holy religion and our free and excellent government." By supporting the French Revolution and embracing Jacobinism, Morse accused the Republican Party of aiming to destroy all the American Revolution had achieved. Forgoing a reasonable assessment of all that Jacobinism actually entailed, Federalist clergymen readily turned the term into a synonym for anarchy, conspiracy, and atheism.[22]

Federalist clergymen, however, used more than Republican support for the French Revolution to justify the Jacobin label for their opponents. Those preaching in the northern states frequently condemned the violence southern slaveholders unleashed upon their human property as deriving from the same "ungodly" spirit that inspired the French Jacobins carrying out the Reign of Terror. In a 1795 Thanksgiving sermon, Reverend Samuel Deane of Portland, Massachusetts (present-day Maine), thanked God for sparing the United States from the violence of the French Revolution but sharply criticized Americans who exhibited similar violence at home by "holding men in chains, in cruel bondage and slavery." Sermons like these echoed the direct connections of slavery to anti-Jacobinism made by their secular counterparts. One such partisan published an anonymous pamphlet in 1796 titled *Reflections on the Inconsistency of Men, Particularly Exemplified in the Practice of Slavery*. The author spared no punches when he called for the total abolition of slavery, asserting that in "the southern [states], where slavery is yet raging in all its horrors, a furious democracy copied from the Jacobin principles of France appears to be the wish of most of the southern gentry." Not all southern slaveholders were Republican, but enough slaveholders supported Jefferson's agrarian vision for such a political strategy to depict the Republicans as the proslavery party and thereby drum up Federalist support in northern states. The anti-Jacobin language of these Federalist clergymen eventually formed a key intellectual foundation for the abolitionist movement of the nineteenth century. But in the 1790s, its immediate intent and effect was to cast the Republican Party as an unsanctified deviation from God's plan for the American nation.[23]

Republicans were hardly Jacobins in any literal sense of the term. In reality, they had far more in common with the Girondins, a group of French revolutionaries from outside of Paris that controlled the government from 1792 to 1793. Substantially more "moderate" than the Jacobins that succeeded them, this group included Thomas Paine and the Marquis de Lafayette. While in control of the Revolution, the Girondins grew wary of Parisian crowds and the penchant of their leaders for violent street demonstrations. They were also more tolerant than the Jacobins of those who opposed the Revolution, including King Louis XVI and Queen Marie Antoinette. The Girondins were in favor of replacing monarchy with a democratic society, but they did not think the execution of the royal family was necessary. Such a "moderate" stance drew the ire of the much more radical Jacobins, and in 1793 they seized control of the revolutionary government, imprisoned prominent Girondins (including Paine and Lafayette) and instituted the Reign of Terror, in which they executed the king and queen along with thousands of aristocrats and others they deemed "political enemies."[24]

Like the Girondins' distrust of Parisian crowds, American Republicans demonstrated concern that public protests and street demonstrations against Federalist policies could go too far. "Radical Democratic-Republicans in the eastern cities were trying to vindicate a new model of politics that comes closer to the condition 'democracy' that modern nations work towards," Jeffrey Pasley explains. They sought "a constitutional order in which public opinion is consulted and freely expressed all the time, at elections but also in between them, in print and in public gatherings and organizations, but in which violence and other forms of physical and economic coercion are strictly forbidden. . . . Outside of a context where power had completely repressed the ability to freely speak, write, and vote," Pasley concludes, "the resort to violence was seen as an irrational, retrograde path." When Democratic-Republicans took to the streets and burned effigies of John Jay in 1795, they did so to express their dissatisfaction with the Jay Treaty, but not to burn Jay himself at the stake. When Republicans in Charleston protested against the Federalists' persistence in maintaining an alliance with Great Britain by dragging a British flag through the dirt to the musical accompaniment of "Yankee Doodle," no one was hurt, and no personal property was destroyed. As one newspaper wrote on this occasion, "We last evening witnessed that a mob could exist without a riot." The public protests Republicans staged during the 1790s were frequently loud and rowdy, but they never approached the level of violence so common in the activism of real French Jacobins.[25]

Thus, when Federalist clergymen followed the lead of their secular allies in labeling Republicans "Jacobins," they were contributing to an acerbic propaganda campaign. Differentiating between the different brands of French revolutionaries would have been an ineffective approach because the Republicans would have appeared measured and thoughtful in their implementation of democratic government. In order to fully discredit and illegitimize their political opponents, Federalists needed to depict Republicans as operating on the absolute extremity of the political spectrum, as a faction composed of men so unruly and irreverent that they knew no bounds in their penchant for violence and their utter disregard for revealed religion. In order to protect their social position and cultural authority, Federalist clergymen grossly exaggerated the social agenda of their political foes.

"How Then Can a Jew but Be a Republican?"

In terms of religious beliefs, the evangelical Christians and the liberal rationalists of the early American republic were miles apart. Evangelicals believed in the divinity of Jesus Christ, while most liberal rationalists—including deists—accepted him as a great moral philosopher but nothing more. Liberal rationalists questioned the authenticity and authority of the Bible, while evangelicals adopted a literal interpretation of scripture. Evangelicals believed that God had frequently instructed mankind through revelation, while many liberal rationalists believed that God had ceased to intervene in the affairs of mankind since the creation of the world.

Yet liberal rationalists and evangelicals found commonalities where the place of religion in politics was concerned. Both groups opposed state sponsorship of churches and the oppressive laws such establishments imposed, particularly ministerial taxes and religious tests for public office holding. Both groups maintained that religion was a personal matter. For evangelicals, this meant that religion transcended politics; it was a higher law and therefore not subject to government regulation. For liberal rationalists, the personal nature of religion meant that it should have no place in the election of office holders or in the daily functions of government. Though they would never see eye to eye on the specific tenets of religious faith, it was in their broad conceptualizations of religion and the philosophy of individual rights of conscience that these two disparate groups found common ground in the emerging Republican Party of the 1790s.

The fact that this common ground was the party of Thomas Jefferson and James Madison was no coincidence. In building an opposition to Federalist policies, the two collaborators purposefully reached out to religious dissenters and all others oppressed by established churches whose hegemony they increasingly associated with Federalist politics. As Jefferson explained amid the tumult of the 1800 presidential election, "I have long labored to rally the Physicians & Dissenting clergy who are generally friends of equal liberty." Religion was certainly not the only factor determining the party affiliation of eighteenth-century Americans, but Jefferson's appeals seemed to work.

For instance, towns dominated by Baptists voted overwhelmingly for Jefferson in the elections of 1796 and 1800. It was Jefferson's social and political opinions that prompted Baptists to flock to the Republican party. Having long been the victims of state-sanctioned religious persecution, no group was more eager than the Baptists to enact a total separation of church and state. According to historian Amanda Porterfield, "Baptists wanted the nation— and the world—to be governed on their own religious, church-based terms, with as little interference as possible from others and support from civic government." Because Jefferson championed religious liberty and the rights of the common man under a limited federal government, Baptists championed Jefferson.[26]

These factors certainly motivated prominent and outspoken Baptist leaders such as Isaac Backus and John Leland to become Republican activists in Massachusetts. For these two ministers, the efforts of the Standing Order to maintain its religious hegemony in their state were part and parcel to the Federalists' broader design of maintaining an oligarchic American society. In a 1792 sermon, Backus argued that governments attempting to control the religious beliefs and practices of a people were, in essence, attempting to regulate the "Kingdom of God," which Jesus had said was "not of this world." "The government of the church should be distinct from all worldly states," Backus averred, "as the power of *truth* on the mind, is from the *sword* on the body." Leland was even more direct in his criticism of the disproportionate religious and social power exercised by elite Congregationalists in the state. In an Independence Day sermon, the fiery minister asked his audience, "What can appear more arrogant, than for fallible men, to make their own opinions, tests of orthodoxy, and force others to yield implicit obedience thereto[?]" Both Backus and Leland supported the Jeffersonian vision of a nation in which the rights of the common man, particularly yeoman farmers, were protected from the undue influence of wealthy manufacturers and speculators, but they left the public promotion of this plan to their secular counterparts. When Backus and Leland preached politics, they focused on depicting the Republicans as the party of social equality through religious liberty.[27]

William Bentley, a Congregationalist-turned-Unitarian minister from Salem, Massachusetts, was not an evangelical, but he nevertheless joined Backus and Leland in promoting the Republican Party in their state. From the start of his career, Bentley was unorthodox in his theology and in his performance of rituals. He went against church rules by baptizing children conceived out of wedlock, as well as those whose parents had not made a "confession of faith." He also dissolved the parish system on the eastern side of Salem in which his church was located. This allowed town residents to attend and financially support whatever church they pleased. In effect, he disestablished the Congregationalist Church in his small section of Massachusetts nearly fifty years before the rest of the state followed suit. He reasoned that the basic tenets of Christianity were what mattered; the differences between the competing sects and denominations were peripheral distractions from the heart of religious faith. Bentley's latitudinarianism placed him on the vanguard of the liberal Congregationalist movement.[28]

Though Bentley was hardly alone in his move away from orthodox Calvinism toward Unitarianism, he was unique among his fellow liberal churchmen in his early support of the Republican Party. As mentioned earlier, the growing chasm between the orthodox and liberal wings of the Congregationalist clergy was bridged momentarily in the 1790s by political unity within the Federalist Party. But Bentley would have no part in Federalist politics. Though he did not officially align himself with the Republican Party until after 1800, his political sermons in the 1790s were decidedly opposed to the policies of the Washington and Adams administrations. In 1792, he called Hamilton's financial plan "depraved" for enabling wealthy merchants and financial speculators "to add to [their] treasures" on the backs of their "fellow mortals." He likewise castigated Federalist attempts to restrict free speech and suppress political dissent. "Man should write and act freely," Bentley declared in one sermon, adding on another occasion that, while "Some books have been written with an ill-effect . . . , we are not to interrupt the stream." But he saved his most intense criticism for Federalist clergymen who justified the Alien and Sedition Acts of 1798 to their congregations, warning the public that paying full intellectual deference to the clergy of the state-sponsored church was dangerous. "It is the power to seize the minds of men that gives such astonishing advantages to eloquence," he preached in 1798. "It is the power to get into men's minds as they are and to lead them by their fears which gives such superior influence to men in other respects undeserving of the least regard." Bentley was calling the bluff of his fellow Congregationalist clergymen who claimed to preach Federalism in order to preserve public morality. Instead, Bentley saw their activism as stripping the men and women in their congregations of their intellectual agency in order to maintain an authoritative cultural and social position that was artificial and undeserved. Bentley was fully in favor of public morality, but believed the Federalist Party was looking for it in all the wrong places.[29]

Bentley's conception of public morality set him apart not only from the majority of Congregationalist ministers but from his fellow Republican preachers as well. Though most Congregationalist ministers insisted that state-sponsored religion was the surest guard of public morality, and Baptist preachers such as Backus and Leland argued that public morality would only thrive when religion was unfettered from government establishments, both groups at least agreed that religion was the principal source of this social virtue. But Bentley looked beyond religion. He believed that morality derived from a variety of sources, of which religion was only one. Bentley saw the teachings of Jesus as an exemplary moral code but grew frustrated with the narrow interpretation and dogmatic implementation of such teachings by his fellow clergymen. Ostracizing men and women for their mistakes and refusing to baptize their children was no way to spread morality or to create a unified moral community. Social division was the effect of such judgments, and this went against the practices of Jesus himself; God's punishments were God's alone to wield. For Bentley, the Bible was helpful in understanding and teaching moral behavior, but it was inadequate by itself. In order to identify the flaws of an individual or an entire society, enlightened reasoning was essential. Bentley did not think that it was detrimental to religion to teach people to think for themselves, investigate the natural laws of the universe, and contemplate the artificial origins of society. Quite to the contrary, Bentley believed Enlightenment philosophy could be a tremendous boon to religion and was essential to the creation of a moral community within a large, imperfect, and religiously diverse society.[30]

Bentley was therefore exceptional as a politicized clergyman. He did not oppose the Federalists out of some agrarian or sectional interest, as did many secular Republicans. Nor did his Republican activism spring from a marked ecclesiastical interest. It was Bentley's philosophical conception of society— and the world at large—that politicized him. As his biographer, J. Rixey Ruffin, explains, "Bentley's priorities lay in preserving the rights of information, ideas, and enlightenment, which he saw as the best sureties of the spread of morality and thus true happiness." It was the pursuit of happiness that drove Bentley into the contentious political discourse of the 1790s, but the path he proposed to such societal bliss was so unconventional and controversial that his congregation drastically diminished in size between 1800 and 1810. Politically and religiously, Bentley stood out. In early-nineteenth-century Massachusetts, this often meant standing alone.[31]

Other Christian denominations that had been marginalized by religious establishments lagged behind the Baptists in terms of partisan mobilization during the 1790s but made up ground in the early nineteenth century. The Methodists are an instructive example of this trend. Following the Revolution, American Methodists were deeply divided theologically and politically. Internal schisms over doctrinal issues such as the scriptural basis for the election of bishops occupied the attention of the Methodist clergy and split the laity. Meanwhile, regional loyalties and commercial interests further prevented political unity. The most concentrated population of American Methodists at the end of the eighteenth century was in Delaware, where the policies of the Washington and Adams administrations were immensely popular. This pitted Delaware Methodists against the denomination's growing population in the rural Kentucky territory that celebrated the agrarian policies of Jefferson. But in the first decades of the nineteenth century, the Methodist Church was invigorated by the revivalism of the Second Great Awakening and experienced rapid growth in membership, especially in western territories. This caused the political pendulum of the denomination to swing decidedly toward the Republicans, and Methodists became an essential part of the voter base for nineteenth-century party leaders such as John Breckinridge of Kentucky. In this way, Methodists, Baptists, and other marginalized religious groups grew together in the nineteenth century through a set of symbiotic relationships within the Republican Party.[32]

This public perception that equated the Republican Party with religious liberty drew support from non-Christians as well. Liberal rationalists, many of whom were prominent in the Democratic-Republican clubs throughout the United States, rallied around the idea of a government led by Jeffersonians. So did the country's Jewish population. Though the rabbis in the five synagogues scattered along the Atlantic coast largely refrained from political activism, lay members of the Jewish community such as Benjamin Nones of Pennsylvania made their political inclinations clear. During the height of partisan contention in the election of 1800, Nones wrote in a Philadelphia newspaper, "I am a Jew, and if for no other reason, for that reason am I a republican. . . . In republics we have rights, in monarchies we live but to experience wrongs. . . . How then can a Jew but be a Republican?" There was a degree of political hyperbole in the way Nones reduced his political allegiance and that of his fellow Jews to a matter of religious affiliation. Yet his point was valid: Republican promises of freedom of conscience for religious minorities were a major selling point for the Jewish community in light of Federalist attempts to maintain the religious hierarchy that had existed under British rule.[33]

Winning the political support of approximately one thousand Jews hardly represented an electoral coup for Republicans, but it illustrates the extent to which the party's liberal religious position attracted support from religiously oppressed communities throughout the country. More importantly, it helps to explain how a religious skeptic such as Jefferson came to lead a party that included thousands of religiously devout Americans and how those religious Americans helped Jefferson ascend to the presidency in 1800 amid claims that his election would rapidly destroy religious life throughout the country.

SIX

The Myth of the Christian President

In March 1801, Thomas Jefferson described to Joseph Priestley the difficulties of his recent electoral contest. "What an effort, my dear Sir, of bigotry in Politics & Religion have we gone through!" the newly inaugurated president wrote. "The barbarians really flattered themselves they should be able to bring back the times of Vandalism, when ignorance put everything into the hands of power & priestcraft." This was a harsh indictment of his Federalist opponents, but Jefferson was not exaggerating.[1]

In 1796 and again in 1800, Federalist politicians and their clerical allies aimed an onslaught of defamatory rhetoric at Jefferson and his deist views in the first two contested presidential elections in United States history. They argued that only Christians should occupy the office of the presidency, consciously disregarding the Constitution's explicit statement that a man's religious disposition could not disqualify him from holding public office. Their impassioned claims did not constitute a formal religious test of office, but rather an informal religious trial administered via the burgeoning nation's newspapers, pamphlets, and pulpits.[2]

But how genuine were expressions of concern over Jefferson's religion in these two election cycles? Can we take such antideist rhetoric in pamphlets, newspapers, and sermons at face value as a citizenry concerned that a non-Christian president would be detrimental to the country's religious liberties and moral fiber? Or was there a strong politically partisan current running just below the surface of these claims against Jefferson's candidacy? Many Federalist clergymen campaigning against Jefferson were motivated by genuine concern over the deterioration of American religious life; but at the same time, they shared the political fears of secular conservatives that the party of social order and hierarchy was losing its hold on national power.

Political anxieties spurred the party's leadership to heighten and manipulate the widespread hysteria that America was in danger of experiencing a destruction of religion similar to that which characterized Revolutionary France. The Federalists' exploitation of Jefferson's deism had as much to do with the ballot box as it did the nation's "soul." The Virginian's detractors feverishly sought secular power by speaking of the sacred.

In many ways, the political participation of clergymen and the infusion of religious concerns in the election of 1800 was a continuation of arguments left unsettled during the ratification debates that divided the country in 1787 and 1788. The apparent disagreement among Americans on the question of whether public morality was reliant upon religion speaks to the malleability and manipulation of supposedly constant values such as republican virtue. For over a century, several colonies established religious tests as prerequisites for office holding, principally as a means of strengthening the position of established churches. Proponents of such tests justified this religious hegemony as necessary to ensure the virtue and morality of public officials. But in the years after the Revolution, experience had convinced many Americans that specific religious affiliation guaranteed neither characteristic, and several states eliminated these tests. Yet tradition has a tendency to linger, and the inclination to elect Christians to public office created by more than 150 years of colonial experience did not disappear overnight. As the election of 1800 approached, Federalists revived the tired trope of religion's inextricable connection to virtue in order to replicate a comfortable picture of elite-dominated structures. In this way, the election of 1800 entailed both continuity and rupture with America's colonial past.

Though presidential elections are by nature national in scope, understanding the full implications of the election of 1800 requires close attention to state and local politics. As this chapter demonstrates, there is a direct correlation between the harshest and most direct criticism of Jefferson's religion and the states or electoral districts where party operatives expected the election to be the closest. The dynamics and idiosyncrasies of local politics present the election of 1800 in an entirely new light, an illumination that necessitates a reassessment of the significance historians have traditionally assigned to the prominence of religious rhetoric in that electoral contest.

The expectation that the American president must be a Christian does not come from the nation's founding documents or from some unspoken rule generally accepted by the country's founders. It arose from the calculated efforts of partisan politicians and their clerical allies during the fractious struggle for power in the decades immediately following independence. The myth of the Christian president was created by desperate Federalists when they resorted to the combustibility of the public's intuitive prejudice in favor of Christian leaders and a fiercely partisan atmosphere. The myth was then crystallized by later generations of Americans with their skewed retellings of the nation's founding era.

"Shall I Continue in Allegiance to God . . . Or Impiously Declare for Jefferson?"

Though the elections of 1796 and 1800 featured the same two candidates, they were very different contests. In 1796, Federalists attacked Jefferson's candidacy from several different angles. Some expressed concern over his personal religious beliefs, but this was typically mixed with concerns over his leadership record and his positions on controversial issues such as the French Revolution. In 1796, Federalists never presented Jefferson's deism as the sole reason Americans should vote for Adams. But by 1800, that changed.[3]

William Loughton Smith's contentious pamphlet *The Pretensions of Thomas Jefferson to the Presidency Examined* is an example of the typical attack on Jefferson in 1796. Smith was an attorney and Federalist congressman from South Carolina. In sixty-four pages, he expressed his aversion to Jefferson on philosophical, political, and religious grounds. Among other criticisms, Smith faulted Jefferson for stirring up party division while serving as Washington's secretary of state, a bold insinuation that America's divided polity could be traced to a Jefferson-led pack of "sycophants" and "interested intriguers." He also criticized Jefferson for generating cultural conflict through his radical philosophies, claiming that "ignorant people" were driven to challenge social order under the influence of aspiring politicians who use the title "philosopher" to mask their "ambitious designs." Furthermore, Smith called Jefferson a coward for fleeing Monticello in 1781 when the British army approached the mountaintop estate. Criticism from fellow Virginians had made Jefferson's flight before British forces a controversial issue in the state at the time it occurred. By recalling the event in his 1796 pamphlet, Smith was attempting to revive the controversy on a national level.[4]

When Smith turned to religious considerations for denying Jefferson the presidency, he referenced Jefferson's *Notes on the State of Virginia* and asked his readers, "do I receive injury, as a member of society, if I am surrounded with atheists . . . on whom there are none of those religious and sacred ties . . . without which ties social society would soon degenerate into a wretched state of barbarism, and be stained with scenes of turpitude, and with every kind of atrocity?" A Jefferson presidency, Smith argued, would bring "anti-Christian" writers such as Thomas Paine to America in large numbers and such men would become "conspicuous figure[s] at the President's table at Philadelphia." Here, Smith treated liberal philosophers as a pestilence, arguing that by placing one at the head of the government Americans would effectively swing open the doors for others until the country was overrun by deists and atheists. In Smith's pamphlet and others authored by Federalists during the election of 1796, religious considerations were certainly pronounced, but they were put forward as just one of many reasons to deny Jefferson the presidency.[5]

Though Smith used a diverse range of talking points in 1796, in several respects his pamphlet paved the way for more focused political attacks four years later. In fact, the way Smith addressed Jefferson's religion in *The Pretensions of Thomas Jefferson*, albeit brief, offered future party operatives a blueprint for making religion a primary focus of the 1800 campaign. First, Smith used images of violence and desolation to tie Jefferson's religious views and his support of the French Revolution to the destruction of religious life in France. Anti-Jefferson pamphleteers in 1800 similarly emphasized words such as "barbarism," "atrocity," and "turpitude," a vocabulary of violence intentionally employed to generate fear and anxiety in the minds of American voters over what a Jefferson presidency would conceivably bring upon the country's religious landscape. Second, Smith emphasized Jefferson's friendship with radical thinkers such as Paine, another strategy commonly adopted by Federalist writers in 1800. By linking Jefferson to some of the most radical philosophers in the Atlantic world at that time and emphasizing these philosophers' alleged (and in some instances, confirmed) atheism, these Federalists portrayed the Virginian as a godless philosopher with aims to replace religious worship with Enlightenment rationalism and to turn Christian churches into "temples of the Supreme Being." Lastly, Smith cited out of context lines from Jefferson's *Notes* and the Virginia Statute for Religious Freedom. Nearly all who wrote against Jefferson's candidacy in 1800 did the same. These sources were essential to Jefferson's detractors because Jefferson had never publicly explained his religious beliefs. But in *Notes* and the Virginia statute, he penned several lines supporting religious liberty that were ripe for misinterpretation as attacks on religion in general. It is impossible to know the precise extent to which Federalists in 1800 directly referenced Smith's pamphlet when constructing their religious-centered attacks on Jefferson. But every one of these published anti-Jefferson diatribes utilized strategies first employed by Smith in 1796.[6]

Adams's electoral victory over Jefferson in 1796 came by the razor-thin margin of three electoral votes, and it was not long before both parties began preparations for the anticipated rematch in 1800. The Federalists' attacks on Jefferson's religious beliefs during the 1796 campaign pale in comparison to the volume and ferocity of those they launched four years later. This rise in frequency and intensity can be accounted for by the increasingly desperate situation of the Federalist party. In 1796, Federalists touted Vice President Adams as Washington's clear successor. Though Washington never officially aligned himself with the Federalist Party, the policies he enacted while in office had a distinct Federalist flavor. But by 1800 the Federalists could no longer lean on Washington's legacy. Adams's presidency had been tumultuous and controversial, to say the least. Though his well-timed release of the identities of the French officials involved in the XYZ affair enabled the Federalists to retain power in both the Senate and the House of Representatives in 1798, the party's future was put into question by several unpopular policies enacted during Adams's administration, most notably the government's handling of the Quasi-War with France and the Alien and Sedition Acts. As historian Robert McDonald describes it, "Federalists found themselves with neither an attractive candidate nor a compelling agenda." Or, in the words of a prominent New York Federalist in 1800, "we have no rallying point." Without a strong candidate of their own, Federalists resorted to tearing down the Republican candidate by any means possible.[7]

If Smith's *The Pretensions of Thomas Jefferson* epitomized the broad attack of Jefferson's candidacy in 1796, then Timothy Dwight's 1798 published address against Enlightenment philosophies and all Americans that espoused them set the tone for the anti-Jefferson publications in 1800 that focused specifically on religious considerations. A devoted Federalist, Dwight spoke from a very influential position as the president of Yale. On July 4, 1798, he marked the twenty-second anniversary of American independence with a sermon he titled "The Duty of Americans at the Present Crisis." He began by reading scriptural passages from Revelation and the First General Epistle of John, which warned of "false prophets" and "false teachers" spreading dissension among Christians in the days leading up to Armageddon. He identified Enlightenment thinkers such as Voltaire, D'Alembert, and Diderot as teachers who "by their doctrines and labours . . . contend against God . . .

and will strive to unite mankind in this opposition." "The labors of this Academy," Dwight warned, were not "confined to religion" but also "morality and government," with the goal of destroying society's "reverence for everything heretofore esteemed sacred." When Dwight declared the Enlightenment the bane of religious, moral, and well-governed societies everywhere, he either forgot or outright denied the role such philosophy had played in the onset of the American Revolution two decades earlier.[8]

As mentioned in previous chapters, this wholesale rejection of Enlightenment philosophy was not relatively common among Americans, lay or clerical. While past generations of historians frequently reduced the Enlightenment to a conflict between religious superstition and rational empiricism, recent scholarship has challenged such narrow generalizations. For instance, historian David Sorkin has argued that while the Enlightenment often pitted religion's most zealous advocates against its most intense skeptics, it was far more common for "religious enlighteners" to attempt reconciling the two extremes, to "renew and articulate their faith, using the new science and philosophy to promote tolerant, irenic understanding of belief." Dwight took an extreme stand against Enlightenment philosophy, whereas clergymen such as Bishop James Madison and Reverend William Bentley embraced it and accordingly adjusted their respective theologies and ideologies. Historians are left to wonder if Dwight always held such animosity toward the Enlightenment or if it was the product of his participation in the fanatically polarized political environment of the 1790s.[9]

Dwight asserted that religious unraveling as a result of the Enlightenment had already taken place in France, where "God was denied and ridiculed . . . Government was asserted to be cursed . . . the possession of property was pronounced to be robbery," and "Adultery . . . and other crimes of the like infernal nature, were taught as lawful, and even as virtuous actions." Dwight declared that these dreadful social changes were "rapidly spreading through the world" and had already made it to America's shores, implying that Republican Virginia was the primary port of landing. If left unchecked, America would soon fall victim to the same plague of irreverence that had stricken France. "Is it, that our churches may become temples of reason[?]" Dwight inquired, painting a dire (and exaggerated) picture of what could befall the country. "Is it that we may see the Bible cast into a bonfire, the vessels of the sacramental supper borne by an ass in public procession[?] . . . [S]hall we, my brethren, become partakers of these sins? Shall we introduce them into our government, our schools, our families? Shall our sons become the disciples of Voltaire . . . or our daughters the concubines of the Illuminati?" Not if Americans stood steadfastly against any of their countrymen associated with such philosophies, Dwight averred. It was the duty of God-fearing Americans "to shun all such connection with them." Dwight was adamant that this was the only way Americans could prevent "partaking in their guilt, and receiving of their plagues."[10]

In this sermon, Dwight exemplified the New England clergy's often selective interpretation of the French Revolution. Since early in America's colonial era, Protestant clergymen throughout the region had maintained that Catholic France was an agent of the Antichrist. The French Revolution forced the closure of Catholic churches throughout that country and the expulsion of many Catholic priests. But instead of sustaining initial celebrations of a major defeat for Protestantism's archenemy, Dwight and many other New England clergymen began to focus almost exclusively on the French revolutionaries' animosity to Christianity in general and their penchant for violence. In this light, France was as threatening to Protestant Christianity as it had ever been. Just as they had done during the Seven Years' War, the New England clergy warned that all things French must be removed from the North American continent.[11]

There was also a decided local perspective in Dwight's sermon, even as he addressed issues of national concern. Though he worried about America's religious character writ large, he seemed more anxious about an unabated spread of Enlightenment secularism, the French democratic spirit, and the Republican party into Connecticut. He urged his listeners to be on guard lest the "ungodly" philosophy he associated with southern Republicans should threaten the position of power Federalists and Congregationalists held in the state. He did not speak of driving this political and philosophical "plague" back to its place of origin. Instead, he argued for a firm stand by Connecticut's citizenry to keep it out of the northern states and out of national power.

At no point in his sermon did Dwight identify Jefferson by name, but he did not have to. The implication was clear. In this midterm election year, Dwight was tying the entire Republican Party to the philosophies embraced by its leader. He was arguing that the Republican Party represented a dire threat to the country's future, that if voters did not thwart Republican ambitions, the United States would share France's fate. In his private correspondence with Federalist senator James Hillhouse in March 1800, Dwight articulated his dislike of Jefferson. "The introduction of Mr. Jefferson will ruin the Republic," the clergyman wrote. "[T]he postponement of his introduction will . . . save it." Dwight warned Hillhouse that the organized and systematic approach of the Republican campaign was proving exceedingly effective and urged him and other Federalist "gentlemen in Congress . . . to imitate [Republicans] in their industry." There is a sense of panic in this letter. Dwight recognized the Republicans' superior party organization and foresaw certain Federalist defeat in the fall election if his party did not follow their opponents' strategy. Other Federalists shared Dwight's panic and similarly turned to the press, but there is no evidence that the spread of Federalist political attacks focused on Jefferson's religion was a coordinated effort stemming from Dwight's pamphlet. Though thematically and rhetorically related, these attacks had separate contemporaneous origins in their respective states. Other partisan pamphleteers and essayists adopted Dwight's anti-France and anti-Republican tone to fit their respective local circumstances, but most were far more direct than the Yale president in publicly decrying Jefferson by name.[12]

It should come as no surprise to anyone that Jefferson's candidacy was strongly opposed in New England. Adams was a New Englander and the region was the Federalist Party's home base. Massachusetts, New Hampshire, Rhode Island, Connecticut, and Vermont had all voted for Adams in 1796 by overwhelming margins, and there was absolutely no doubt that they would vote for his reelection in 1800. Hence, the political activity of New England clergymen in 1800 raises an interesting question: if the chances that a Republican candidate could carry any one of these states ranged from slim to nonexistent, why did the region's Federalist writers bother to publish pamphlets and newspaper articles that demonized Jefferson based upon his religious beliefs locally? Why expend the effort? The answer has less to do with national electoral politics and more to do with the politics of local religion.

At the heart of the matter was an effort to maintain a religious establishment. While many states had permitted religious tolerance before the Revolution and others, such as Georgia and South Carolina, had followed Virginia's example and passed laws disestablishing religion shortly after the country secured independence, Massachusetts and Connecticut remained obstinate on the issue. Communities in these two states were still largely organized around the church, a characteristic that set them apart from their counterparts south of New England at this time. Yet Congregationalist clergymen in these states felt that their religious hegemony was under assault, and Jefferson personified the many threats to their social position and cultural influence. Though the federal government had no constitutional power to disestablish churches in individual states, many Connecticut and Massachusetts clergymen worried that a Jefferson presidency would push the tide of public action against religious establishments into the country's last holdouts. It seemed quite plausible to these men that placing the country's greatest champion of religious freedom at the head of the government nationally would encourage and inspire minority faiths locally. Their pamphlets and essays served to remind New England Congregationalists that their religious establishment was vulnerable to attacks from outside the region. Congregationalist clergymen wanted to keep their congregations alert.[13]

Accordingly, a Connecticut resident writing as "A Humble Citizen" expressed concern that if Jefferson and the "democrats could acquire control of our religious establishments . . . they would destroy them." In Massachusetts, an anonymous contributor to the *Western Star* declared that the Federalists, unlike "the Virginia Jacobins," would "never consent to prostrate our Government for the visionary theories of speculating philosophists." For New England Federalists generally, the status quo was good and ought to be maintained at all costs. For Congregationalist clergymen in Massachusetts and Connecticut particularly, the election of 1800 was as much about protecting the favored status of their sect within their states as it was about choosing the next head of the national government.[14]

Just as Federalists were virtually assured victory in New England, the Republicans could count on Virginia. Yet, despite the Old Dominion's status as a Republican stronghold, it was not immune to published invective against Jefferson and his deism. For instance, Accomack, Norfolk Borough, and Westmoreland Counties consistently elected Federalists to the U.S. House of Representatives. Other counties such as Princess Anne, James City, New Kent, and the city of Williamsburg were sharply divided politically. Located along the shores of Chesapeake Bay and more reliant upon trade with Great Britain than other regions of the state, many voters in these counties were attracted to Federalist policies. In 1796, the election was closely contested in these places, and a significant number of freeholders voted for Adams and would do so again in 1800. In fact, these counties remained areas of Federalist resistance to the state's Republican majority well into the first decade of the nineteenth century.[15]

It is significant that essays attacking Jefferson's candidacy in 1796 and 1800 based upon his religion were more prevalent in these electoral districts than any others in Virginia. Usually, such writings were published in newspapers with a strong Federalist bias. In the *Columbian Mirror and Alexandria Gazette*, for instance, "A Freeholder" from James City County argued that no man "ought to be President, who does not profess and practice the Christian religion—Does Mr. Jefferson profess to be of the society of Christians? If he does, pray inform the public what sect he belongs." In a different issue of the same paper, another partisan writer operating under the pen name "A Friend of the Government" insisted that "many countries at various times have fallen into abject vassalage, in consequence of abandoning the principles of virtue and common good, which has always been the dire and baneful effect of infidelity." This Federalist presented a partisan view of what constituted the "common good," insisting that what was good for his party and in the interest of its adherents was good for the entire country.[16]

Though these pockets of Federalist opposition were far too small to move Virginia from the Republicans' electoral column, their existence in the election of 1800 is significant. In Jefferson's home state, the only counties publishing religious-based invectives aimed at the Republican candidate were those in which the Federalists had a real chance of winning, a correlation that further evidences the partisan origins of this political strategy. Virginia Federalists in these counties apparently knew they stood no chance of carrying the election statewide but believed they had a real chance of maintaining and increasing control at the local level. In this instance, local political interest motivated the movement to construct a Christian identity for the office of the presidency. On election day, however, even many of the most religiously concerned Virginia Republicans ignored the Federalist propaganda and continued to follow the advice of ministers such as David Barrow to continually guard against "all false doctrines and heretical principles," while simultaneously remembering that when it came to statesmen and politics, "all religious tests, and ecclesiastical establishments, are oppressive, and infring[e] the rights of conscience." Accordingly, Jefferson won his home state by an overwhelming margin of approximately 14,800 votes, or 77 percent for Jefferson versus 23 percent for Adams.[17]

However, the most compelling evidence of the strong partisan motives for Federalists making Jefferson's religion the center of attacks can be found in the states that were not solidly Federalist or Republican, what we deem "swing states" in today's political jargon. In 1800, there were three: New York, Pennsylvania, and South Carolina. These states were the wild cards of the Electoral College, and each party was determined to place them squarely in its column. Accordingly, Federalists bombarded citizens of these three states with pamphlets and essays to an extent that greatly exceeded electioneering elsewhere.[18]

Of these three "swing states," none presented party leaders with a more complex political dynamic than New York. In 1796, the state awarded all twelve of its electoral votes to Adams. In 1800, the Republicans' impressive party organization made the state the primary target of its efforts. But New York voters were fractured in a way that went far beyond a simple Federalist-Republican dichotomy, with Republicans themselves divided over local issues and allegiances into three factions: the Clintonians, the Livingstons, and the Burrites. The only way the Republicans could overtake the Federalists in the presidential election was to temporarily unite, or at least appease, these factions. To this end, Aaron Burr displayed a high level of organizational ingenuity and political industry, working tirelessly to assemble and promote a slate of candidates to the state's House and Senate (where New York selected its presidential electors) that would secure Jefferson's victory. Burr's efforts did not go unnoticed by the opposition, and the Federalists launched their counterattack in the state's printed pages. Their pitch was less about Adams's merits than it was about Jefferson's vices, as these pamphlets and newspaper essays unabashedly played off religious fears in an effort to tear down the public's support for Jefferson specifically and the Republicans generally.[19]

Among the many tirades against Jefferson that originated in New York, Reverend William Linn's *Serious Considerations on the Election of a President* stands out as the most damning. Linn made the standard references to *Notes* and the Virginia Statute for Religious Freedom to demonstrate Jefferson's "rejection of the Christian Religion and open profession of Deism" and was especially critical of the vice president for his objections to young children being taught from the Bible while in school. This, Linn claimed, proved that Jefferson desired to make the United States "a nation of Atheists." Linn made the extreme prediction that should Jefferson win the presidency, he would "get rid of religion and the clergy," while other nations would look down upon Americans as a faithless people. But above all else, a Jefferson presidency would incur upon the country the "displeasure" of God. "Though there is nothing in the Constitution to restrict our choice," Linn explained, speaking directly to the idea of an extraconstitutional religious test, "yet the open and warm preference of a manifest enemy to the religion of Christ, in a Christian nation, would be an awful symptom of the degeneracy of that nation, and I repeat it, a rebellion against God. . . . The question is not what he will *do*," Linn concluded, "but what he *is*." Linn was arguing that it was Thomas Jefferson's religious identity that mattered above all else, and in doing so he tied the identity of the president to that of the nation at large. To speak of the Adams administration's track record would have been counterproductive with many New Yorkers, so Linn dismissed the Constitution's embrace of religious liberty and deemed America "a Christian Nation" in order to narrow his readers' focus to religious considerations over all others.[20]

Even in these early instances of its American use, the term "Christian nation" was politicized. The idea and language of a "Christian Nation" was not uniquely American. During the process of nation-state formation that characterized early modern Europe, declaring a nation "Christian" had multiple implications, some more politically benign than others. It could serve as a designation based merely upon demographics, describing the predominant religious practices of a people. The label could similarly inform a nation's orientalism by religiously differentiating the nations of "Christendom" from those of Africa and Asia. The idea of distinctively Christian nations also grew out of the development of national providentialism (the idea that God punishes and rewards his chosen nations just as he does individuals) in seventeenth-century England. As described in earlier chapters, this was an idea readymade for political exploitation. Linn did not use the phrase in a demographic or orientalist vein. Instead, he was following the long-established pattern of using the language of national providentialism to achieve partisan goals.[21]

If Linn were attempting to describe a demographic fact, he could have stated that Americans at that time practiced Christianity more than any other religion. Statistically, he would have been correct and could have argued that electing a Christian president would better represent the religious preferences of a plurality of Americans. Instead, Linn declared the United States a "Christian Nation," averring that in order to be a full member of the nation a person must be a Christian. Non-Christians were somehow less American, free to reside in the country but barred from full participation in its government. Defining a nation's identity is not simply about describing the characteristics associated with an imagined community. The process inherently includes declarations of who is excluded from full membership. The fiercely partisan election of 1800, then, is an instance in which partisan politics encouraged a battle of religious demarcation in America's ongoing process of national formation.[22]

Pennsylvania was another sharply divided state in 1800 and, like New York, it experienced a heated debate over the presidential election. The western regions of the state were decidedly Republican, the eastern portions strongly Federalist, and Philadelphia was largely split between the two. In this environment, "A Layman" asked the public, "*Shall* THOMAS JEFFERSON be chief magistrate of these states? . . . —GOD FORBID!" There was no room for compromise in this pamphleteer's view, as he declared that electing a non-Christian president was "an open renunciation of your faith." Then, writing in a manner that suggested a desire to institute formal religious tests as a prerequisite for federal office holding, he insisted that the absence of a formal profession of Christian beliefs from Jefferson or "his allies" was evidence enough that he was either a deist or an atheist. No amount of beneficial "measures [Jefferson was] expected to pursue, [were] so essential to the welfare of our country . . . as to outweigh every moral consideration flowing from his *unbelief.*" But certainly none contested Jefferson's election more extremely and succinctly than John Fenno's *Gazette of the United States* in which the proadministration editor declared that Americans could "continue in allegiance to God—and a Religious President; Or impiously declare for Jefferson—and No God!!!"[23]

This rhetoric was typical of other anti-Jefferson publications then circulating throughout the state. Like Reverend Linn in New York, the Pennsylvania Federalists aimed to demonize Jefferson, to degrade his character to such an extent that no political platform touting greater individual freedom and support for yeoman farmers could redeem him. Less a coordinated assault on Jefferson than fellow partisans adopting what appeared to be an effective political strategy in a desperate moment, Federalists in swing states used antideist rhetoric as though the entire election depended on generating fear and panic over what a Jefferson presidency *might* bring upon the country.

Of all the states in the South, the Federalists were strongest in South Carolina. Burdened by Revolutionary War debt, many of the state's political leaders welcomed Alexander Hamilton's plan of assumption in 1790. Merchants in Charleston and other coastal settlements also benefited greatly from the Federalists' economic policies, while many of the wealthy political leaders espoused the party's elitist perspective on government. The population in the state's backcountry relied heavily on farming and was inclined to favor the Republican party. In 1798 the state sent one Federalist and one Republican to the Senate and a delegation to the House of Representatives comprising one Republican and five Federalists. In 1800 it sent two Republican senators, but its delegation to the House was evenly divided. In an attempt to attract greater southern support, the Federalists tapped South Carolinian Charles Cotesworth Pinckney as their choice for vice president (though many in the party more loyal to Hamilton than Adams considered Pinckney a viable replacement for Adams atop the party's ticket). Under these circumstances, South Carolina was very much in play in the election of 1800.[24]

So the Federalists went to work trying to secure South Carolina's six electoral votes. Because South Carolina's electors were selected by the state legislature, Federalist pamphleteers aimed their antideist rhetoric at voters before the state elections hoping that fear of a non-Christian president would bring the Federalist Party greater sway in the statehouse. After these elections, the same religiously oriented language continued to fill the state's papers but focused instead on the already elected state representatives.

No South Carolinian wrote more adamantly against Jefferson than Henry W. DeSaussure. In Charleston, he published multiple political pamphlets during 1800, alternating between the pseudonyms "A South-Carolina Federalist," and "A Federal Republican." "The Laws tolerate the professors of all religions, as well as those of no religion at all," DeSaussure wrote, alluding to Jefferson's language in *Notes*. "But when one of these believers in twenty gods, or unbelievers in *any* God, claims the supreme magistracy in a country, where only *one true and ever living God* is worshipped, the people of that country, surely have the right to object [to] being ruled by such a believer, or by such an unbeliever." He followed this ironically intolerant take on religious tolerance with a warning in another pamphlet "that the election of Mr. Jefferson to the office of President . . . will place us nearly in a revolutionary state." DeSaussure's essays exemplify the strategy of South Carolina Federalists for an Adams victory in that state: conflate Jefferson with irreligion, and irreligion with disorderly societies.[25]

The anti-Jefferson publications in these "swing states" are essential to understanding the partisan elements in the creation of the myth of the Christian president. Federalist political leaders and like-minded clergymen in Massachusetts and Virginia warned Americans to guard against the election of a deist such as Jefferson, maintaining that any attractive policies supported by the Virginia philosopher were greatly outweighed by the threat he presented to American religious life. But in New York, Pennsylvania, and South Carolina, published declarations against Jefferson were more direct and damning. As these three states teetered on the fence between the two candidates, the Federalists grew increasingly desperate and brought out the big guns. Framing the election as an outright contest between "God" and "the ungodly" gave them their best shot of winning. Had their hyperbolic rhetoric gone unchallenged, their strategy might have worked.[26]

"If Your Civil Privileges Are Once Gone . . . What Shall Protect Your Religious Ones?"

But the Republicans fought back effectively. Some defended Jefferson against charges of atheism and deism. DeWitt Clinton, writing under the pen name "Grotius," insisted that "An open profession [of deism] means a full and unequivocal acknowledgement" and that since Jefferson had made no such statement publicly, such charges were false. Instead, Clinton insisted without clear substantiation, "we have the strongest reasons to believe that [Jefferson] is a *real Christian.*" Benjamin Pollard, a twenty-year-old Massachusetts Republican, similarly wrote "that Mr. Jefferson is at least as good a Christian as Mr. Adams, and in all probability a much better one." An anonymous Maryland Republican published extracts from *Notes* and the Virginia Statute for Religious Freedom in a pamphlet cleverly titled *A Test of the Religious Principles of Mr. Jefferson* in which he restored the controversial passages to their proper context (supporting freedom of conscience, not opposing religion) and accused Federalists of trying to disqualify Jefferson from the presidency on religious grounds as a way of masking their political weakness. John Beckley, a Virginian and an early American pioneer in the practices of electioneering and campaign management, even went so far as to exhort Americans to "practice the RELIGION OF JEFFERSON" as displayed in *Notes* and the Virginia statute, as they were written as "sublime truths" and in "inspired language." Interestingly, Jefferson had not made any of these men his confidants on matters of his personal religious beliefs, a fact that made it difficult for them to defend him with detailed descriptions of what he really believed. The few Republican portrayals of Jefferson as a devout Christian based upon his published writings were, in reality, as much guesswork as many of the Federalists' claims.[27]

Other Republicans did not focus on Jefferson's faith but instead criticized Federalists for making religion an election issue in the first place. Rhode Island merchant and dedicated Republican Jonathan Russell argued that the public should "preserve a distinction between the moral qualities which make a man amiable in private life, and those strong virtues which alone fit him for elevated public station." A public office holder is "answerable to society for his actions only," Russell asserted. "[F]or his faith, we will trust him with his God." Tunis Wortman, a New York City attorney and active participant in the New York Democratic Society, responded to William Linn's scathing attack on Jefferson by accusing Federalist clergymen of exercising too much political influence. "Will you tell the patriot whose understanding convinces him that the liberty of the people, and the very existence of the Constitution, depends upon the election of Mr. Jefferson," Wortman wrote, "that he is placed in a dilemma in which he must either abjure his country or his religion? . . . If your civil privileges are once gone, my countrymen, what shall protect your religious ones?" Though Jefferson was not orthodox in his Christian worship or beliefs, he was "a decided friend to the republican constitution." Pinckney and Adams, on the other hand, were Christians, but "friends of aristocracy." Wortman asked, "Which of the three would be the most dangerous man?" To Republicans such as Russell and Wortman, the Federalists had set up Jefferson's deism as a straw man intended to distract from the real issues at stake in the election.[28]

Still other Republicans went on offense by turning Federalists' claims that they were God's party back on the writers making such insinuations. Abraham Bishop of Connecticut called Federalists "agents of delusion" and urged the public "to repel the first attempts to bind us with ecclesiastical fetters; and to say to the clergy, 'your business is to teach the gospel; the sheep will never thrive, if the shepherd, instead of leading them to green pastures, is to be constantly alarming them with the cry of wolves.'" Bishop then encouraged Jefferson's supporters to be confident in continuing their support of the Republican, insisting that "However you may be agitated on the subject of religion, rest assured, that you are not to depend on any administration of government for the prosperity of Zion." An anonymous writer from Delaware lamented that "the man who could pen the Declaration of Independence," was the subject "of incessant slander and abuse" with "no Sedition Law to protect him." He predicted this campaign of bigotry "like waves that dash against a rock . . . will recoil on [its] authors." Just as the Federalists were trying to portray the election of 1800 as a choice between God and the ungodly, these Republicans framed it as a battle against religious bigotry and oppressive religious establishments.[29]

The Federalists' strategy failed. Jefferson won all of South Carolina's and New York's electoral votes and split Pennsylvania's with Adams, eight to seven. In reality, the odds were stacked pretty heavily against Adams. The organization and coordination of the Republican campaign far surpassed the

Federalists' efforts. Adams, who remained bitter over the election for several years, believed the many religious-based attacks on Jefferson waged by Federalists had indeed backfired on the party and cost him reelection. Because the Federalists depicted Adams as the "Christian" candidate and the protector of American religion, Republicans accused Federalists of wanting to establish a national church. Writing to Jefferson about the election thirteen years later, Adams spoke derisively of both Federalists and Republicans. "Both parties have excited artificial terrors," Adams lamented, "and if I were summoned as a Witness to say upon Oath, which Party had excited, Machiavillialy, the most terror . . . I could not give a more sincere Answer, than in the vulgar Style, 'Put Them in a bagg and shake them, and then see which comes out first.'" In Adams's estimation, the Republicans were guilty of framing the election as a fight against bigotry and religious hegemony (and *he* had represented neither) just as the Federalists were guilty of framing it as a fight against irreligion (which *Jefferson* did not represent). Adams believed both parties had acted dishonorably and that the important issues in the election were ignored in favor of party-generated hysteria.[30]

The injection of religion in the political exchange between Federalists and Republicans distinguishes the election of 1800 as a pivotal moment in the ongoing debate over the severability of religion and public virtue examined in earlier chapters. Though the campaign's religious rhetoric had partisan origins, it once again raised the question of whether or not Christianity, or religion generally, held a monopoly on virtue and morality. Though it was not the central theme in this election, the Federalists' attacks and the Republicans' defense forced the public to consider anew this important issue. Though the election of 1800 was hardly the end of the debate, Jefferson's victory represented a major moment of political-religious "trust-busting."

Still, it is important to remember that the election was about far more than the religious preferences of Americans. Devout Christians and non-Christians in the Federalist Party voted for Adams, while devout Christians and non-Christians in the Republican Party voted for Jefferson. In retrospect, the Federalists' strategy of attacking Jefferson personally based upon his religion has been far more influential to presidential politics in the long term than it was effective in the short term. In the centuries that have passed, rival parties have regularly made personal religious beliefs a prominent feature in presidential politics, and the way many Americans understand the qualifications for the presidency can be traced back to the rhetoric employed in the election of 1800. As for Jefferson, his electoral victory in 1800 did not end the public debate over the details of his personal religious convictions. The question of whether or not he was a Christian rose to the public's attention once more in the final decade of the third president's life.

"Say Nothing about My Religion"

Fifteen years after the election, Jefferson was retired from public life and spending the bulk of his days at his mountaintop home, Monticello. Throughout the year 1816, a biographer named Joseph Delaplaine peppered Jefferson with letters seeking details about his life and the lives of other leaders of the Revolutionary generation. In a letter dated November 23, Delaplaine inquired about rumors circulating in Philadelphia and other northern cities of a change in Jefferson's religious belief. He explained that Charles Thomson, former secretary of the Continental Congress and one of Jefferson's political allies, had freely shown friends and acquaintances a letter from Jefferson in which the retired president had purportedly avowed himself "a *perfect believer in the Christian Religion*" and "in the *Divinity of Our Saviour*." Delaplaine explained that this news was in "general circulation" and had "gained such ground" that another biographer, James Wilkinson, had already included the "news" of the former president's conversion in his biographical work. Wanting to verify the alleged conversion of the former president whose deist beliefs had once been the source of political controversy, Delaplaine asked Jefferson to describe "precisely what [he] believed" for the purpose of including an accurate description in his forthcoming biographical repository.[31]

When confronted by Delaplaine, Jefferson clearly stated how he wanted to be represented in terms of his religiosity. "Say nothing about my religion," the Virginian wrote. "It is known to my god and myself alone. It's [sic] evidence before the world is to be sought in my life. If that has been honest and dutiful to society, the religion which has regulated it cannot be a bad one." A retired Jefferson was adamant: he did not want his personal religious beliefs to once again become the subject of public speculation.[32]

An impatient Jefferson described to Adams his exchange with Delaplaine. "One of our fan-colouring biographers, who paints small men as very great, enquired of me . . . whether he might consider as authentic, the change in my religion spoken of in some circles." Then, expressing what was likely the most frustrating part of the reports he received from Delaplaine, Jefferson fumed: "Now this supposed that they knew what my religion was before, taking for it the word of their priests, whom I certainly never made the confidants of my creed." Jefferson did not trust the clergy or their false represen-tation of his personal beliefs. In 1800 they had attempted to halt his public career and derail his political aspirations for the country as encompassed in the Republican party. Now, in his retirement, he was not going to let them hijack his reputation and legacy by "converting" him in the minds of his fel-low Americans.[33]

The letter Jefferson wrote to Thomson has survived, though it is hard to see how those who read it could so completely misunderstand Jefferson's statement. Responding to the recent publication of Thomson's translation of the Septuagint from Greek into English, Jefferson described some of his own experimentations with scripture. "I, too, have made a wee-little book from the same materials, which I call the Philosophy of Jesus," Jefferson wrote. "[I]t is a paradigm of his doctrines, made by cutting the texts out of the book, and arranging them on the pages of a blank book, in a certain order of time or subject." Then Jefferson penned the line that set in motion the rumor mills of northern social circles: "A more beautiful or precious morsel of ethics I have never seen; it is a document in proof that *I* am a *real Christian,* that is to say, a disciple of the doctrines of Jesus." Had Jefferson stopped there, Thom-son and others might be justified in proclaiming that Jefferson's *Philosophy of Jesus* (which none of them had seen) was in fact solid evidence of the third president's Christian conversion. But Jefferson continued, making clear that when he called himself "a real Christian," it was not a signal of approbation of any Christian sect then organized in America. Instead, Jefferson declared that his "Christian" discipleship was "very different from the Platonists, who call *me* an infidel and *themselves* Christians and preachers of the gospel, while they draw all their characteristic dogmas from what its author never said nor saw." Such preachers had "compounded from the heathen mysteries a sys-tem beyond the comprehension of man." Jefferson declared that had Jesus returned to life at that moment, "he would not recognize one feature" of the several churches then claiming to be teaching his true doctrine.[34]

Jefferson's exchanges with Delaplaine and Thomson are often quoted by those seeking to explain Jefferson's personal religious beliefs, but there is a meaningful angle that, until now, historians have ignored. Why was a rumored change in Jefferson's religion such a hot topic in the social circles of the North? Why were Thomson and the friends to whom he showed Jef-ferson's letter so willing to blatantly misread the intended irony of Jefferson's claim to be a Christian? Jefferson had been retired from the presidency for nearly a decade, so the political concerns that influenced the antideist rhetoric of his political opponents in 1796 and 1800 cannot explain it. Besides, Thomson had been a political ally of Jefferson's since the 1770s. So why the concern and excitement over Jefferson's beliefs in 1816?

In part, the answer lies in Jefferson's celebrity and eighteenth-century Americans' keen interest in the lives and lifestyles of the famous. Part of the answer also lies in the symbolism Americans assigned to the Revolutionary leadership and their desire to project their Revolutionaries as moralists. Lastly, the answer to these questions lies in the persistent belief among many Americans that the presidency should be occupied by a Christian. Jefferson's political opponents had attempted to discredit his candidacy by questioning his religiosity, insisting that electing a "deist" would spell ruin for America, religiously, morally, socially, and politically. Yet, their dire predictions proved wrong during Jefferson's two terms. The apocalypse did not occur as a result of Jefferson's presidency, and the country did not fall to pieces. Under Jefferson's leadership and that of his like-minded successors, a Republican ascendency had occurred to the extent that the Federalists had been relegated to the status of a regional faction (though Jefferson never ceased to suspect that Federalists in Republican clothing were conspiring to restore the rival party). It is very possible that northern Christians grew excited about Jefferson's rumored conversion as a way of theologically justifying his success. They were, in effect, retroactively converting his "secular" presidency into a "Christian" presidency.[35]

Such efforts were not limited to Jefferson, but extended to George Washington as well. During his presidency, Washington was not subjected to allegations of atheism or of desiring to banish religion from America as Jefferson was. But for decades after the first president's death, many became intent on proving the devoutness with which Washington practiced Christianity. Accordingly, dozens of Americans in the early nineteenth century wrote Bishop William White requesting information on the first president's worship habits, specifically the taking of communion. To one such correspondent, White wrote that "Washington never received the communion in the churches of which I am the parochial minister," but "Mrs. Washington was an habitual communicant." Concluding his letter, White explained, "I have been written to by many on that point, and have been obliged to answer them as I now do you." Historians continue to argue over White's account and what it means about Washington's religious beliefs. But what White's commentary says about attempts to retroactively establish a president's Christianity is also important. The fact that dozens of Americans were interested enough in establishing Washington's religious "credentials" that they wrote a prominent Philadelphia clergyman for information suggests that it was a point of debate in several American cities. To many in the second generation of Americans, the religious disposition of the president mattered, even several decades after the fact.[36]

This persistent interest in determining past presidents' religiosity was influenced in part by the Second Great Awakening. Several historians argue that the first generation of Americans born after independence was more religious than the preceding generation had been. This increase in religious participation was the result of both the general democratization of American Christianity and the pressing need felt by many Americans to instill some sense of order in an increasingly democratic society. Historian Joyce Appleby describes the Second Great Awakening as "a cohort of youthful revivalist ministers . . . driving the irreligion of the Revolutionary era out of the public space." Several people willfully misreading Jefferson's letter to Thomson and attempting to prove Washington's religious devoutness are examples of the "inheriting generation" attempting to drive irreligion out of the nation's historical memory as well.[37]

This concern for past presidents' religious beliefs, particularly as it pertained to Jefferson, is historically significant for three main reasons. First, it is an early example of what historian Merrill D. Peterson labeled "the Jefferson image in the American mind." Peterson persuasively argued that since the third president's death in 1826, Jefferson's image has frequently been appropriated by individual candidates, special interest groups, and political parties. Individuals and groups make such appropriations (or misappropriations) of Jefferson's life, ideas, and politics as a way of establishing their legitimacy by claiming to be the true heirs of Jefferson's political and ideological legacy. However, Peterson only offered posthumous examples of Jefferson's "image" being adopted. The way many groups of Christians willfully misinterpreted Jefferson's statements about his own "Christianity" in 1816 is an early example of this phenomenon, one that occurred while Jefferson still lived. The aging statesman did not approve.[38]

Secondly, the celebrations of Jefferson's rumored conversion came at a time when nostalgia and a keen desire to find comfort in the historical legacy of the founders preoccupied the new generation of Americans. In the years leading up to the country's jubilee, celebrations of founding figures were commonplace. But these occurrences did more than display respect and gratitude for those who established American independence. These celebrations created a founding mythology, where Revolutionary leaders such as Washington and Franklin were transformed from ordinary men who had accomplished something remarkable into demigods whose Revolution and experiments with republicanism had been foreordained by a higher power and destined to succeed from the outset. In this cultural atmosphere, it is no surprise that people in Christian circles were ready to accept rumors of Jefferson's conversion as fact. This appropriation created a historical myth wherein the real history of the election of 1800, a deist ascending to the presidency, was erased. Such mythmaking enabled the new generation to fit the third president and author of the Declaration of Independence neatly in the American pantheon.[39]

Lastly, the excitement with which Christians heard and passed on news of Jefferson's conversion speaks to religion's continuing influence in America's political culture. It also suggests that uneasiness existed among Christians who *needed* Jefferson to be converted in order to construct an American identity that privileged Christianity as a chief characteristic. The Federalists did not create the notions among many Americans that the country's political leaders needed to be religious and moral men. Nor did they create the hysteria many Americans experienced in response to the French Revolution or pertaining to the fear of deism's spread. In the election of 1800, Jefferson's opponents merely manipulated and strained extant prejudices. Even though their dire political prophesies of the tribulations a non-Christian president would bring upon the country had proven false, the mythical idea remained imbedded in the fabric of America's political culture, to be exploited again and again by political partisans as their various quests for power demanded.

Indeed, religion has played a significant role in presidential politics on several occasions since the elections of 1796 and 1800. Notable examples include attacks by Whig leaders against Andrew Jackson's anticlericalism in 1832, anti-Catholic rhetoric leveled against Al Smith in 1928 and John F. Kennedy in 1960, mutually exclusive claims in 2008 that Barack Obama was simultaneously a follower of a radical Christian preacher and a closet Muslim, and assertions from conservative evangelical pundits in 2012 that Mitt Romney's membership in the Church of Jesus Christ of Latter-day Saints made his candidacy objectionable. It is important to note that in 1832 dozens of office holders in federal and state governments shared Jackson's anticlericalism. In 1928, several Catholic men were serving as senators and congressmen while Al Smith was being sharply castigated during his presidential run. Furthermore, when Kennedy sought the presidency in 1960, Catholic inclusion in government had grown substantially from what it had been in 1928. Nor have Mormons been strangers to House and Senate chambers or gubernatorial mansions in the late 1900s and early 2000s. The trend displayed here is clear. Americans have held the office of president in special reserve, closed to men and women of faiths outside "mainstream" Protestant Christianity, even as increased religious toleration opened lower offices to men and women adhering to a greater variety of personal religious creeds.

Though each of these post-1800 religion-infused presidential campaigns unfolded under unique circumstances, collectively they represent the perpetuation of cultural and historical myth. In each instance, party leaders exaggerated and exploited genuine religious concerns within certain sectors of America's citizenry in order to disqualify opposing candidates in the eyes of religious Americans. The election of 1800 was the first manifestation of the myth of the Christian president, a myth that persists in twenty-first-century American political culture.[40]

Conclusion

More Than a Question of Church and State

Religion never purified politics in America's founding era. If anything, politics tainted religion. As the political and spiritual leaders of the country forged alliances with each other, they did so out of a mixture of genuine religious belief and ambitious self-interest. Furthermore, the fact that many Americans opposed the active role of clergymen in national politics from the outset demonstrates that the founding generation never reached a consensus on the proper relationship of religion and politics. We can credit the founders, then, with initiating the enduring American tradition of mixing religion and politics while simultaneously debating the proper balance of the two.

But why do twenty-first-century Americans care so deeply about the role religion played in the political processes that created the United States? Can all the heated arguments over the issue really be about finding the "correct" or "intended" degree of separation of church and state? Surely the crux of the issue lies deeper than a fight over if and when political leaders can pray publicly or comment on religious-based morals. Indeed, the issue's full historical context tells us that there is much more to the equation than simple, pragmatic questions of the proper role religion should play in the country's political sphere. The clamor and passion twenty-first-century Americans exhibit in their public debate over the relationship of religion to politics during the nation's founding era is indicative of a far more personal and internal conflict. At its core, it is an issue of identity.

For better or for worse, identity is tied to the past. Americans care about the details of their country's founding in large part because that process represents a key component in America's ever-evolving self-image. Such logic maintains that the "type" of nation America *is* determines what it means for individuals *to be* American. National identity, then, is simultaneously communal and individual; it is both abstract and personal. As an aging Benjamin Rush observed in 1811, "all historians delight in making the history of their nations as ancient as possible . . . for all men wish their Religions to be perpetual and universal, and patriots wish their governments or their country to last to the end of time." Through this statement, Rush implied that many of his contemporaries had assigned historical significance to the Revolutionary events of their era in order to legitimize and perpetuate their own religious and political endeavors. Yet Rush's assessment also serves as an apt description of the reasons twenty-first-century Americans continue to battle over historical interpretations, particularly where the relationship of religion and politics in the founding era is concerned.[1]

From the early nineteenth century to the present, politicians seeking power have opportunistically presented to Americans a skewed version of their country's religious and political history. By privileging the role religion played in the country's founding, these partisans declare themselves and their religiously laced political agendas the true inheritors of the founding legacy and label all others as detrimental departures from the principles that made America "great." These historical myths gain traction because they play off the genuine religious belief of many Americans. Many religious Americans quite reasonably exhibit a sincere desire to establish a government and society based on their ideas of what constitutes morality. Additionally, many Americans—religious or not—understandably seek a government made up of men and women who mirror their own social backgrounds, values, and priorities. These are all real and significant contributing factors to the controversy over religion's place in the politics of the country's founding, and we should not dismiss them. Yet such sentiments among a portion of the American populace do not justify distorting the past in order to manipulate the present.

For years, historians and other academics have argued that individual, communal, and national identities are socially constructed. They are not inherent but relative and artificial, developed by social and cultural forces. At times the cultural processes by which such identities are created occur consciously; at other times, they unfold unconsciously. Yet, despite theorists' elaborate and cogent claims of the artificial conceptual origins of an identity, more often than not the default perception that identity is innate seems to prevail among the general public, when nonacademics even consider such topics at all. Inasmuch as the study of the past informs the identities of people in the present, it is incumbent upon professionally trained historians to relate the past in all its complexity. Hence we see the inadequacy of the "Christian Nation" question as a historical framework. This question of whether the United States was founded as a Christian or a secular nation only serves to produce misleading and inaccurate history. It forces advocates to approach the topic as a zero-sum game, leaving no room to explore the interplay of politicized religion and religiously infused politics, as well as the institutional complexity and cultural ambiguity at play in the founding era. Rather than determine whether or not America was a "Christian Nation," we should engage broader themes and pose narrower questions that get at the complexity of the subject.[2]

Our new thinking will not be as neatly packaged as the answers provided by ideologues, but the approach will illuminate more. The relationship of religion to politics in America's founding era was complex and at times riddled with ambiguity. This is because, like people today, eighteenth-century Americans *were* complex and the motivations for their actions frequently *were* ambiguous. As much as individuals fully engaged in the "Christian Nation" debate would like simple and clear answers on the subject, they are not always available.

This book preserves the ambiguity of the past. A delegate in Congress could believe in the supernatural power of fasting and prayer while simultaneously recognizing its political utility, just as another delegate could spew religious language for political purposes without necessarily believing in its spiritual efficacy. Chaplains in Congress and in the Continental Army were men burdened with both spiritual and pragmatic expectations. America's Revolutionary leadership relied on them to keep Americans in the war and to preserve civility among congressional delegates as much as it depended on them to preach the gospel of Jesus Christ. Furthermore, the preceding chapters demonstrate how the loyalist-patriot division among the colonial clergy and the extreme variations in such men's individual experiences during and after the war stand as strong evidence against popular conceptions of the Revolution as a war over religion. Religion was an important issue in the conflict, but it was just one of many.

As the Revolution came to a close and the related processes of state and national formation commenced, religion continued to play an important role. But religion's role did not become any simpler. Though clergymen participated in the process of ratifying the new federal Constitution in 1787 by speaking out either for or against its passage, what resulted was not a religious document. Still, the Constitution impacted American religious life, and its primarily secular nature did not preclude religious influence in its ratification. The complexity of religion's impact in American political culture is further demonstrated by the significant involvement of politicized clergymen in the formation of political parties and the myriad motivations behind such partisan activity. While many clergymen preached party because they shared the ideological vision of their fellow partisans, others participated in the divisive contests of the 1790s in an attempt to shore up an eroding social influence. And finally, the interplay of religion and early American political culture is further complicated in the way the extraconstitutional expectation that the president should be Christian was invented by the Federalists in the election of 1800 in a manner that manipulated existing fears and anxieties among the population concerning religious life in America. Whether looking at the political figures of America's past or those operating in the present, we should be wary of accepting at face value the religious utterances of political power brokers.

Regarding the laws and constitutions the founding generation adopted in the aftermath of the Revolution, Thomas Jefferson reminded his peers that "the earth belongs in usufruct to the living." In making such a plea, Jefferson hoped to prevent the binding of future generations to inflexible laws and intransigent forms of government. But Jefferson's statement applies to informal political traditions as well. The founders were empiricists. Though their creation of a republican government was in many ways based on an assortment of political philosophies, they largely operated on a system of trial and error. When twenty-first-century Americans assume that the founders discovered and agreed upon the place religion should have in national politics, they misunderstand their country's past. Religious expression was common in the political culture of the Revolutionary era, yet it was as much the calculated design of ambitious men seeking power as it was the natural outgrowth of a devoutly religious people.[3]

Notes

Introduction

1. For examples of high-profile narratives of the American Revolution that omit any significant examination of clergymen as political actors, see Middlekauf, *The Glorious Cause,* and McCullough, *1776.* On the dearth of historical studies of politicized clergymen during the Revolution and early republic, see Jeffrey L. Pasley, "The Cheese and the Words: Popular Political Culture and Participatory Democracy in the Early American Republic," in Pasley, Robertson, and Waldstreicher, eds., *Beyond the Founders,* 31–56, 52–53n.

2. The clergy's role in translating legal and philosophic justifications for the Revolution and the formation of party politics that followed is an important subject and, until now, an understudied one. Gordon S. Wood correctly identifies the clergy's intermediary role between elite and common men but does not recognize the elite-versus-elite power struggle inherent in the Revolution and says nothing of the clergy's continuance in this role during the decades immediately following the Revolution. See Gordon S. Wood, "Religion and the American Revolution," in Stout and Hart, eds., *New Directions in American Religious History,* 173–205, 175; and Bailyn, Wood, et al., *The Great Republic,* 1:291. James P. Byrd is thorough in his examination of the ways in which clergymen and political leaders alike used scripture to inspire patriotism. Byrd demonstrates that America's Revolutionary leadership, both clerical and secular, turned to scripture in order to depict the Revolution as a "sacred war" but writes under the assumption that all leaders who used religious rhetoric to drum up patriotism were genuine in their expressions. Neither Wood nor Byrd critically examines the motives behind the Revolutionary alliances of America's political and religious leaders. See Byrd, *Sacred Scripture, Sacred War.* Rhys Isaac emphasizes the politicization of the Virginia clergy on the eve of the Revolution, but he stresses clergymen's role as instigators of antipatriarchal expressions that subsequently became Revolutionary protest and not as willful intermediaries between elite and average Americans. See Isaac, *The Transformation of Virginia.*

3. For examples of books on the United States in the Revolutionary and early republic eras that largely overlook the political significance of religious language and symbols used by early national leaders, see Middlekauf, *The Glorious Cause;* and Pasley, *"The Tyranny of Printers."* For an example of books that overemphasize the same, see Kidd, *God of Liberty.* On the concessions made by the Anglican establishment in Virginia during the Revolution, see Ragosta, *Wellspring of Liberty.*

4. On the concept of "chosen land" as a nationalizing theme in the seventeenth- and eighteenth-century Atlantic world, see Colley, *Britons;* Smith, *Chosen Peoples;* and Guyatt, *Providence and the Invention of the United States.*

5. The debate over the Great Awakening as a cause of the American Revolution is long and complicated. It is mentioned here only as an example of historians identifying changes in Christian theology as a principal source of change in American politics. Works that address both sides of the debate over the Great Awakening and the American Revolution include Heimert, *Religion and the American Mind;* Isaac, *The Transformation of Virginia;* Butler, "Enthusiasm Described and Decried"; Lambert, *Inventing the "Great Awakening";* and Kidd, *The Great Awakening.* For an example of historians privileging the role and impact of evangelical Christians in the American Revolution and the process of nation building that followed, see Kidd, *God of Liberty.* Kidd acknowledges the role of both evangelical Christians and deists in the Revolution, but in depicting this alliance of American patriots coming from an assortment of religious backgrounds, he pays special attention to evangelicals. For more on Kidd's use of the label evangelical, see Mark David Hall, review of Kidd, *God of Liberty,* in *The Journal of American History* 98, no. 1 (June 2011): 191. For examples of historians placing significant emphasis on "evangelical" characteristics of American founders who would never have considered such a label for themselves, see Gaustad, *Sworn on the Altar of God,* 212–17; Kidd, *Patrick Henry,* 30; and Isaac, *The Transformation of Virginia,* 266–69.

6. Paine, *Common Sense,* in *The Complete Writings of Thomas Paine,* 1:45. On the intellectual transition from notions of the divine right of kings and the divine origins of civil society to concepts of social compacts as the origins of governments, see Hobbes, *De Cive;* Hobbes, *Leviathan;* Locke, *Two Treatises on Government;* and Locke, *Letter Concerning Toleration.* Enlightenment works in which philosophers considered the connection between religion and morality include Voltaire, *Dictionnaire Philosophique;* Baron D'Holbach, *The System of Nature;* and Rousseau, *Emile.*

7. Victor Hugo Paltsits, ed., *Washington's Farewell Address,* 151.

8. Ibid.; Tocqueville, *Democracy in America,* 298.

ONE   Congress and the Courtship of Providence

1. John Adams to Abigail Adams, June 11 and 17, 1775, *Adams Family Papers* (hereafter *AFP*); Rakove, *The Beginnings of National Politics,* is a thorough examination of the creation of a national governing body. However, Rakove omits any discussion of the role fast days played in this process.

2. Several works ably discuss the religious elements of the fast days proclaimed by Congress during the Revolution. Derek Davis claims Congress proclaimed fast days because it was "convinced that God was fighting its battles." See Davis, *Religion and the Continental Congress,* 88. James H. Hutson argues that fast days are evidence of congressional "concern for the spiritual condition" of its constituents and the army. See Hutson, *Religion and the Founding of the American Republic,* 55. Thomas S. Kidd pays little attention to fast days themselves but instead focuses on a vague and ill-defined "public spirituality" as a unifying force among Americans. See Kidd, *God of Liberty.* But Davis, Hutson, and Kidd do not consider the political motivations and reverberations of fast days. Only relatively recently have historians begun to directly engage with the political implications of fast days. David Waldstreicher expounds the political elements of such observances in general, arguing that patriots "linked an increasingly interregional war effort to their local experiences by holding 'continental' fasts." See Waldstreicher, *In the Midst of Perpetual Fetes,* 34–35. Nicholas Guyatt looks to providentialism as the key ingredient in the creation of American exceptionalism and traces the connection between providentialism and fast days back to the earlier Puritan rituals. See Guyatt, *Providence and the Invention of the United States.* Benjamin H. Irvin discusses the Revolutionary fast days more specifically, arguing that by taking upon itself the privilege of proclaiming fast days, Congress was sending a message to the king about its authority to govern. Irvin also contends that the congressionally appointed fast days demonstrate the faith many delegates placed "in the utility of emblems and rituals." See Irvin, *Clothed in the Robes of Sovereignty,* 7–8. Irvin, Guyatt, and Waldstreicher have laid a foundation for the study of fast days' political implications upon which this study builds.

3. On nations as ideological communities, see Anderson, *Imagined Communities.* Patricia Bonomi addresses the significance of the clergy's political sermons in mobilizing American patriots. Yet she does not address the political implications of fast days or delve into the full meaning and implication of the providential language utilized by the clergy and Congress alike. See Bonomi, *Under the Cope of Heaven,* 209–16.

4. William Perkins, *A Godly and Learned Exposition of Christ's Sermon in the Mount,* 330; Henry Mason, *Christian Humiliation,* 24–26. See also Hall, *Worlds of Wonder, Days of Judgment,* 166–72.

5. On the development and variety of American providentialism as an ideology, a theology, a worldview, and a language, see Guyatt, *Providence and the Invention of the*

United States. On the connection between millennialism and providentialism, see Ernest Lee Tuveson, *Redeemer Nation,* and Ruth Bloch, *Visionary Republic.*

6. Hall, *Worlds of Wonder, Days of Judgment,* 170–71; Boorstin, *The Genius of American Politics,* 60–61. For an almost encyclopedic compendium of New England's fast and thanksgiving days during the colonial, Revolutionary, and early republic eras, see Love, *Fast and Thanksgiving Days of New England.*

7. Bloch, *Visionary Republic,* 13–15; Edwards, *An Humble Attempt to Promote an Explicit Agreement.* For more on Edward's call for a concert of prayer, see Bloch, *Visionary Republic,* 17. On early uses of providentialism outside of New England, including the Virginia Company's attempts to attract settlers from England, see Guyatt, *Providence and the Invention of the United States,* 19–23.

8. Berens, *Providence and Patriotism in Early America,* 32–35; Isaac, *The Transformation of Virginia,* 243–45. John Ragosta demonstrates how, as fighting began in New England, religious dissenters originating from the Great Awakening increasingly linked their religious beliefs, practices, and hopes for religious liberty to the patriot's cause. See Ragosta, *Wellspring of Liberty,* 48–50.

9. "Resolution of the House of Burgesses Designating a Day of Fasting and Prayer," in *The Papers of Thomas Jefferson,* 1:105–6 (hereafter *PTJ*); *The Autobiography of Thomas Jefferson,* 11–13. On the Puritans' fast days during the English Civil Wars, see H. R. Trevor-Roper, "The Fast Sermons of the Long Parliament," in *Essays in British History,* ed. Trevor-Roper, 85–138.

10. Edward Rutledge to John Jay, June 29, 1776, in *Letters of Delegates to Congress,* 1:455–56 (hereafter *Letters*); George Washington to Lund Washington, August 20, 1775, in *The Papers of George Washington: Revolutionary War Series,* 1:334–37 (hereafter *PGW-RWS*); George Washington to Richard Henry Lee, August 29, 1775, *PGW-RWS,* 1:372–75. For an abundant collection of examples of the colonial regions' negative views of each other, see Merrill Jensen, "The Sovereign States: Their Antagonisms and Rivalries and Some Consequences," in Hoffman and Albert, *Sovereign States in an Age of Uncertainty,* 226–50. On the exploitation of sectional differences as a key component of British strategy during the war, see Julie Flavell, "British Perceptions of New England and the Decision for a Coercive Colonial Policy, 1774–1775," in Flavell and Conway, *Britain and America Go to War,* 95–115.

11. In the seventeenth and eighteenth centuries, new understandings of the physical body and its senses arising from the medical enlightenment were changing the way theologians wrote about the "body Christian" and the way political leaders wrote about the body politic. This fast day episode is but one of many that demonstrate the influence of philosophers such as René Descartes and John Locke, as the language of sensibility that they appropriated in their seventeenth-century writings was being applied by civic and spiritual leaders in the eighteenth century to both religious and political discourse. See Porter, *Flesh in the Age of Reason;* and Burstein, *Sentimental Democracy.*

12. For a record of acts, writings, and declarations of the Continental Congresses,

see *Journals of the Continental Congress* (hereafter *Journals*). On assuming the right to proclaim fast days, see Waldstreicher, *In the Midst of Perpetual Fetes*, 145; and Irvin, *Clothed in the Robes of Sovereignty*, 113. On the political legitimacy of Congress, see Marston, *King and Congress*, and Rakove, *The Beginnings of National Politics*. Both Marston and Rakove describe in depth the creation of national politics and the assumption of power by Congress; however, neither discusses the role of fast days in these processes.

13. John Adams to Abigail Adams, June 17, 1775, *AFP*. In Isaiah 35, Isaiah prophesies that "the desert . . . shall blossom as the rose," and the verses that follow indicate that this refers to the gathering and building up of Zion prior to the millennial era. Other themes from this chapter pertinent to the imperial crisis as Adams saw it were deliverance, redemption, and persuasion in which the blind can now see and the deaf can hear. The text of Duffield's sermon has not survived, but Adams's remark that he applied the entire prophesy to America suggests that the sermon that inspired Adams pertained to American millennialism.

14. As an example of Americans' unfamiliarity with new national political figures in Congress, when Jefferson visited Rhode Island in 1784, a Providence newspaper included a description of Jefferson's recent accomplishments in order to explain to their readers precisely who their distinguished visitor was. Coincidently, this is also the first instance on record of Jefferson being publicly credited with authorship of the Declaration of Independence. Original dateline, Providence, June 19, 1784. Reprinted in several New England newspapers, such as Boston's *American Herald*, June 28, 1784. See also Burstein and Isenberg, *Madison and Jefferson*, 110.

15. On the education of clergymen and the politicization of college faculties in the 1750s and 1760s that precipitated and encouraged the politicization of students during the Revolution, see Robson, *Educating Republicans*, 22, 29–50; and Hoeveler, *Creating the American Mind*, 347–49. For examples of the political activism of clergymen during the Stamp Act crisis, see Throop, *A Thanksgiving Sermon*, and Charles Chauncey, *A Discourse On "the Good News from a Far Country,"* in Thornton, *The Pulpit of the American Revolution*, 105–45. On the role of clergymen in the diffusion of information in colonial New England, see Brown, *Knowledge Is Power*, 65–81.

16. Dennis, *Red, White, and Blue Letter Days*, 40–41. On the role of ritual in the Revolution, see Shaw, *American Patriots and the Rituals of Revolution*. On the appearance of consensus for festive rites, see Waldstreicher, *In the Midst of Perpetual Fetes*, 8–9, 14. For more on the role of regions in the creation of national identities, see Ayers et al., *All Over the Map*, 1–10. For an analysis of Galloway's "Plan of Union," see Jasanoff, *Liberty's Exiles*.

17. Colley, *Britons*, 54.

18. Benjamin Rush to John Adams, June 27, 1812, in *Letters of Benjamin Rush*, 2: 1144. Rush writing that Adams "arose to defend the motion" suggests that Adams may not have been the delegate to propose the fast day. Either way, Adams's strong support for the motion was evident.

19. *Diary and Autobiography of John Adams,* 3:335. Nearly all of Jefferson's biographers describe Jefferson's aversion to public speaking and his typical reticence during congressional debates. For example, see Burstein and Isenberg, *Madison and Jefferson,* 44–45; and Ellis, *American Sphinx,* 36–38.

20. For composition of the committee, see *Journals,* 1:81. For a description of Hooper's draft, see *Letters,* 1:455–56 (the quotation is the editor's commentary on "William Hooper's Draft Resolve").

21. William Hooper, "William Hooper's Draft Resolve," in *Letters,* 1:455–56.

22. On the goals of reconciliation in 1775, see Maier, *American Scripture,* 21.

23. "Resolution for a Fast," June 12, 1775, *Journals,* 2:87.

24. Ibid.

25. *Journals,* 2:87, 22:138, 16:252.

26. Maier, *American Scripture,* 144.

27. On the authorship of the Declaration on the Causes and Necessity, see Boyd, "The Disputed Authorship of the Declaration on the Causes and Necessity of Taking up Arms, 1775." On the Quaker influence manifested in John Dickinson's political theory, see Calvert, *Quaker Constitutionalism and the Political Thought of John Dickinson,* 18–19, 233–34. Also see Irvin, *Clothed in the Robes of Sovereignty,* 81.

28. On the reasons for removing passages on the slave trade from Jefferson's draft of the Declaration of Independence, see Maier, *American Scripture,* 146–47. A comparison of Jefferson's draft with the final version of the Declaration comprises appendix C in ibid., 236–41.

29. John Adams to Abigail Adams, July 3, 1776, *AFP.* For more on the speech and Adams's use of biblical language, see Shaw, *The Character of John Adams,* 98–102; note 68 is especially comprehensive in listing sources by which aspects of Adams's speech can be reconstructed.

30. Royster, *A Revolutionary People at War,* 25–53; "Resolution for a Fast," March 20, 1779, *Journals,* 13:342–44; see Ecclesiastes 11:9. See also James G. Williams, "Proverbs and Ecclesiastes" in Alter and Kermode, *The Literary Guide to the Bible,* 263–82. There is no explanation in the congressional record of why Congress did not appoint a fast day in 1777. Entries in *Journals* for that year make no mention of any motions to this end. But the first day of thanksgiving appointed by Congress was in the fall of 1777. For a complete table of fast and thanksgiving days appointed by Congress between 1775 and 1784, see Irvin, *Clothed in the Robes of Sovereignty,* 116.

31. "Resolution for a Fast," March 20, 1779, *Journals,* 13:342–44. On anti-Catholicism in the American Revolution, see Cogliano, *No King, No Popery.*

32. "Resolution for a Fast," March 20, 1779, *Journals,* 13:343. For more on the depiction of Great Britain as working against God's plan for the world and throwing off their once favored status therein, see Bloch, *Visionary Republic,* 54–56. On the use of the Old Testament as a political text during the Revolution, see Shalev, *American Zion,* 15–49. Shalev devotes brief but specific attention to the Exodus narrative in the Revolution. See ibid., 6–7, 19–21.

33. On the proposed seals of the United States, see Hutson, *Religion and the Founding of the American Republic*, 50–51.

34. On British critiques of American slaveholders' complaints about imperial policy aimed at "enslavement," see Waldstreicher, *Runaway America*, 195–98. For Franklin's rebuttal to these British criticisms, see Benjamin Franklin, "Conversation Between an Englishman, a Scotchman, and an American, on the Subject of Slavery," in *The Papers of Benjamin Franklin*, 17:37–44.

35. J. P. Fokkelman, "Exodus," in Alter and Kermode, *The Literary Guide to the Bible*, 56–65 (quotation at 60).

36. Bloch, *Visionary Republic*, 60. Bloch quotes from Hitchcock, *A Sermon Preached at Plymouth December 22d, 1774*, and Samuel West, *A Sermon Preached Before the Honorable Council . . . May 26, 1776*, in Thornton, *The Pulpit of the American Revolution*, 319.

37. Bernard McGinn, "Revelation," in Alter and Kermode, *The Literary Guide to the Bible*, 523–41.

38. *British Royal Proclamations Relating to America*. The particular proclamations cited here were issued on January 23, 1778; January 1, 1779; December 13, 1779; January 12, 1781; and January 9, 1782.

39. For a detailed examination of the role fast days played among other celebratory rituals during the partisan battles of the 1790s, see Waldstreicher, *In the Midst of Perpetual Fetes*, 146–48. On the continuation of congressionally appointed fast and thanksgiving days during the Revolution and the discontinuation of the annual fast after 1783, see Davis, *Religion and the Continental Congress*, 88–90.

40. Despite the recent increase in the number of historians examining fast day rituals, surprisingly little has been written on how average Americans observed such occasions on a national and local scale or on how fast day observance varied from colony to colony or from urban spaces to rural spaces. Until now, the most detailed account of popular fast day observance is Irvin, *Clothed in the Robes of Sovereignty*, 110–15, in which Irvin focuses on the ritual's practice in the military and mentions the decisions of local governing bodies, both secular and ecclesiastical, to cancel previously appointed fasts in favor of the continental day in 1775. He also writes of Samuel Seabury as an example of partisan protest against the fast. In Davis, *Religion and the Continental Congress*, 67–68, the author argues that Congress took its fast days seriously and that "the American people took Congress's pronouncements with equal seriousness." But Davis only offers scant evidence of this, citing the decision of the Presbyterian synod of New York and Philadelphia to replace its fast day with the congressionally appointed day and the journal of one Philadelphian who comments on the city's calmness on these occasions. The reaction of Philadelphians to the 1775 and 1776 fast days is briefly described in isolation from the rest of the continent in Jane E. Calvert, "Thomas Paine, Quakerism, and the Limits of Religious Liberty during the American Revolution," in *Selected Letters of Thomas Paine*, 602–29. In Guyatt, *Providence and the Invention of the United States*, 96, 105, 116–21, the author primarily focuses on the popular observance of British fast days during the war to

compare the diverging British and American forms of providentialism but does not undertake a careful examination of how Americans responded to congressional fast days. In Hutson, *Religion and the Founding of the American Republic*, 51–54, Hutson takes John Adams at his word that the fast "did not disappoint" those in Congress, confident in the ritual's efficacy in bringing millions of Americans to pray at once, without verifying such claims with reports from across the country.

41. On the sociopolitical functions of "Revolutionary Rituals," see Shaw, *American Patriots and the Rituals of Revolution;* Waldstreicher, *In the Midst of Perpetual Fetes*, 27–52; and Irvin, *Clothed in the Robes of Sovereignty*, 1–18. On loyalty oaths utilized by local and state governments during the Revolution (discussed in greater detail in chapter 3), see Jasanoff, *Liberty's Exiles*, 21–23, 28, 40–41.

42. John Adams to Abigail Adams, July 23, 1775, *AFP*.

43. On the destruction of Quaker property on the 1775 fast day in Philadelphia, see Christopher Marshall Diary, July 20, 1775, Christopher Marshall Papers, 1774–1781, Historical Society of Pennsylvania; Irvin, *Clothed in the Robes of Sovereignty*, 115. On Adams's use of hyperbolic rhetoric, see Farrell, "John Adams and the Rhetoric of Conspiracy," 55–72.

44. Committee of Inspection and Observance, *In Committee Chamber, May 16, 1776;* Strauch, "Open for Business."

45. Calvert, "Thomas Paine, Quakerism, and the Limits of Religious Liberty." This chapter builds upon Calvert's description of Paine's use of the "common cause" rhetoric; see ibid. Also see Crabtree, "Holy Nation," 61. On the "common cause" rhetoric as it was generally employed by America's Revolutionary leaders, see Robert G. Parkinson, "'Manifest Signs of Passion': The First Federal Congress, Anti-Slavery, and Legacies of the Revolutionary War," in Hammond and Mason, *Contesting Slavery*, 49–68. On the power struggle between Philadelphia's Quakers and other non-Quaker elites, see Hanna, *Benjamin Franklin and Pennsylvania Politics*.

46. Steiner, *Samuel Seabury*, 159–64.

47. *The Diary of Reverend Ebenezer Parkman;* Jacob Bailey to anonymous, no date, quoted in Leamon, *The Reverend Jacob Bailey*, 110. More than eleven hundred loyalists fled Boston with the British army in 1776. See Jasanoff, *Liberty's Exiles*, 29.

48. Reverend John Newton Diary, Hargrett Rare Book and Manuscript Library, University of Georgia.

49. Entry for 1780, St. Thomas and St. Denis Parish Records, 1693–1778, South Caroliniana Library, University of South Carolina; Diary of Sermon Topics, Oliver Hart Papers, South Caroliniana Library, University of South Carolina.

50. *The Literary Diary of Ezra Stiles*, 1:591. On Newport's religious pluralism and the strain the Revolution placed upon it, see Carp, *Rebels Rising*, 99–142. In Leamon, *The Reverend Jacob Bailey*, 101, Leamon similarly comments that in the frontier settlement of Pownalborough (present-day Dresden, Maine), "the crisis drawing the town into the Revolution tended to politicize animosities that up to then had been largely religious and personal in nature."

51. Carp, *Rebels Rising*, 5–9, 13–17, 225. Also relevant to this study is Carp's description of the difficulty most American cities experienced in maintaining effective communication with the "rural hinterlands"; see ibid., 12–13.

52. Samuel Edward Butler Diary, Hargrett Rare Book and Manuscript Library, University of Georgia.

53. Numerous thanksgiving sermons were preached, published, and circulated throughout the country after the British surrender at Yorktown in 1781 and the signing of the Treaty of Paris in 1783, many of which used providential language to describe the battle and surrender at Yorktown, as well as to depict the character of British officers (particularly Cornwallis and Tarleton) as sinful. Two examples of Thanksgiving sermons with rhetoric very similar to Butler's poetry are Robert Smith, *The Obligations of the Confederate States of North America to Praise God*, and George Duffield, *A Sermon Preached in the Third Presbyterian Church*.

54. On the general practice of governments using religion to advance the aims of the state and the corresponding creation of American "civil religion," see Bellah, *The Broken Covenant*, 1–35.

TWO   Revolutionizing Chaplains

1. The causes of the political and social divide of South Carolina's tidewater and backcountry (piedmont) regions, particularly as they apply to Drayton, Tennent, and Hart's mission, are examined in Rachel N. Klein, "Frontier Planters and the American Revolution: The South Carolina Backcountry, 1775–1782," in Hoffman, Tate, and Albert, *An Uncivil War*, 40–47; Klein, *Unification of a Slave State*; Krawczynski, *William Henry Drayton*, 153–59; and Dabney and Dargan, *William Henry Drayton and the American Revolution*, 89–93. The lingering effects and presence of the North Carolina Regulators in this region are described in Butler, *Awash in a Sea of Faith*, 205–6.

2. For much of the expedition, the three men traveled separately. Hart was the first to commence his travels and the first to return home, citing discomfort with his prolonged travels and suggesting discouragement that his message was not universally well received. Hart and Tennent each recorded their experiences during the expedition in their respective diaries. See "Oliver Hart's Diary of his Mission through the Backcountry," Oliver Hart Papers, South Caroliniana Library, University of South Carolina; and William Tennent Journal, William Tennent Papers, South Caroliniana Library, University of South Carolina. Hart wrote his diary in code. The typescript cited above is the decoded version. Detailed descriptions of the political expedition to the South Carolina interior include Krawczynski, *William Henry Drayton*, 153–95; and Dabney and Dargan, *William Henry Drayton and the American Revolution*, 89–106.

3. William Tennent Journal, August 14, 1775, William Tennent Papers, South Caroliniana Library, University of South Carolina.

4. The expectations and duties of chaplains serving in the British army are described in detail in Holmes, *Redcoat*, 115–20. Historians have approached the role of chaplains in the Continental Army from various perspectives. Charles Royster explains how chaplains helped turn continental soldiers into a professional army. See Royster, *A Revolutionary People at War*, 161–74. Derek Davis briefly summarizes the activity of chaplains in the army. See Davis, *Religion and the Continental Congress*, 80–83. Thomas Kidd limits his description of the primary purpose and historical significance of chaplains in the army, claiming they served solely to "inculcate virtue among the soldiers." See Kidd, *God of Liberty*, 115–30. Jon Butler describes chaplains' frustration with the at times indifferent response of the soldiers to their sermons. See Butler, *Awash in a Sea of Faith*, 209–12. James P. Byrd thoroughly examines the specific Bible verses chaplains used most frequently. See Byrd, *Sacred Scripture, Sacred War*.

5. Historians have approached the role of congressional chaplains from various perspectives. James Hutson continues the overall theme of his book by claiming that the appointment of congressional chaplains is evidence of congressional piety. See Hutson, *Religion and the Founding of the American Republic*, 50–52. Derek Davis views the congressional chaplaincy merely as a continuation of colonial tradition in his larger effort to explain how the early actions of Congress should contribute to the way present-day jurists should attempt to understand the founders' "original intent." See Davis, *Religion and the Continental Congress*, 71–80, 91–92. Christopher C. Lund examines the history of congressional chaplains largely to uncover the historical background of significant twentieth-century legal decisions pertaining to the institutional relationship of church and state. He argues, in part, that the appointment of several Anglicans as chaplains was intended as a direct response to Parliament's Quebec Act, thereby portraying Congress as a strong supporter of Protestantism compared to a Parliament that was permissive to Catholicism. See Lund, "The Congressional Chaplaincies."

6. Nathanael Greene to John Adams, May 2, 1777, in *The Papers of General Nathanael Greene*, 2:64 (hereafter *PNG*); John Adams to Nathanael Greene, May 9, 1777, *PNG*, 2:74.

7. Notable among the European military experts upon whom Congress and the army relied was the Prussian-born Baron von Steuben, who served as a major general in the army and wrote a training manual, *Regulations for the Order and Discipline of the Troops of the United States*, which Congress published in 1779 and subsequently distributed to the army's officers. See Royster, *A Revolutionary People at War*, 213–54. The colonists realized their own martial disorder when compared to the British regulars more than a decade earlier during the Seven Years' War, and it had a lasting impact on Americans' sense of identity within the British Atlantic world. See Anderson, *A People's Army*, 135–41.

8. On the expanding presence of the urban working class in the British army and the pay rates for enlisted men compared to other professions, see Holmes,

Redcoat, xxi–xxiii, 75. The nature of desertion from the British army is described in ibid., 316–18. The resistance of the British army to the idea of the citizen-soldier during the Revolutionary era is detailed in ibid., 36–39. On the impact the idea of the citizen-soldier had in the American army, see Royster, *A Revolutionary People at War*, 42–44, 62–63.

9. Washington, "General Orders," August 3, 1776, *PGW-RWS*, 5:551; Washington, "Circular Instructions to the Brigade Commanders," May 26, 1777, *PGW-RWS*, 9:533; Royster, *An American People at War*, 76–77, 162; Hutson, *Religion and the Founding of the American Republic*, 55–56.

10. Washington to John Hancock, June 28, 1776, *PGW-RWS*, 5:134. The resulting resolution by Congress is in *Journals*, 4:61; Washington, "General Orders," July 9, 1776, *PGW-RWS*, 5:246.

11. Royster, *A Revolutionary People at War*, 153. On the frequent use of the Old Testament as a political text during the Revolutionary and early republic eras, Eran Shalev writes, "This Old Testament biblicism, the identification of the United States as a God-chosen Israel, provided a language to conciliate a modern republican experiment with the desire for biblical sanction; it could thus help alleviate anxieties related to the limits of human authority and legitimize the unprecedented American federal and republican endeavor." See Shalev, *American Zion*, 2 (quote), 7, 19–21.

12. Patrick Henry to Richard Henry Lee, June 18, 1778, in *Official Letters of the Governors of the State of Virginia*, 1:292; Hatch, *The Sacred Cause of Liberty*, 12. Eran Shalev cogently argues that while the Exodus narrative was extremely popular with Americans as a biblical typological trope by which to understand the historical significance of the Revolution, it was just one part of a much larger Hebraic revolutionary political imagination that enabled the Old Testament to function as a political text. See Shalev, *American Zion*, 19–21. James P. Byrd examines patriot use of Exodus scripture. See Byrd, *Sacred Scripture, Sacred War*, 45–72.

13. On the Bible as ancient history and the prominence of ancient texts in the American cultural imagination at this time, see Shalev, *American Zion*, and Shalev, *Rome Reborn on Western Shores*.

14. *Journals*, 2:119; see Deuteronomy 25:1–3 and 2 Corinthians 11:24. The total number of lashes permitted was changed to one hundred when the Articles of War were revised in 1776.

15. On the consistent lack of discipline in the Continental Army and the slim prospects of it ever being obtained, see Royster, *A Revolutionary People at War*, 164–65, 168–69. On the praise for the army as a whole for its success but the ultimate criticism for its failures directed at its officers, see ibid., 176–77, 188–89.

16. Isenberg, *Fallen Founder*, 22–23.

17. Nathanael Greene to John Adams, May 2, 1777, *PNG*, 2:64–65; Adams to Greene, May 9, 1777, *PNG*, 2:74; Greene to Adams, May 28, 1777, *PNG*, 2:98.

18. Nathaniel Folsom to New Hampshire Committee of Safety, July 1, 1775, in *New Hampshire Provincial Papers*, 7:557; Washington to Hancock, January 31, 1777,

PGW-RWS, 8:201–2. The different causes of desertion, as well as the desertion rates for the entire war, are discussed at length in Edmonson, "Desertion in the American Army during the Revolutionary War," ix–x, 217–61; Royster, *A Revolutionary People at War*, 60–61, 66, 71–72; and Ruddiman, *Becoming Men of Some Consequence*. For examples of other officers lamenting the rate of desertion from the Continental Army, see William Irvine to Washington, January 4, 1780, in *Pennsylvania Archives*, 8:74; William Heath to Washington, July 23, 1782, William Heath Papers, Massachusetts Historical Society, 25:379–80; and Edmonson, "Desertion in the American Army during the Revolutionary War," x–xi.

19. McDonnell, *The Politics of War*, 281–88.

20. Adams to Greene, June 2, 1777, *PNG*, 2:102–3. For a thorough accounting of the various punishments Congress affixed to desertion throughout the war, see Edmonson, "Desertion in the American Army during the Revolutionary War," especially chapter 4; and *Journals*, 3:330–34.

21. Washington to Jonathan Trumbull Sr., December 15, 1775, *PGW-RWS*, 2: 555–56.

22. "Petition from Sundry German Officers," May 6, 1778, Papers of the Continental Congress, no. 42, V, folio 69, Manuscript Division, Library of Congress; *Journals*, 11:507–8. At the time of Miller's appointment, Congress was assigning one chaplain per brigade. However, Miller's case was special, as he was not attached to a specific brigade but was to minister to all German-speaking soldiers.

23. Alexander McDougall to Washington, December 30, 1776, *PGW-RWS*, 7: 485–86.

24. Washington to Hancock, December 31, 1775, *PGW-RWS*, 2:624; *Journals*, 4:61.

25. Washington to Hancock, December 31, 1775, *PGW-RWS*, 2:624. For examples of clergymen delinquent in their duties as chaplains, see *Journals*, 14:659. On congressional legislation raising chaplains' pay, see *Journals*, 3:383–84.

26. *Journals*, 8:390, 14:978. This change in the distribution of chaplains in the army resulted in the denial of several chaplains' requests to serve. See *Journals*, 14: 773. Washington to Hancock, June 8, 1777, *PGW-RWS*, 9:644–45; Hancock to Washington, May 27, 1777, *PGW-RWS*, 9:540.

27. "Journal of Dr. Lewis Beebe," 343; William Tennent Journal, September 2–3, 1775, South Caroliniana Library, University of South Carolina; "Diary of Jabez Fitch, Jr.," 69; Royster, *A Revolutionary People at War*, 21, 162–63.

28. David Avery to David McClure, May 23, 1778, McClure Papers, Dartmouth College Library, quoted in Cunningham, *Timothy Dwight*, 81. For a detailed narrative of Dwight's service as a chaplain, see ibid., 59–87. Brigadier General Samuel Parsons was one of Washington's most trusted officers, and Washington leaned heavily upon him throughout the war. See Hall, *Life and Letters of Samuel Holden Parsons*.

29. For Washington's appeals to the First Congregationalist Church in Wood-

stock, Connecticut, see Washington to the First Church of Woodstock, March 24, 1776, *PGW-RWS*, 3:531–32.

30. For a brief narrative of Leonard's chaplain service, including examples of the respect various Revolutionary leaders had for him and his myriad bouts with mental illness, see Royster, *A Revolutionary People at War*, 170–74.

31. Evans, *A Discourse Delivered at Easton;* see Royster, *A Revolutionary People at War*, 166–68. For Benjamin Boardman's activity as a chaplain, see "Diary of Benjamin Boardman," 400–413.

32. *The New-York Diary of Lieutenant Jabez Fitch*, 27; "Journal of Dr. Lewis Beebe," 337–38.

33. John Adams to Abigail Adams, September 16, 1774, *AFP*. An earlier version of the discussion in this chapter of Jacob Duché and the politics of congressional prayer was published as McBride, "A 'Masterly Stroke of Policy.'"

34. Historians have typically looked to the practice of congressional prayer during the Revolution as evidence of the religious piety of the Continental Congress as a governing body, nothing more than a political entity engaging in religious worship. For instance, James H. Hutson argues that prayer in the Continental Congress simply demonstrates that America was "a deeply religious society," which had sent to Philadelphia "deeply religious leaders" and that instances of congressional prayer were merely moments when "anxious and penitent men" reached out to God in a moment of personal and collective peril. See Hutson, *Religion and the Founding of the American Republic*, 50–51, 76–77. One of Samuel Adams's biographers, Ira Stoll, uses the motion for prayer in the first meeting of Congress anecdotally as a way of demonstrating his subject's persistent piety even in political matters. While one would find it difficult to disprove this depiction of Adams as a devoutly religious man, Stoll infers that the rest of Congress supported the fiery Massachusetts delegate for similarly pious reasons. See Stoll, *Samuel Adams*, 133–36. Several works have been published on the faiths of America's founders. Some, such as Mapp, *The Faiths of Our Fathers*, argue that the founders were, by and large, devout Christians. Others, such as Frazier, *The Religious Beliefs of America's Founders*, and Holmes, *The Faiths of the Founding Fathers*, take more balanced approaches to the subject and place individual founders on a spectrum between orthodox Christianity and affirmed deism.

35. For the most part, records of what was said in the individualized prayers offered in Congress have not survived. Besides the first congressional prayer in 1774, the only surviving texts of individualized congressional prayers are those included in published fast day sermons clergymen preached to the delegates. Historians, then, must look to other sources to understand what prayer meant to Congress. The *Journals of the Continental Congress* is one such source and aids in reconstructing the circumstances in which these prayers were offered. Another valuable source is the personal correspondence of congressional delegates, which provides insight into how such prayers were generally received.

36. Neill, "Rev. Jacob Duché," 58–73. The quote is on page 60 and is from Reverend Smith in a letter of recommendation to the administration at Cambridge University. The only full-length biographical volume on Duché is Dellape, *America's First Chaplain.*

37. Psalm 35:1–4, 20; *The Book of Common Prayer,* 24.

38. The full text of Duché's prayer can also be located on the official website of the Office of the Chaplain, United States House of Representatives, under the title "The First Prayer of the Continental Congress, 1774," http://chaplain.house.gov /archive/continental.html. Also see Dellape, *America's First Chaplain,* 71–94.

39. In 1774, Myles Cooper, then president of Kings College, as well as Rev. Jonathan Boucher and Henry Addison of Maryland, visited Philadelphia to confer with Duché and other Anglican ministers there to discuss the conflict between the colonies and their parent government; see Neill, "Rev. Jacob Duché," 63. A chart depicting the political allegiance of each Anglican minister in America during the Revolution can be found in Bell, *A War of Religion,* 222–40.

40. John Adams to Abigail Adams, September 16, 1774, *AFP;* Samuel Adams to Joseph Warren, September 9, 1774, *Letters,* 1:26–27.

41. John Adams Diary, no. 22, September 10, 1774, *AFP.*

42. Abraham Clark to the Rev. James Caldwell, August 2, 1776, *Letters,* 4:605.

43. *Journals,* 1:25. Franklin's remarks are described in *The Debates in the Several State Conventions on the Adoption of the Federal Constitution,* 5:253–55. Franklin's motion that the convention pray was subsequently debated, and it was stated that the reason prayer had not hitherto been called for was because the convention had no funds with which to procure a chaplain. The motion was debated, and several delegates objected that to start inviting a clergyman to pray at that point in the convention would signal to those outside that there was severe contention and would also put the secrecy in which their deliberations were held in jeopardy. The convention adjourned without voting on Franklin's motion.

44. Duché, "The First Prayer of the Continental Congress, 1774." For the official record of how delegates were elected to Congress in 1774, see *Journals,* 1:14–24. Perhaps the most direct challenge to Congress's legitimacy and authority was the White Plains Protest, signed by dozens of American loyalists deeming illegal all colonial assemblies, committees, and congresses operating without the express sanction of the king. A patriot's report of the White Plains Protest was published in *Rivington's New-York Gazetteer,* April 20, 1775. See Steiner, *Samuel Seabury,* 155–62.

45. Duché, *The American Vine,* iii–vii.

46. Examples of positive comments on Duché's prayer and sermon include Silas Deane to Elizabeth Deane, July 20, 1775, *Letters,* 1:640; Connecticut Delegates to John Trumbull Sr., July 22, 1775, *Letters,* 1:647. *The American Vine* was first published by the Philadelphia printer James Humphrey in 1775 and subsequent editions by Benjamin Franklin, which attests to the esteem in which Franklin held Duché's sermon.

47. Neill, "Rev. Jacob Duché," 66–67. Duché wasted no time in announcing this liturgical change, doing so on July 4, 1776. Congress approved of Duché's alteration to the standard form of prayer, and many delegates mailed copies of the altered form to friends at home. For example, see Thomas Jefferson to John Page, August 5, 1776, *Letters*, 4:623. Benjamin Rush clipped a copy of the altered prayer published in a Philadelphia newspaper and preserved it in his scrapbook; see Rush Family Papers, 79:182, Library Company of Philadelphia.

48. *Journals*, 6:886–87.

49. Jacob Duché to George Washington, October 8, 1777, *PGW-RWS*, 11:430–36. Some delegates suggested that Duché's letter was dictated by General Howe and then written in Duché's hand; see *Letters*, 8:155. The label of Duché as an "apostate" comes from a letter from John Adams to Abigail Adams, October 25, 1777, *AFP*. The label of Duché as "the first of Villains" comes from a letter from John Penn and Cornelius Harnett to Richard Caswell, October 21, 1777, in *Letters*, 8:155–56. Henry Laurens's comments come from a letter dated October 25, 1777, in Henry Laurens Papers, Historical Society of Pennsylvania, 1:14.

50. *Journals*, 9:822.

51. *Journals*, 9:887. Duché subsequently donated the money to widows of Pennsylvania soldiers killed in the war. On Congress and its conscious efforts to project a particular image to the public, see Irvin, *Clothed in the Robes of Sovereignty*.

52. On Congress's 1775 fast day observance, see John Hancock to the New York Committee of Safety, July 20, 1775, *Letters*, 1:638.

53. On presidents of William and Mary College accepting appointment as chaplain in the House of Burgesses as a point of honor and public distinction, see Tyler, *The College of William and Mary in Virginia*.

54. *Records of the Presbyterian Church in the United States of America, 1706–1788*, 468; Paine, *Common Sense*, in *The Complete Writings of Thomas Paine*, 1:37.

55. On Congress's experience at Catholic mass, see Holmes, *The Faiths of the Founding Fathers*, 2–3. On the role Catholics played in the Revolution more generally, see Farrelly, *Papist Patriots*; Ragosta, *Wellspring of Liberty*, 3–13.

56. A contemporary copy of the *Westminster Confession of Faith* can be found in Early English Books Online, Cambridge University Library. Both Duffield and White remained influential religious figures after the Revolution. White became the first presiding bishop of the American Episcopal Church in 1789. Duffield remained prominent in the American Presbyterian Church before he died in 1794. Despite the increase in individualized prayers that accompanied Duffield's appointment, the delegates still wrote very little about the prayers they heard in Congress. Again, this could be because the frequency of congressional prayer turned it into a mundane ritual or merely a part of traditional legislative procedure. It is hard to know for sure.

57. Kevin J. Dellape demonstrates that Duché's growing discomfort with the Revolution was, in part, the product of class warfare in which radical Revolutionaries in Pennsylvania used the war with Great Britain as an opportunity to displace

the proprietary gentry that had served as the colony's ruling elite. See Dellape, *America's First Chaplain*, xv.

58. Thomas Paine, *The Crisis*, in *The Complete Works of Thomas Paine*, 1:91. The details of Duché's defection are briefly discussed in several secondary sources, but among the earliest and most thorough is Neill, "Rev. Jacob Duché." Duché discreetly returned to Philadelphia in 1792 and lived there quietly until his death in 1798.

59. Jacob Duché to George Washington, October 8, 1777, *The Washington-Duché Letters*. Examples of brief mentions or cursory descriptions of the content of this infamous letter appear in Neill, "Rev. Jacob Duché"; Burnett, *The Continental Congress*, 252–54; and William Pencak, "Out of Many, One: Pennsylvania's Anglican Loyalist Clergy in the American Revolution," in Pencak, *Pennsylvania's Revolution*, 97–102, 105–6. Also see Dellape, *America's First Chaplain*, 117–36. For the letter Francis Hopkinson wrote to his brother-in-law, see *The Washington-Duché Letters*.

60. Duché to Washington, October 8, 1777, in *The Washington-Duché Letters*.

61. Ibid. On the general concern among many Revolutionaries about the competency of the delegates in Congress to manage the Revolutionary War and establish an adequate government, see Burnett, *The Continental Congress*, 204–6, 650–51; and Irvin, *Clothed in the Robes of Sovereignty*, 245–51. For contemporaries' descriptions of Virginia's first delegations to Congress, see Burnett, *The Continental Congress*, 29–30. It is important to note that Peyton Randolph did not leave Congress for Virginia but rather died in 1775 while serving as the president of the representative body. Duché officiated at his funeral.

62. Duché to Washington, October 8, 1777, in *The Washington-Duché Letters*.

63. Ibid.

64. On the plight of Thomas Coombe, see High, "Thomas Coombe, Loyalist," 284–86; and Pencak, "Out of Many, One," 103–4.

65. Brydon, "Revision of the Prayer Book by an American Civil Legislature," 133–38. On Reverend Bass and other Boston Anglican clergymen who agreed to patriot demands that they stop praying for the king, see Leamon, *The Reverend Jacob Bailey*, 115–16.

THREE   Navigating Revolution

1. Though several historical works focus on the complexity involved in choosing sides during the Revolution (many of which are listed in the next note), some popular surveys on the Revolution continue to assume a strict ideological determinism in the process and pay little attention to the matter. For example, see Wood, *The American Revolution*.

2. On the tension caused by the choice between Revolution and loyalty, see Jasanoff, *Liberty's Exiles*, 5–17; Skemp, *William Franklin*, xii–xiv; and Tiedemann, *Reluctant Revolutionaries*. Some have taken a quantitative approach to analyzing how Americans chose sides. See Hull, Hoffer, and Allen, "Choosing Sides."

3. In Skemp, *William Franklin*, 267–73, the author identifies the loyalists as the ultimate losers of the Revolution, even more so than the British, citing (among other things) their struggles with the Loyalist Claims Commission. While no one could rightfully declare this group "winners" in any sense of the word, works such as Jasanoff's *Liberty's Exiles* and the experiences of loyalists such as Samuel Seabury present significant exceptions to this notion.

4. Several historians have argued that religious affiliation was a major factor in determining which side Americans supported during the Revolution. Examples include Thornton, *The Pulpit of the American Revolution;* Ireland, "The Ethnic-Religious Dimension of Pennsylvania Politics, 1778–1779"; and Steiner, *Connecticut Anglicans in the Revolutionary Era.* Some have even gone so far as to argue that religion was one of the primary factors over which the Revolutionary War was fought, including Bell, *A War of Religion*, x–xvi; and Doll, *Revolution, Religion, and National Identity*, 11–31. For an explanation of why many Anglican ministers supported the Revolution, see Brydon, "The Clergy of the Established Church in Virginia and the Revolution," 11–17. On Anglican dissenters negotiating with patriot leaders for religious liberty in Virginia, see Ragosta, *Wellspring of Liberty.* For an instance of an entirely Quaker regiment being formed in the Continental Army, see letter from John Tyler, May 12, 1775, Carter-Blackford Papers, 1736–1908, Albert and Shirley Small Special Collections Library, University of Virginia. Accounts of disciplinary action being taken against Quaker men joining the army can be found in Davis, *Quaker Records in Georgia*, 47–69.

5. A fair amount has been written on Samuel Seabury. The best book-length biography of the loyalist clergyman is Steiner, *Samuel Seabury.* Other informative and insightful works detailing Seabury's life as well as his political and ecclesiastical activities include Thomas, *Samuel Seabury*; E. E. Beardsley, *Life and Correspondence of the Right Reverend Samuel Seabury*; and Gould, "Wit and Politics in Revolutionary British America."

6. Much has been written about cultural, social, and religious retention in post-colonial societies, including the United States, in the late eighteenth and early nineteenth centuries. See Gould, *The Persistence of Empire*, and Gould, "A Virtual Nation."

7. Steiner, *Samuel Seabury*, 23–25, 34, 45–51, and 79–87. There is evidence that Seabury owned slaves, though on a small scale; see "Certificate of Transfer of Three Negros by S. Seabury to E. Hicks," November 1, 1765, Samuel Seabury Papers, General Theological Seminary, New York City.

8. Steiner, *Samuel Seabury*, 127–32.

9. Samuel Seabury, "Proposals for Establishing the Church of England in America," undated, Samuel Seabury Papers, General Theological Seminary. Also see Samuel Seabury, "Letter of Address to the Archbishop of York," November 24, 1783, Samuel Seabury Papers. On the earlier "plot" to appoint an English bishop over the church in America, see Bell, *A War of Religion*, and Bonomi, *Under the Cope of Heaven*, 199–216. Seabury explained in his proposal, "the easiest and most effectual

Method of encouraging & promoting Loyalty in the Colonies, is to encourage & promote the Church of England"; see Steiner, *Connecticut Anglicans*, 26.

10. The initials "A.W." in Seabury's pen name stood for "A" and "Westchester," as in "A Westchester Farmer." On Seabury's refusal to leave his clerical post, see Samuel Seabury to the Society for the Propagation of the Gospel in Foreign Parts secretary, November 14, 1775, Society for the Propagation of the Gospel in Foreign Parts Manuscripts B 2, Manuscript Division, Library of Congress, 644. On political divisions within his congregation, see Steiner, *Samuel Seabury*, 165.

11. Seabury, *Free Thoughts on the Proceedings of the Continental Congress*, 5, 18. Historians have written extensively on the slavery metaphor in Revolutionary rhetoric, arguing that it was used to elicit an emotional response from Americans and to tap into the Whig political tradition. Even more significantly, historians have described the hypocrisy of slaveholders using the slavery metaphor and the ways in which it was observed and criticized by English writers condemning the Revolution. See Dorsey, *Common Bondage*; Fliegelman, *Declaring Independence*, 140–47; and Waldstreicher, *Runaway America*, 181–82.

12. *New-York Gazetteer*, January 12, 1775. The political disposition of King's College faculty and students, as well as their respective political actions during the Revolution, are described in Roche, *The Colonial Colleges*, 36–39, 55–56, 62–63. On Hamilton's early political ambitions and the way they influenced his participation in the public sphere, see Chernow, *Alexander Hamilton*, 55–61; and Randall, *Alexander Hamilton*, 27–28, 56, 82–86.

13. Hamilton, *A Full Vindication of the Measures of Congress*, 8. Hamilton's use of the imagery of slavery tapped into the emotional power of such language demonstrated by the popularity of earlier patriotic pamphlets and the prominent place of such in the Declaration of Independence a year later. For examples, see Church, *Liberty and Property Vindicated*; Hopkins, *Rights of the Colonies Examined*, 41–48; and Thomas Jefferson, *A Summary View of the Rights of British America*, 9, 14–15.

14. Hamilton, *The Farmer Refuted*; Gould, "Wit and Politics in Revolutionary British America"; Steiner, *Samuel Seabury*, 155–67. "The White Plains Protest" appeared in Lewis Morriss, "To the PUBLIC," *New-York Gazetteer*, May 7, 11, and 18, 1775.

15. Steiner, *Samuel Seabury*, 165–69; Polf, *Garrison Town*.

16. Samuel Seabury to the British Treasury, undated, Samuel Seabury Papers, General Theological Seminary; William Franklin to British Treasury, October 31, 1783, Samuel Seabury Papers; T. B. Chandler to British Treasury, October 31, 1783, Samuel Seabury Papers. Detailed accounts of the Loyalist Claims Commission and the outcomes of many making their appeals include Jasanoff, *Liberty's Exiles*, 120–48; and Skemp, *William Franklin*, 267–73.

17. Abraham Jarvis to John Moore, William Markham, and Robert Lowth, April 21, 1783, Samuel Seabury Papers, General Theological Seminary; Thomas Bradbury Chandler to Samuel Seabury, July 5, 1777, Samuel Seabury Papers; Steiner, *Connecticut Anglicans*, 70–71; Steiner, *Samuel Seabury*, 184–90.

18. "Minute Book of the College of Bishops in Scotland," quoted in "Intercommunion of the American and Scottish Churches," *Scottish Ecclesiastical Journal* 1 (October 1851): 215; Skinner, *The Nature and Extent of the Apostolic Commission.*

19. Steiner, *Samuel Seabury*, 253–54. In a letter from Stephen James DeLancey to Seabury on October 26, 1785, Samuel Seabury Papers, General Theological Seminary, DeLancey informed Seabury that New York was experiencing a severe shortage of clergymen and personally appealed to the newly ordained bishop to help remedy the situation.

20. The plan for a united Episcopal Church to replace the Church of England's ecclesiastical structure was proposed in White, *The Case of the Episcopal Churches in the United States Considered.*

21. Rufus King to Elbridge Gerry, May 8, 1785, in *The Life and Correspondence of Rufus King*, 1:95; *The Diaries of George Washington*, October 10, 1785, 4:203–4.

22. James Rivington to Seabury, July 25, 1785, Samuel Seabury Papers, General Theological Seminary. William White attempted to resolve Seabury's concerns in a letter, specifically his dissatisfaction with the inclusion of laity in church conventions; see White to Seabury, October 18, 1785, Samuel Seabury Papers. For a thorough description of Seabury's disdain for many church leaders in the southern states, see Steiner, *Samuel Seabury*, 234–40.

23. Lohrenz, "The Advantage of Rank and Status."

24. Ibid.

25. Isenberg, *Fallen Founder*, 88–89; Alexander Hamilton to Robert Livingston, August 13, 1783, and Alexander Hamilton to Governeur Morris, February 21, 1784, in *The Papers of Alexander Hamilton*, 3:430–31, 512. The experiences of attorneys Andrew Ronald, John Warden, and John Wickham clearly demonstrate how loyalist attorneys in Virginia were able to criticize and even openly mock Revolutionary leaders, but because Virginia needed experienced attorneys, all three were allowed to continue practicing in the state simply by making disingenuous apologies. For more on Ronald and Warden, see Shepard, "Sketches of the Old Richmond Bar: Andrew Ronald"; Shepard, "Sketches of the Old Richmond Bar: John Warden"; Sabine, *Biographical Sketches of Loyalists of the American Revolution*, 2:427–28; Harrell, *Loyalism in Virginia*, 162–65; and Mays, *Edmund Pendleton, 1721–1803*, 2:192–93.

26. All of Seabury's extant sermons (manuscript and published) are in the Samuel Seabury Papers, General Theological Seminary. In 1786, Seabury revised the church's prayers without a struggle to reflect the country's political changes. On Seabury's altering the church's prayers after the Revolution, see Seabury, "Pastoral Letter," August 12, 1785, Samuel Seabury Papers. Samuel Seabury died on April 4, 1796, less than an hour after feeling sudden sharp pains in his chest; see Abraham Jarvis to Rev. S. Peters, April 4, 1796, Samuel Seabury Papers.

27. No full-volume biography of Bishop James Madison exists, but biographical sketches of the man and his influence on America's political, civil, religious, and educational history are included in numerous books and articles. For an account

of Madison's ecclesiastical activity, see Brydon, *Virginia's Mother Church and the Political Conditions under Which It Grew*, 2:474–91. On Madison's activity as an educator and college president, see Roche, *The Colonial Colleges*, 41, 73–74, 134–35; and Robson, *Educating Republicans*, 106–7, 158–59, 171. On Madison's political views, see Crowe, "Bishop James Madison and the Republic of Virtue." For an edited collection of many of Madison's letters on politics, see Gwaltney, "Bishop James Madison's Letters on Politics, 1787–1809."

28. On Jefferson's ambition and connection to George Wythe and Edmund Pendleton, see Burstein and Isenberg, *Madison and Jefferson*, 6–8, 15–16; and Ellis, *American Sphinx*, 26–27. On James Madison Jr.'s ambition and connection to Pendleton and John Witherspoon, see Burstein and Isenberg, *Madison and Jefferson*, 10–15; and Rakove, *James Madison and the Creation of the American Republic*, 2–7.

29. Boucher, *Reminiscences of an American Loyalist, 1738–1789*, 48; Rev. James Madison, *An Oration*.

30. Madison, *An Oration*, 6–8; Locke, *Two Treatises on Government*.

31. Madison, *An Oration*, 6–8.

32. Ibid., 8–9, 13–14. On the invocation of the Glorious Revolution to justify and encourage political resistance in the 1770s, see Tuckness, "Discourses of Resistance in the American Revolution," 555–56. For another example of a clergyman referencing the Glorious Revolution in his political sermons, see Emerson, *A Thanksgiving Sermon Preach'd at Pepperel*, 9–10. Preaching on the day of thanksgiving appointed in Massachusetts after the repeal of the Stamp Act, Emerson directly linked the resistance of 1669 to that of 1785, the latter a continuation of the tradition of the former. Interestingly, Thomas Paine negatively depicted the arrival of William of Orange in England as "A French bastard landing with an armed banditti and establishing himself King of England against the consent of the natives." His intent was to demonstrate that the English monarchy was derived from "very paltry rascally" origins and not divine appointment. Coupled with Madison's versions, it certainly demonstrates the flexible utility of English history as propaganda. See Thomas Paine, *Common Sense*, in *The Complete Works of Thomas Paine*, 1:14.

33. On the willingness to speak out against the king that came relatively late in the Revolutionary conflict, see Marston, *King and Congress*, and Eric Foner, *Tom Paine and Revolutionary America*, 74–87.

34. Madison, *An Oration*, 9–10.

35. Ibid., 11–12. For Madison's private declaration that state-established religion was tyrannical during the debate in Virginia in 1785, see "Bishop James Madison on Assessment, c. 1785," Breckinridge Family Papers, 1752–1965, Manuscript Division, Library of Congress.

36. Thomas Jefferson, "Act for Establishing Religious Freedom," January 16, 1786, manuscript, Records of the General Assembly, Enrolled Bills, record group 78, Library of Virginia. Detailed accounts of the movement to disestablish the Anglican Church include Peterson and Vaughan, *The Virginia Statute for Religious Freedom*,

and Ragosta, *Religious Freedom*. On Reverend Madison's activity during that debate, see Brydon, *Virginia's Mother Church*, 474–75.

37. On Madison's aversion to violence and warfare, see Madison, *A Form of Prayers to be used by the Ministers of the Protestant Episcopal Church*, and Madison, "Prayer at Jamestown," in William Meade, *Old Churches, Ministers and Families of Virginia*, 1:423–24.

38. Word of Madison's espionage was discovered too late by British customs officials but was reported in a letter from John Robinson to John Powell, September 15, 1775, Public Records Office, Colonial Office 5/146, f. 117, as cited in Wickwire, *British Subministers and Colonial America, 1763–1783;* also see Bell, *A War of Religion*, 173. On Madison's opinions of George Washington, see the bishop's memorial eulogy for the deceased president, *A Nation Mourns: Bishop James Madison's Memorial Eulogy on the Death of George Washington*.

39. James Madison to St. George Tucker, September 20 and 22, 1775, Tucker Coleman Papers, Swem Library, College of William and Mary.

40. The political temperaments of the faculty at William and Mary are best described in Robson, *Educating Republicans*, 40–43, 104–9; and Roche, *The Colonial Colleges*, 39–41, 133–34.

41. On the fate of the loyalist faculty at William and Mary (some of whom fled the country, while others remained in Virginia) and the dismissal of John Camm, see Robson, *Educating Republicans*, 41–42, 106–8; and Roche, *The Colonial Colleges*, 133–34.

42. Tyler, *The College of William and Mary in Virginia*, 57–58.

43. Ibid. Andrews was appointed in 1777, McClurg and Wythe in 1779. On the appointment of new faculty members at William and Mary by Madison, see Roche, *The Colonial Colleges*, 134–36. On Jefferson's plans for education reform, see ibid., and Robson, *Educating Republicans*, 106–9.

44. Reverend Madison to James Madison Jr., January 18, 1781, in *The Papers of James Madison*, 2:294.

45. Tyler, *The College of William and Mary in Virginia*, 58.

46. Though Madison's vision for an empire of republics mirrored that of Jefferson in many ways, a key difference between the two was that Madison viewed organized religion as having an essential (though not central) place therein, and Jefferson did not. See Crowe, "Bishop Madison and the Republic of Virtue." On Jefferson's views of the United States' potential for imperial expansion, see Onuf, *Jefferson's Empire*, 1–2, 7–9, 56–57; and Burstein and Isenberg, *Madison and Jefferson*, 387–92.

47. Meade, *Old Churches, Ministers, and Their Families*, 1:28–29; Issac A. Coles to Henry St. George Tucker, July 20, 1799, *William and Mary Quarterly*, 1st series, 4, no. 2 (October 1895): 105–8, quote at 107. For a broad study of the common ground of religious belief and enlightenment rationalism, see Sorkin, *The Religious Enlightenment*.

48. The only full-length biography of John Zubly is Martin, *John J. Zubly*, which

was published as an unrevised dissertation. Martin's book offers insight into Zubly's political writings but takes liberties in describing the moods and emotional reactions of Zubly to events based purely on speculation. The best brief biographical sketch of Zubly is in the introduction to an edited volume of his writings, *"A Warm & Zealous Spirit,"* ed. Randall M. Miller. Also see Daniel, "John Joachim Zubly—Georgia Pamphleteer of the Revolution" and Perkins, "John Joachim Zubly." On Zubly's status as Georgia's sole patriotic pamphleteer, see Adams, *American Independence,* which consists of a bibliography of all American pamphlets published about the Revolution.

49. On Zubly's early life, see Martin, "John J. Zubly Comes to America," 125–39. On the local church politics preventing Zubly's ecclesiastical appointment in South Carolina, see Martin, *John J. Zubly,* 12–17. On attempts to attract Swiss emigrants to South Carolina, see Smith, "Purrysburg."

50. Zubly recorded that shortly after meeting George Whitfield, the latter remarked to a crowd, "I am afraid of nobody at Savannah but this little man." See John J. Zubly to Ezra Stiles, October 10, 1768, in *Extracts from the Itineraries and Miscellanies of Ezra Stiles, 1775–1794,* 599. Adam's description of Zubly and his personality comes from "John Adams' Diary," September 15, 1775, in *Letters,* 1:194–95.

51. *The Colonial Records of the State of Georgia,* 9:144. By the time of his death in 1781, Zubly owned upwards of twenty-six hundred acres of land and several houses. See Cordle, "The Will of John Zubly," and Martin, *John J. Zubly,* 40–41. Zubly's first wife, Anna, died in 1765. He wed Anne Pyne sometime thereafter, but they had no children together. Both of Zubly's sons participated in the Revolution: John Zubly [Jr.] fought for the Americans, David Zubly for the British. For Muhlenberg's description of Zubly's library, see *Journals of Henry Melchior Muhlenberg,* 2:645, 679, 682.

52. Martin, *John J. Zubly,* 27–28. The bestowal of the honorary AM degree upon Zubly was recorded in Dexter, ed., *Extracts from the Itineraries and Miscellanies of Ezra Stiles,* 71. The honorary DD degree was awarded to Zubly by Princeton in 1774; see *Georgia Gazette,* December 7, 1774. Zubly eventually had a falling out with Whitfield, as he disagreed with the way the latter ran the orphanage at Bethesda and the at times condescending manner in which he and the orphanage's staff interacted with the community at large; see Martin, *John J. Zubly,* 62–65, 90–91.

53. John Joachim Zubly, *The Stamp Act Repealed,* in *"A Warm & Zealous Spirit,"* 32–49; Daniel, "John Joachim Zubly—Georgia Pamphleteer of the Revolution." *The Stamp Act Repealed* was Zubly's second publication. His first was a book on the last words of dying men and women, titled *The Real Christian's Hope in Death, Or, An Account of the Edifying Behavior of Several Persons of Piety in their Last Moments,* collected and published by J. J. Zubly; see Cohen, *South Carolina Gazette, 1732–1775,* 74.

54. Zubly, *An Humble Enquiry Into the Nature of the Dependency of the American Colonies Upon the Parliament of Great-Britain,* in *"A Warm & Zealous Spirit,"* 51–82.

55. Zubly, *Calm and Respectful Thoughts on the Negative of the Crown,* in *"A Warm*

& Zealous Spirit," 95–119. On the friction between the Georgia Commons House and Governor Wright, see Abbot, *Royal Governors of Georgia, 1754–1775*, 126–61.

56. Zubly, *The Law of Liberty*, in *"A Warm & Zealous Spirit,"* 123–61. *The Law of Liberty* was reprinted in Philadelphia and, because of its warning to Lord Dartmouth, in London. Other Americans then using language similar to Zubly's in urging their fellow colonists to be moderate in their approach to the crisis with Great Britain include John Dickinson and Joseph Galloway.

57. Zubly, *The Journal of the Reverend John Joachim Zubly* August 10–25 1775, 35–39.

58. John Adams to Abigail Adams, September 17, 1775, *AFP; The Literary Diary of Ezra Stiles*, 1:446.

59. *The Journal of the Reverend John Joachim Zubly*, September 16 and October 24, 1775, 40–43. Zubly's statement that republican government was "little better than government of Devils" is recorded in *Journals*, 3:491. On Zubly's opinions of Swiss politics and the larger political discourse from which it sprang, see Martin, *John J. Zubly*, 169; Oechsli, *History of Switzerland, 1499–1914*, 249; and Thürer, *Free and Swiss*, 69–72.

60. The debate on American trade policies during the Revolution is recorded in *Journals*, 3:471–504, the verbal exchange between Chase and Zubly being primarily contained on pages 481–83, 493–94, and 500–501.

61. Examples of historians retelling the story of Chase revealing in Congress a secret correspondence between Zubly and Wright include Zubly, *"A Warm & Zealous Spirit,"* 21–22; and Hazelton, *The Declaration of Independence*, 50–51. These authors maintain that fellow Georgia delegate Archibald Bulloch was dispatched home to prevent Zubly from sabotaging the patriot cause in the southernmost colony, but Archibald had been assigned to return to Savannah even before Zubly left. This is evidenced by a letter Zubly wrote to Bulloch on November 10, mentioning that he was leaving "greatly indisposed" but adding that his fellow delegate would "doubtless reach home before [him] tho' you should not depart these 10 days." Zubly promised "not to make any report to our council of safety till we are all present." See Zubly to William Houstoun and Archibald Bulloch, November, 10, 1775, John J. Zubly Manuscripts and Letters, 1770–1781, Georgia Historical Society. The origins of this myth appear to be a misreading of a passage in Ezra Stiles diary wherein the Connecticut clergyman wrote (several months after the fact) that Zubly had left Congress hastily and that Congress "sent one after him." Stiles then records a rumor that Zubly's 1776 imprisonment in Georgia resulted in part because he was suspected of maintaining a secret correspondence with the exiled royal governor of South Carolina, Lord Campbell; see *The Literary Diary of Ezra Stiles*, 2:10.

62. *Georgia Gazette*, January 3, 1776.

63. An official list of enemies to the United States residing in Georgia was created by the Provincial Congress; see *The Revolutionary Records of the State of Geor-*

gia, 1:47. The oaths of loyalty required by patriotic councils and their effects on confirmed loyalists and political neutrals alike are detailed in Jasanoff, *Liberty's Exiles,* 21–23, 28, 40–41; and Irvin, "Tar, Feathers, and the Enemies of American Liberties, 1768–1776," 216–17.

64. John J. Zubly, "To the Grand Jury of the County of Chatham," in *"A Warm & Zealous Spirit,"* 165–70, quote at 169.

65. *The Journal of the Reverend John Joachim Zubly,* May 8, 1779, 75–76.

66. The quotations from Zubly's diary are dated June 27, 1779; December 14, 1777; April 2, 1777; and March 4, 1781, in *The Journal of the Reverend John Joachim Zubly,* 64, 71, 78, and 93. The confiscation of patriot lands was based upon the Disqualifying Act of 1780, in *The Revolutionary Records of the State of Georgia,* 1:348–63.

67. John J. Zubly, "Helvetius Essays," in *"A Warm & Zealous Spirit,"* 171–99. This series consists of seven essays, each published separately in the *Royal Georgia Gazette* between July 27, 1980, and October 12, 1780.

68. Ibid., 173–77, 185, 187–88.

69. Ibid., 187, 197. For the passage of *Common Sense* Zubly found so reprehensible, see Paine, *Common Sense,* in *The Complete Works of Thomas Paine,* 1:22–23.

FOUR   Clergymen and the Constitution

1. Works that describe in detail the composition of the Constitutional Convention of 1787 and its secular focus include Beeman, *Plain and Honest Men;* Berkin, *A Brilliant Solution;* Burstein and Isenberg, *Madison and Jefferson,* 133–65; and Rakove, *Original Meanings.*

2. Several works briefly comment on the role clergymen played in the ratification process. Nicholas Guyatt devotes a short section of his analysis of providentialism to religious claims made in support of the Constitution. See Guyatt, *Providence and the Invention of the United States.* Pauline Maier periodically quotes individual clergymen in her examination of the ratification debates but does not give them attention as a significant (albeit divided) special interest group. See Maier, *Ratification.* Saul Cornell provides one of the most expansive and insightful examinations of Anti-Federalists and their legacy in American politics, but he does not include clergymen as a significant political group in the debates of 1787–88. See Cornell, *The Other Founders.* Thomas Kidd puts forth a brief account of the ratification debates and argues that evangelical clergymen played a major role in ensuring that the Constitution would not be hostile to Christianity and would ensure public virtue. Yet, because Kidd is so focused on a poorly defined category of evangelical clergymen, his account does not give a complete account of the role clergymen played as political actors with institutional and individual interests in the Constitution's adoption, and evangelical ministers are overly privileged therein. See Kidd, *God of Liberty,* 219–24. In Ericson, *The Shaping of American Liberalism,* and Siemers, *Ratifying the Republic,* the respective authors make passing references to individual clergymen participat-

ing in the ratification debates without examining the significant role they played collectively. The examination of the ratification debates that most directly addresses religious concerns is Stephen A. Marini, "Religion, Politics, and Ratification," in Hoffman and Albert, *Religion in a Revolutionary Age*, 184–219. Marini is less concerned with the political activism of clergymen than he is with demonstrating that religion mattered in the ratification process inasmuch as the religio-political alignments of delegates to state ratifying conventions influenced votes for and against the Constitution at a regional level.

3. Saul Cornell argues that the Federalists were a much more organized and cohesive group than their opponents. In fact, it was the Federalists who assigned the "Anti-Federalist" label to the opponents of the Constitution. Though the Anti-Federalists were hardly a cohesive group launching a coordinated campaign against ratification, Federalists found it easier to combat them by lumping them together under a single negative title. See Cornell, *The Other Founders*, 26–34.

4. Wood, *The Creation of the American Republic*, 606; H. J. C. Grierson, "Classical and Romantic: A Point of View," in Gleckner and Enscoe, *Romanticism: Points of View*, 41–54, quotes at 52. Since Wood made these claims, historians have written extensively on the Enlightenment and its place in America's intellectual, political, and social development. Henry F. May divides the Enlightenment as experienced in America into five distinct and chronologically ordered categories and not as a singular event. See May, *The Enlightenment in America*. Scholars have since largely abandoned the idea of the Enlightenment as a singular movement and a coherent body of thought. Instead, historians focus on a variety of enlightenments, each situated in a unique intellectual, political, and cultural context. Though these enlightenments informed one another, they were essentially autonomous intellectual movements; see Porter and Teich, *The Enlightenment in National Context*, and Conrad, "The Enlightenment in Global History." From this view, the American Enlightenment was not merely a European Enlightenment extending to North America but instead an individual movement, related to but distinct from its European counterparts. This conceptual framework is demonstrated in Ferguson, *The American Enlightenment*, in which Ferguson analyzes the American Enlightenment's distinctiveness as Americans receiving European ideas but using them "to express their own needs in the prolonged crisis of the Revolution and national formation" (25).

5. On William Bentley's sympathy for the Anti-Federalist position, see William Bentley Diary, October 3, 1787, in *The Documentary History of the Ratification of the Constitution*, 4:32–33 (hereafter *DHRC*). Bishop James Madison's opinion of the Constitution can be reconstructed from a series of letters on politics. See Bishop James Madison to Thomas Jefferson, March 28, 1787, Bishop James Madison Papers, Earl Gregg Swem Library Special Collections; Bishop James Madison to James Madison Jr., October 1, 1787, Bishop James Madison Papers; Bishop James Madison to Thomas Madison, October 1, 1787, Bishop James Madison Papers.

6. James Madison to Archibald Stuart, December 14, 1787, in *DHRC*, 8:237–

38; Madison to Edmund Pendleton, February 21, 1788, in *DHRC*, 8:398–99. For a detailed account of Madison's political calculations as he observed the ratification process in each state from his home in Virginia, see Rakove, *James Madison and the Creation of the American Republic*, 70–79.

7. "Marcus," *New York Daily Advertiser*, October 15, 1787, in *DHRC*, 19:85–87; "Letter V," in *DHRC*, 19:238. For examples of others arguing that clergymen supported the Constitution solely to provide financial stability include "Atticus IV," December 27, 1787, *Independent Chronicle*, in *DHRC*, 5:531; and Hugh Ledlie to John Lamb, January 15, 1788, in *DHRC*, 3:580–81. On Anti-Federalist charges that the Constitution was designed solely for the profit of speculators and property owners, see Beard, *An Economic Interpretation of the Constitution of the United States*.

8. "Convention Debates, 6 February, A.M.," in *DHRC*, 6:1454–55.

9. "Artisides," *New York Daily Advertiser*, September 10, 1787, in *DHRC*, 19: 22–23; "Convention Debates," in *DHRC*, 9:931.

10. "Berkeley County Meeting," September 28, 1787, in *DHRC*, 8:22; "Extract of a Letter from a Gentleman . . . in Fairfax County," *Providence United States Chronicle*, April 24, 1788, in *DHRC*, 9:756–57; "Timon," *New York Daily Advertiser*, March 22, 1788, in *DHRC*, 20:877–78. Richard Terrill to Garret Minor, December 6, 1787, in *DHRC*, 8:208.

11. *Philadelphia Freeman's Journal*, November 7, 1787, in *DHRC*, 19:185–86; "A Baptist," *New York Journal*, November 30, 1787, in *DHRC*, 9:331–37. The Baptist association's circular letter was published as a pamphlet titled *Minutes of the Baptist Association Held at New York, October 1787* . For an example of Federalist praise for the circular letter, see "Curtius III," *Daily Advertiser*, November 3, 1787, in *DHRC*, 19:174–75.

12. "Demosthenes Minor," *Gazette of the State of Georgia*, November 15, 1787, in *DHRC*, 3:234–36.

13. "Agricola's Opinion," *Poughkeepsie Country Journal*, April 1, 1788, in *DHRC*, 20:884–87.

14. Joseph Huntington, *A Discourse Adapted to the Present Day*, 9–11; Shalev, *American Zion*, 63; Paine, *Common Sense*, in *The Complete Writings of Thomas Paine*, 1:45. Huntington further extrapolated upon these biblical comparison in *God Ruling the Nations for the Most Glorious End*. For another example of a clergyman comparing America under the Articles of Confederation to Israel under the Hebrew constitution, see John Murray, *Jerubbaal, or Tyranny's Grove Destroyed*.

15. Samuel Langdon, *The Republic of the Israelites and Example to the American States*, 7–12. See Shalev, *American Zion*, 66–68.

16. Eran Shalev observes that comparisons of the new Constitution to the "Mosaic Constitution" provided Federalists "powerful historical vindication for their own political endeavor." See Shalev, *American Zion*, 75. Shalev specifically exams the influence of political Hebraism on the Constitution. Ibid., 50–69. Guyatt, *Provi-*

dence and the Invention of the United States, 142–46. On the political models Madison studied and the Constitutional Convention actually referenced, see James Madison, "Notes on Ancient and Modern Confederacies," in *The Papers of James Madison*, 9:3–24; also see Burstein and Isenberg, *Madison and Jefferson*, 136; and Rakove, *Original Meanings*, 45–46.

17. "Convention Debates, P.M.," December 12, 1787, in *DHRC*, 2:592–96. The development of Rush's religious beliefs throughout his life is discussed in Hawke, *Benjamin Rush*, 33–42, 259–61, 310–12, 320, 336. On the publication of Rush's speech in other states during the ratification debates, see ibid., 353–55.

18. Hawke, *Benjamin Rush*, 338–57.

19. Ibid., 351; "Newspaper Reports of Proceedings and Debates," in *DHRC*, 2: 366–68. For a thorough account of Rush's participation in the ratification debates, see Hawke, *Benjamin Rush*, 338–57.

20. *The Autobiography of Benjamin Rush*, 334–36. On the "Christianization" of the Enlightenment and the "enlightenment" of Christianity as a common theme in other countries' experience of enlightenments, see Sorkin, *The Religious Enlightenment*.

21. Hobbes, *De Cive*; Hobbes, *Leviathan*; Locke, *Two Treatises of Government*. On the prevalence of the liberalism of philosophers such as Hobbes and Locke in eighteenth-century American society, particularly as it pertained to the idea of the social contract, see Bailyn, *The Ideological Origins of the American Revolution*, 28–29, 229; and Rakove, *Original Meanings*, 18.

22. "Americanus II," *Virginia Independent Chronicle*, December 19, 1787, in *DHRC*, 8:244–48; *Pennsylvania Gazette*, October 17, 1787, in *DHRC*, 2:186. Though Rush did not speak out against such misuses and abuses of his pro-Constitution appeals, the use of the Constitution as a "test" of Americans' religious devoutness did not mesh with Rush's personal views on religious liberty; see Hawke, *Benjamin Rush*, 159–60.

23. On the Constitution as a tool by which Americans could "close the floodgates of morality," see *Middlesex Gazette*, October 22, 1787, in *DHRC*, 3:394–96.

24. Rousseau, *The Social Compact*, III, xi. Also see Slauter, *The State as a Work of Art*, 10–11.

25. On the inherent lack of cohesiveness and a clear-cut ideology among Anti-Federalists, see Cornell, *The Other Founders*, 1–15, 26–34; and Maier, *Ratification*, 93.

26. "Denatus," *Virginia Independent Chronicle*, June 11, 1788, in *DHRC*, 10:1600; Thomas Wilson to Archibald Stuart, November 4, 1787, in *DHRC*, 8:144–45.

27. "Agrippa XVI," *Massachusetts Gazette*, February 5, 1788, in *DHRC*, 5:863–68; "Samuel," *Independent Chronicle*, January 10, 1788, in *DHRC*, 5:678–80. The inclusion of "a Bankrupt" as a religiously undesirable individual in the same league as a pagan or a Muslim derived from the prevalent opinion in eighteenth-century American society that bankruptcy denoted the negative way society viewed debtors. Some were termed honest bankrupts and others fraudulent, the latter bringing debt

and sustained poverty upon themselves by hearkening to "Satan's temptations," principally pride, luxury, and lust. See Mann, *Republic of Debtors*, 36–44.

28. "Lycurgus," *American Herald*, October 29, 1787, in *DHRC*, 2:161–62.

29. "A Countryman II," *New York Journal*, November 23, 1787, in *DHRC*, 19:291–93. For a biographical sketch of Hughes and descriptions of his other Anti-Federalist publications, see Waldstreicher, *Slavery's Constitution*, 128–30; and Wakelyn, *Birth of the Bill of Rights*, 1:95–96. Other examples of Anti-Federalists critical of the Constitution's protection of slavery on religious grounds include DeWitt Clinton; see "A Countryman II," *New York Journal*, December 13, 1787, in *DHRC* 19:406–9.

30. Waldstreicher, *Slavery's Constitution*, 3–19, 107–51, quotes at 19 and 114. Some Anti-Federalists attacked the Constitution's protection of slavery from a purely secular perspective, including Benjamin Gale, Consider Arms, Malachi Maynard, and Samuel Field. See "Speech by Benjamin Gale, November 12, 1787," in *DHRC*, 3: 421–28, and *Hampshire Gazette*, April 9 and 16, 1788, in *DHRC*, 7:1733–1742. Waldstreicher argues that as an Anti-Federalist strategy, antislavery "typified the Constitution's tightly interwoven problems" of its "aristocratic, insufficiently republican, and possible deceitful character." See Waldstreicher, *Slavery's Constitution*, 117. In addition to Waldstreicher, several other historians have examined the role of slavery in the ratification debates, paying close attention to the antislavery arguments of the Anti-Federalists in particular. For instance, Robin L. Einhorn argues that the use of slavery-related issues to oppose the Constitution varied in each state and that this variety revealed the core of the issue for Federalists and Anti-Federalists alike: the relative treatment of northern and southern white men under the proposed federal government. See Einhorn, "Patrick Henry's Case against the Constitution." John P. Kaminski provides insightful commentary on the variations of Federalist and Anti-Federalist discourse over slavery and the Constitution in his published collection of primary source documents on the subject. See Kaminski, *A Necessary Evil?* However, none of these works focuses to any significant degree on the religious language used in these debates. On the Clintons' political interest in opposing the Constitution, see the biographical profiles of DeWitt Clinton and George Clinton in Wakelyn, *Birth of the Bill of Rights*, 1:49–54.

31. Charles Cotesworth Pinckney, "Debates in the Legislature and in Convention of the State of South Carolina, on the Adoption of the Federal Constitution," January 16, 1788, quoted in Kaminski, *A Necessary Evil?*, 158; George Mason, "Virginia Ratifying Debates," June 11, 1788, quoted in Kaminski, *A Necessary Evil?*, 161. Pauline Maier explains that Federalists used the inconsistency of Anti-Federalists on the slavery issue against their opponents by arguing that the Constitution could not be at once promotive and destructive of slavery. See Maier, *Ratification*, 284.

32. There were several prominent antislavery spokesmen among the clergy prior to the ratification debates. Perhaps the most notable was Reverend Samuel Hopkins, who published pamphlets directed at the Continental Congress urging it to

take action against slavery in the country's formative years. See Hopkins, *A Dialogue Concerning the Slavery of Africans*. Several late-eighteenth-century clergymen who supported the Constitution became leaders in the abolitionist movement of the nineteenth century, as did many of their children and parishioners. See Cleves, *The Reign of Terror in America*, 230–75. The theological tradition of the colonial New England clergy, in connection with theological developments of the Second Great Awakening, continued to fuel the abolitionist movement in antebellum America. See Minkema and Stout, "The Edwardsean Tradition and the Anti-Slavery Debate, 1740–1865," and Perry, *Radical Abolitionism*.

33. Richard Henry Lee to Edmund Randolph, October 16, 1787, in *DHRC*, 8:61. Many Americans joined Lee in his call for amendments, particularly a bill of rights. For an overview of the fight in the various states for the Bill of Rights, see the individual accounts of each state's ratifying process in Maier, *Ratification*, and Burstein and Isenberg, *Madison and Jefferson*, 166–208. On Lee's political background and the relative absence of religion as an influence on his political thought and writings, see McGauhy, *Richard Henry Lee of Virginia*.

34. "Valerius," *Virginia Independent Chronicle*, January 23, 1788, in *DHRC*, 8:313–15. On the idea of the Constitution as a "living," changeable document, and on the generational theory of constitutionalism espoused by men such as Jefferson, see Rakove, *Original Meanings*, xv; and Burstein and Isenberg, *Madison and Jefferson*, 167–69, 390. On the development of American "political theology" and how it differs from concepts of "civil religion," see Rounes, *Civil Religion and Political Theology*, and Bellah and Hammond, *Varieties of Civil Religion*.

35. The most extensive study of the origins, development, and political manipulation of the myth of American religious freedom is Sehat, *The Myth of American Religious Freedom*.

36. Sehat, *The Myth of American Religious Freedom*, 1–10, 227–54.

37. James Madison to Thomas Jefferson, October 24 and November 1, 1787, in *DHRC*, 8:103–4.

38. Isaac Backus Diary, January 1788, in *DHRC*, 4:983; "Massachusetts Convention Debates," February 4, 1788, in *DHRC*, 6:1421–22. For thorough examinations of Backus and his efforts to bring about religious liberty in Massachusetts, see McLoughlin, *Isaac Backus on Church, State, and Calvinism* ; and McLoughlin, *Isaac Backus and the American Pietistic Tradition*.

39. "Truth," *Massachusetts Centinel*, November 24, 1787, in *DHRC*, 4:234–35.

40. "A Landholder VII," *Connecticut Courant*, December 17, 1787, in *DHRC*, 3:497–501.

41. For examples of Federalists calling for an amendment instituting religious tests as a requirement for federal office holding, see "Summary of Alterations Proposed in the Revised Constitution," in *DHRC*, 9:771; and "Belchertown Preliminary Instructions," in *DHRC*, 5:901–2. On the initial hesitancy of Samuel Adams to

endorse the Constitution because it prohibited religious tests, see James Madison to Edmund Randolph, October 7, 1787, in *DHRC*, 4:58; and Edmund Pendleton to James Madison, October 8, 1787, in *DHRC*, 10:1774.

42. "A Friend to Good Government," *Poughkeepsie Country Journal*, April 8, 1788, in *DHRC*, 20:902–5. John Leland's objections to the Constitution were recorded by Joseph Spencer in a letter to James Madison; see *DHRC*, 8:424–27. Some politicians saw the fight for religious liberty as extending to Christianity only and called for a general expectation, if not an outright requirement, that federal office holders be Christian (though the particular denomination to which they belonged would not matter). For an example of this, see "Townsend Middlesex Country [Mass.], December 24," in *DHRC*, 5:1055–57; and "Convention Debates, 6 February, p.m.," in *DHRC*, 6:1471–73.

43. "A Watchman," *Worcester Magazine*, February 7, 1788, in *DHRC*, 5:879–81; "Curtiopolis," *New York Daily Advertiser*, January 18, 1788, in *DHRC*, 20:625–29; "Report of Convention Debates, 19 January," *New York Morning Post*, February 4, 1788, in *DHRC*, 6:1264–65.

44. Spellberg, "Could a Muslim Be President?" 494–96; also see Bradley, "The No Religious Test Clause and the Constitution of Religious Liberty," 710. For a thorough examination of the role Islam had in the political-religious thought and government policy at the time of America's founding, see Spellberg, *Thomas Jefferson's Qur'an*. On the size of Catholic populations in eighteenth-century America, see Carey, *Catholics in America*. On the size of the Jewish population in America at the same time, see Holmes, *The Faiths of the Founding Fathers*, 1–2. On the estimates of the Muslim population, see Spellberg, "Could a Muslim Be President?" For an examination of Islamic beliefs among African slaves in early America, see Gomez, *Black Crescent*, 143; and Diouf, *Servants of Allah*.

45. The term "Christian Sparta" was coined by Samuel Adams in 1780 when he wrote that he hoped Boston would come to deserve the title by the virtue of its residents after the Revolution. "They will be free," Adams declared, "no longer than while they remain virtuous." Samuel Adams to John Scollay, December 30, 1780, in *The Writings of Samuel Adams*, 4:237–38. Examples of historians arguing that Americans largely saw religious virtue as essential to republican virtue include Kidd, *God of Liberty*, 108–16; and Byrd, *Sacred Scripture, Sacred War*, 17–18.

FIVE   Preaching Party

1. John Trenchard, "Number III: Of the Contempt of the Clergy," *The Independent Whig*, in Trenchard and Gordon, *The English Libertarian Heritage*, 6–7.

2. On the popularity of Trenchard's *The Independent Whig* in Revolutionary America, see Bailyn, *The Ideological Origins of the American Revolution*, 35–37, 43–45.

3. For a thorough examination of the rise and fall of the Standing Order in Massachusetts, see Field, *The Crisis of the Standing Order*.

4. On religious liberty as a threat to the Standing Order from within and without Massachusetts, see Sassi, *A Republic of Righteousness*, 21–33; and Ruffin, *A Paradise of Reason*, 79–89. As late as 1760, the Congregationalist establishment represented approximately 40 percent of all Christian congregations in the thirteen colonies, most of which were in New England. In 1790, that proportion had dropped to 23 percent. Despite an increase in total membership, the position of the Congregationalist Church was weakening throughout the entire country with the growth of other denominations, and even its rate of growth within New England began to slow dramatically. See Marini, "Religion, Politics, and Ratification," in Hoffman and Albert, *Religion in a Revolutionary Age*, 190–96.

5. Weld, *A Sermon, Delivered on the Day of the Annual Fast;* Hooker, *The Moral Tendency of Man's Accountableness*, 24; Ely, *The Wisdom and Duty of Magistrates*, 26. Also see Sassi, *A Republic of Righteousness*, 88–91.

6. On the schism within the Standing Order, see Field, *The Crisis of the Standing Order*, 8–9, 49–81; and Sassi, *A Republic of Righteousness*, 25–26.

7. For the history of the Reign of Terror, see *The Oxford History of the French Revolution*, 247–71. For a statistical analysis of those killed and imprisoned during the Reign of Terror, see Greer, *The Incidence of the Terror during the French Revolution*. Many Americans in the southern states continued to support the French Revolution instead of turning to Great Britain as the country's principal European ally and trading partner because of the indebtedness of the planter class to British merchants and earlier attempts by the British to foment slave rebellion. See Fox-Genovese and Genovese, *The Mind of the Master Class*, 11–40. On the American response to the Reign of Terror, see Cleves, *The Reign of Terror in America*. On the rejection and tempering of radical political ideology in America that resulted in part from the violent turn of the French Revolution, see Cotlar, *Tom Paine's America*.

8. John Prince, *A Discourse, Delivered at Salem*, 14. On the ways the apprehensions of New England clergymen about the French Revolution played out in national and in local politics, see Sassi, *A Republic of Righteousness*, 75–83; and Cleves, *The Reign of Terror in America*, 73–94. On the temporary political unity of orthodox and liberal ministers within the Standing Order, see Field, *The Crisis of the Standing Order*, 7, 86–92.

9. Stephen Higginson to Timothy Pickering, May 27, 1797, Timothy Pickering Papers, Massachusetts Historical Society. On the 1833 demise of the Congregationalist establishment in Massachusetts, see Field, *The Crisis of the Standing Order*, 208–35.

10. Brydon, *Virginia's Mother Church*, 2:247. On the political choices and post-Revolutionary careers of individual Anglican clergymen in Virginia, see Brydon, "The Clergy of the Established Church in Virginia and the Revolution," 11–23, 123–43, 231–43, 297–309.

11. See Ragosta, *Wellspring of Liberty*, for a thorough examination of the negotiations between Anglicans and dissenting sects during the Revolution.

12. On Jefferson and Madison acting in the best interest of Virginia when they were engaged in national politics, see Burstein and Isenberg, *Madison and Jefferson*, 3–6.

13. Steiner, *Samuel Seabury.*

14. On the calculated efforts of Hamilton and others to create talking points for Federalists throughout the country, see Pasley, *The First Presidential Contest*, 221–22, 230–74.

15. Federalists in Congress such as Representative William Loughton Smith of South Carolina published newspaper essays and pamphlets that used the opposition's attachment to the ideas of French radicals as a means of depicting Republicans (and Thomas Jefferson in particular) as men with their heads in the clouds, too soft and effeminate to lead the United States to its rightful place among the powers of the earth. See Smith, *The Pretensions of Thomas Jefferson to the Presidency Examined;* and Stiles, *The United States Elevated to Honor and Glory*, 70. As an example of the claims Stiles was rejecting, a deist newspaper editor named Denis Driscol argued that deists were "the best citizens" because "the more the deists despise the superstitions that surround them, the more they impose upon themselves the agreeable task of being just and humane." See Driscol, *Temple of Reason*, June 3, 1801.

16. Belknap, *Dissertations on the Character, Death & Resurrection of Jesus Christ*, 8; Vestry Minutes, 1799–1816, St. Michael's Church Records, South Carolina Historical Society.

17. Paine, *The Age of Reason;* Palmer, *The Examiners Examined.*

18. Schlereth, *An Age of Infidels*, 4–5.

19. On the radical Enlightenment, see Israel, *Radical Enlightenment.*

20. Hume, *A Treatise on Human Nature*, part I, section XI; Pasley, *The First Presidential Contest*, 238–40. Also see Federici, *The Political Philosophy of Alexander Hamilton.*

21. Pasley, *The First Presidential Contest*, 231, 239–40; Burke, *Reflections on the Revolution in France;* Green, *A Sermon Delivered in the Second Presbyterian Church*, 25–26.

22. Dwight, *The Duty of Americans, at the Present Crisis*, 19–21; Morse, *A Sermon, Exhibiting the Present Dangers, and Consequent Duties of the Citizens*, 13.

23. Deane, *A Sermon Preached February 19th, 1795*, 11–16, quote at 16; Buel, *Reflections on the Inconsistency of Man, Particularly Exemplified in the Practice of Slavery* (New York, 1796). Rachel Hope Cleves explains that "the Federalist attack on southern opposition leaders as aristocratic slave owners resonated with attacks on southern Republicans as Jacobins and partisans of violence, despite the seeming incongruity of the two charges. Charges of slaveholding aristocracy did not undermine the Federalist argument that southerners were Jacobins, because the Federalists did not define Jacobinism by its democratic ideals. American anti-Jacobins redefined the French Revolution as a cataclysm of anarchic violence and the Jacobins as men of blood." See Cleves, *The Reign of Terror in America*, 104–52, quote at 112.

24. Pasley, *The First Presidential Contest*, 63–72. For a thorough examination of how Federalist clergymen criticized and warned against the unrestrained violence of the French revolutionaries and applied their criticisms to their Republican opponents (as well as to southern slaveholders in general), see Cleves, *The Reign of Terror in America*.

25. *American Daily Advertiser*, July 27, 1995. On Republican uses of street demonstrations and protests versus "Jacobin" violence, see Pasley, *The First Presidential Contest*, 91–92; and Waldstreicher, *In the Midst of Perpetual Fetes*, 108–15.

26. Jefferson to Gideon Granger, October 18, 1800, *PTJ*, 32:228. Porterfield, *Conceived in Doubt*, 9–10, 137–46, 150–54, quote at 139. Also see Paul Goodman, *The Democratic-Republicans of Massachusetts*, 93–95.

27. Backus, *The Kingdom of God*, 11–12; John Leland, *Politics Sermonized Exhibited in Ashfield*, 8. On Leland's career as a politicized clergyman, see Butterfield, "Elder John Leland, Jeffersonian Itinerant," 142–252. On Baptists (including Backus and Leland) as Republican activists, see Porterfield, *Conceived in Doubt*, 150–54.

28. Ruffin, *A Paradise of Reason*, 79–89.

29. William Bentley Sermon Collection, #530, #699, #806, #1099, Digital Collections and Archives, Tufts University. On Bentley's political preaching in the 1790s and 1810s, see Ruffin, *A Paradise of Reason*, 119–52.

30. J. Rixey Ruffin argues that Bentley's "Christian Naturalism," as well as his willingness to accept and baptize individuals the orthodox and liberal wings of the church rejected, was hardly "moral relativism." Instead, he was motivated by a sense that "Human frailty, though lamentable, should not prevent basically good people from joining his, and God's, family." See Ruffin, *A Paradise of Reason*, 79–89, quote at 86.

31. Ibid., 133 (quote), 164.

32. Porterfield, *Conceived in Doubt*, 163–75.

33. Benjamin Nones, *Aurora and General Advertiser*, August 13, 1800. For a biographical sketch of Benjamin Nones that highlights his political opinions, see Murastin, "Benjamin Nones." On the role of Jews and anti-Semitism in the early American republic, see Nathans, "A Much Maligned People"; Pencak, *Jews and Gentiles in Early America*; and Rock, *Haven of Liberty*. Rock also demonstrates that in New York City, at least, the division between Federalists and Republicans contributed to a schism within the Jewish community, as evidenced by a break away from the city's first synagogue, Shearith Israel. On the prominence of liberal rationalists in the Democratic-Republican clubs, see Pasley, *The First Presidential Contest*, 82–100.

SIX   The Myth of the Christian President

1. Thomas Jefferson to Joseph Priestley, March 21, 1801, *PTJ*, 33:393.

2. Numerous books and articles examine the religious aspects of the elections of 1796 and 1800. Edward J. Larsen examines the interplay and competition between

religion and science in the election. See Larsen, *A Magnificent Catastrophe*. Robert M. S. McDonald describes the actual effects Jefferson's election had on the American religious life after so many dire predictions concerning the religious ramifications of a Jefferson presidency. See McDonald, "Was There a Religious Revolution of 1800?," in Horn, Lewis, and Onuf, *The Revolution of 1800*, 173–98. Frank Lambert highlights the strategic aspects in the Federalist's attacks on Jefferson's religious beliefs. See Lambert, "'God—and a Religious President . . . [or] Thomas Jefferson and No God.'" Thomas S. Kidd argues that many evangelical Christians celebrated Jefferson's election in 1800 as the triumph of religious freedom, but he gives scant attention to the political motivations behind the antideist rhetoric leveled at Jefferson by Federalists. See Kidd, *God of Liberty*, 229–43. Other more general works on these elections that touch on their religious components to varying degrees include Ferling, *Adams vs. Jefferson*, 153–55; and Sharp, *The Deadlocked Election of 1800*, 104–5. In Freeman, "The Election of 1800," Freeman explains that a "crisis mentality" was pervasive in the country in the 1790s and was an influence on the extreme rhetoric and political maneuvering of both parties.

3. On elections and the expected behavior of candidates in the electoral process, see Elkins and McKitrick, *The Age of Federalism*, 721–22, 732–36; Sharp, *American Politics in the Early Republic*, 232–33; and Cunningham, *The Jeffersonian Republicans*, 275–98. The most thorough examination of early American newspapers and their role in the formation of political parties is Pasley, *"The Tyranny of Printers."*

4. Smith, *The Pretensions of Thomas Jefferson*, 18–19. See Pasley, *The First Presidential Contest*, 255–73. Other examples of anti-Jefferson publications organized in a fashion similar to Smith's include "From a Correspondent in Connecticut," as well as "Remarks on the Aurora, No. 1," in *Minerva, & Mercantile Evening Advertiser* (hereafter *Minerva*), September 3, 1796, and "An American," as well as "Of Religion," in *Minerva*, September 26, 1796. For detailed examinations of Jefferson's flight from Monticello in June 1781 and its political ramifications in the decades that followed, see Burstein and Isenberg, *Madison and Jefferson*, 78–84; and Kranish, *Flight from Monticello*.

5. Smith, *The Pretensions of Thomas Jefferson*, 36–39; Jefferson, *Notes on the State of Virginia*, Query XVII, 159.

6. Thorough examinations of the hostility toward religion displayed by French revolutionaries and the effect of Enlightenment philosophy upon religious life in France include Roche, *France in the Enlightenment*, 579–95; and Lewis, *Life in Revolutionary France*, 36–57. On the American perception of the antireligious elements of the French Revolution and fears of the violence it could bring to American shores, see Cleves, *The Reign of Terror in America*. On the reception of Paine in America after the publication of *The Age of Reason*, see Foner, *Tom Paine and Revolutionary America*, 118, 245–49; and Cotlar, *Tom Paine's America*, 1–17. For a historical analysis of Jefferson's views and reasons for publishing *Notes*, see Wilson, "The Evolution of Jefferson's 'Notes on the State of Virginia.'" For the Virginia Statute for Religious

Freedom, see Thomas Jefferson, "Act for Establishing Religious Freedom," January 16, 1786, manuscript, Records of the General Assembly, Enrolled Bills, record group 78, Library of Virginia. Detailed accounts of the statute's drafting, debate, and long-term effects are in Ragosta, *Religious Freedom*, and Peterson and Vaughan, *The Virginia Statute for Religious Freedom*.

7. McDonald, "Was There a Religious Revolution of 1800?," 181; Robert Troup to Rufus King, October 1, 1800, in *The Life and Correspondence of Rufus King*, 3:315. On the partisan battle for public opinion during the Adams administration, see Elkins and McKitrick, *The Age of Federalism*, 719–26; and Pasley, *"The Tyranny of Printers,"* 119–31.

8. Dwight, *The Duty of Americans, at the Present Crisis*, 4–7. Earlier that year, Dwight published two sermons that he preached at Yale's commencement exercises in September 1798, under the title *The Nature, and Danger, of Infidel Philosophy: Exhibited in Two Discourses, Addressed to the Candidates for the Baccalaureate, in Yale College.* As the title suggests, this pamphlet contained diatribes against Enlightenment philosophy similar to those contained in *The Duty of Americans.* Biographies of Dwight that include examinations of his politics include Fitzmier, *New England's Moral Legislator*, and Cunningham, *Timothy Dwight, 1752–1817.* On the movement of New England clergymen away from liberal philosophies in the decades following their involvement in the American Revolution, see Ruffin, *A Paradise of Reason*, 119–32.

9. Sorkin, *The Religious Enlightenment*, 6. Though Sorkin's study primarily focuses on the enlightenments of Europe, his claims can be applied to the popular reaction to Enlightenment philosophy throughout the Western world, including America. For examples and explanations of how eighteenth-century Americans negotiated Enlightenment rationalism with religious tradition, see Ferguson, *The American Enlightenment*, 42–79.

10. Dwight, *The Duty of Americans, at the Present Crisis*, 8, 16–17.

11. On the complex religious framework through which New England clergymen viewed the French Revolution's violence as well as its animosity toward religion (particularly the disestablishment of Catholicism), see Cleves, *The Reign of Terror in America*, 7–8. Cleves demonstrates how the clergy nationwide (but particularly in New England) disagreed on how the French Revolution fit in their providential view of the past and providential prophesies of the future.

12. Timothy Dwight to James Hillhouse, March 1, 1800, Hillhouse Family Papers, Sterling Memorial Library, Yale University.

13. McDonald, "Was There a Religious Revolution of 1800?," 174; Rhys Isaac, "'The Rage of Malice of the Old Serpent Devil': The Dissenters and the Making and Remaking of the Virginia Statute for Religious Freedom," in Peterson and Vaughan, *The Virginia Statute for Religious Freedom*, 139–69. Connecticut did not disestablish the Congregationalist Church until 1818. The Congregationalist Church in Massachusetts remained the state's established church until 1833. On changes to Connecti-

cut's social order and the ecclesiastical presence therein before, during, and after the Revolution, see Bushman, *From Puritan to Yankee*, and Beasley, "Emerging Republicanism and the Standing Order." Though Bushman demonstrates an increase in individual liberty during Connecticut's colonial era and Beasley makes a strong case for an emerging opposition party in the state during the 1790s, both admit that the Congregationalist establishment remained firmly in place before 1800. On developments within Massachusetts's social order, see Field, *The Crisis of the Standing Order.* Field examines how an alliance of clerical-intellectuals and merchants united to maintain traditional Congregationalists' cultural and political authority well into the early nineteenth century despite an increasingly heterogeneous citizenry and an emerging capitalist economy.

14. "A Humble Citizen," *Connecticut Courant*, March 17, 1800; "Political Miscellany," *Western Star*, October 27, 1800. Even Rhode Island, another Federalist stronghold, experienced antideist rhetoric aimed at Jefferson during this election cycle, but this appears to have come largely in response to Republicans attempting to make inroads in that state. Aaron Burr prematurely reported to Madison and Jefferson that the latter's political fortunes were rising in that state just as Rhode Island papers began to publish claims that Jefferson was "a man who has, in his writings, proclaimed himself to the world a *Deist*, if not an Atheist," whereas it could not be declared that Adams "was an infidel in principle . . . or a dupe to the wild anti-Christian, and demoralizing theories of the age, which have corrupted mankind." See "Investigator," *Newport Mercury*, September 30, 1800.

15. For congressional and presidential election results by county and congressional district, see Lampi Collection of American Electoral Returns, 1788–1825, American Antiquarian Society, 2007; and Martis, *The Historical Atlas of Political Parties*, 73–77. Many Virginian Federalists accused their in-state Republican rivals of rigging the election of 1800 by altering the state's electoral legislation, awarding all of Virginia's electoral votes to the candidate that won the state as a whole, thereby eliminating the small but potentially significant handful of electoral votes Adams may have won in Federalist districts; see "Alexandria, November 4," *Columbian Mirror and Alexandria Gazette*, November 4, 1800.

16. "A Freeholder," *Columbian Mirror and Alexandria Gazette*, October 27, 1796; "A Friend of the Government," *Columbian Mirror and Alexandria Gazette*, May 7, 1795. In Thomas C. Thompson, "Perceptions of a 'Deist Church' in Early National Virginia," in Sheldon and Dreisbach, *Religion and Politics in Jefferson's Virginia*, 41–58, Thompson argues that there was far more discontent among Virginians over Jefferson's religion in 1796 than in 1800 and that the difference can be explained as a popular belief that deism was no longer a threat to Christians in the state by the latter date. Yet numerous works, including Cleves, *The Reign of Terror in America*, and Walters, *The American Deist*, indicate that apprehension of philosophies associated with France in general, and deism in particular, remained strong until the final years of Jefferson's second term. In reality, the drop off in antideist campaign publi-

cations in Virginia is better explained by a population growing increasingly Republican than one that was growing less concerned for the preservation of religion.

17. Allen, "David Barrow's *Circular Letter* of 1798." For Virginia's election returns in 1800, see Lampi Collection of American Electoral Returns, 1788–1825.

18. A search of the inclusive databases of the period's pamphlets and newspapers, Early American Imprints, series 1, and the American Antiquarian Society's "Clarence" database, reveals that nearly twice as many pamphlets and newspaper essays criticizing Jefferson's candidacy based upon his religious beliefs originated in the swing states of New York, Pennsylvania, and South Carolina than all the other states combined.

19. Isenberg, *Fallen Founder*, 196–202; Freeman, "The Election of 1800." When the deadlocked election went to the House of Representatives, several Federalists in Congress continued to use religious rhetoric to support Burr over Jefferson, emphasizing that Burr was neither "a professed deist; nor a scoffer at religion." See Burstein and Isenberg, *Madison and Jefferson*, 359–60. The use of such arguments among elected officials suggests that Federalists leaders believed attacks on Jefferson's religion could be effective in states where electors were selected by state legislators as well as in those where electors were chosen by popular vote.

20. Linn, *Serious Considerations on the Election of a President*, 14, 18, 23–25, 28, 32.

21. On medieval and early modern European conceptions of nations as "Christian" as it relates to the development of European orientalism, see Obolensky, "Nationalism in Eastern Europe in the Middle Ages"; and Said, *Orientalism*, 64–71. On the development of national providentialism in early modern England, see Anthony Fletcher, "The First Century of English Protestantism and the Growth of National Identity," in Mews, *Religion and National Identity*, 309–17; Patrick Collinson, "England and International Calvinism, 1558–1640," in Prestwich, *International Calvinism, 1541–1715*, 196–223; and Guyatt, *Providence and the Invention of the United States*, 14–17.

22. Historians largely agree that the number of Americans practicing non-Christian religions was small in the late eighteenth century, with an estimated Jewish population just over one thousand and a marginal populations of Muslims, Hindus, and Buddhists estimated at less than ten each (though an unknown number of African slaves may have been Muslims). See Spellberg, "Could a Muslim Be President?"; Hutson, *Forgotten Features of the Founding*, 111–12, 128; and Austin, *African Muslims in Antebellum America*. However, statistics concerning religious adherence among Christians in the years before and immediately after the Revolution have long been a contentious subject among American historians. It is important to note that church membership is not the only indicator of Christian belief, yet religious historians have pored over these statistics as important indicators of where the religious landscape stood at various points in America's history. In Stark and Finke, "American Religion in 1776," the authors offer a complex analysis of church attendance to determine a low religious adherence of between 10 and 12 percent of

Americans in 1776. James H. Hutson contests the numbers and ratios upon which Stark and Finke's study is based and argues for a much higher (though unspecified) percentage of Americans adhering to Christian denominations. See Hutson, *Forgotten Features of the Founding*, 111–24. Other historians have approached statistical analyses of church adherence in ways that take into account the varying fortunes of different denominations before and after the Revolution, as well as an assortment of reasons Americans attended church beyond or in addition to individual belief in a denomination's theology: social, cultural, economic, political, geographic, and so forth. See Bonomi, *Under the Cope of Heaven*, 87–127; and Butler, *Awash in a Sea of Faith*, 206–24.

23. *The Claims of Thomas Jefferson to the Presidency*, 8, 10, 17, 52; *Gazette of the United States*, September 10, 1800.

24. Elkins and McKitrick, *The Age of Federalism*, 523–24; Martis, *The Historical Atlas of Political Parties*, 76–77.

25. DeSaussure, *Citizens of South-Carolina on the Approaching Election of President and Vice-President of the United States*, 17n; DeSaussure, *Answer to a Dialogue Between a Federalist and a Republican*, 21.

26. It is important to note that not all clergymen in swing states were against Jefferson's candidacy in 1800. Even in Massachusetts and Virginia, Federalist and Republican strongholds, respectively, many clergymen either ignored allegations of his disregard for religion or looked past it to what they believed were more pressing issues. Notable examples of outspoken clergymen promoting Jefferson's candidacy include Unitarian minister William Bentley of Salem, Massachusetts, and Baptist minister David Barrow of Virginia and Kentucky.

27. Clinton, *A Vindication of Thomas Jefferson*, 1; Pollard, *Serious Facts, Opposed to "Serious Considerations,"* 7; *A Test of the Religious Principles, of Mr. Jefferson*, 5–6; Beckley, *An Address to the People of the United States*, 6. Beckley's political activity and effectiveness as a party organizer (as well as his admiration for Jefferson) is explained in Cunningham, "John Beckley," and Pasley, "'A Journeyman, Either in Law or Politics.'"

28. Russell, *To the Free Men of Rhode-Island*, 2; Wortman, *A Solemn Address to Christians and Patriots*, 12–13. For a brief biographical sketch of Wortman, see *Political Sermons of the American Founding Era*, 2:1478.

29. Bishop, *An Oration on the Extent and Power of Political Delusion*, 6, 24, 67; *Address to the Citizens of Kent*, 4.

30. John Adams to Benjamin Rush, August 28, 1811, in *The Works of John Adams*, 9:635–40; Adams to Rush, June 12, 1812, in *Old Family Letters*, 391–96; Rush to Adams, June 4, 1812, in *Letters of Benjamin Rush*, 2:1138–39; John Adams to Thomas Jefferson, June 30, 1813, in *The Adams-Jefferson Letters*, 346–47.

31. Joseph Delaplaine to Thomas Jefferson, November 23, 1816, Thomas Jefferson Papers, Manuscript Division, Library of Congress. The other biography Delaplaine claimed was running with unconfirmed rumors of Jefferson's conversion to Chris-

tianity was Wilkinson, *Memoirs of My Own Time*. Wilkinson had served in the Continental Army as an officer and had been involved in the "Burr Conspiracy" that had captured the nation's attention a decade earlier. Despite Delaplaine's claim, Wilkinson made no mention of Jefferson's rumored conversion in any volume of his memoirs. For a description of Jefferson's efforts to dispel rumors that he was an enemy of religion during his presidency, see McDonald, "Was There a Religious Revolution of 1800?," 187–94.

32. Jefferson to Delaplaine, December 25, 1816, Thomas Jefferson Papers, Manuscript Division, Library of Congress.

33. Jefferson to Adams, January 11, 1817, in *The Adams-Jefferson Letters*, 505–6.

34. Jefferson to Thomson, January 9, 1816, Thomas Jefferson Papers, Manuscript Division, Library of Congress. Thomson's translation of the Septuagint was published as Charles Thomson, *The Holy Bible, Containing the Old and New Covenant, Commonly Called the Old and New Testament, Translated from the Greek*. Jefferson's own reworking of the four gospels was posthumously published as *The Life and Morals of Jesus of Nazareth*. The correspondence among Jefferson, Delaplaine, and Thomson is discussed in detail in Burstein, *Jefferson's Secrets*, 225–27, 245–47; and in Gaustad, *Sworn on the Altar of God*, 123–24.

35. On the successes and failures of Jefferson's administration, see Burstein and Isenberg, *Madison and Jefferson*, 423–25, 463–65; also see McDonald, "Was There a Religious Revolution of 1800?," 187–94. On the demise of the Federalist party, see ibid., 547–84, 586–87; and Buel, *America on the Brink*, 219–35.

36. The quote from Bishop White is taken from his response to a letter from a Colonel Mercer in 1835 as recorded in Wilson, *Memoir of the Life of the Right Reverend William White*, 197–98. On Washington's religious beliefs and practices, see Holmes, *The Faiths of the Founding Fathers*, 59–71; Chernow, *Washington*, 131–32; and Thompson, *"In the Hands of Good Providence,"* 52. On Washington's refusal to take communion, Chernow explains that the president displayed "an Enlightenment discomfort with religious dogma," as he was "sober and temperate in all things, distrusted zealotry," and "would have shunned anything, such as communion, that might flaunt his religiosity." Holmes suggests that it derived more from a matter of personal conscience, even the inclusion of elements of deism in his personal Christian beliefs.

37. This idea of driving irreligion out of the public space, expressed in Applebee, *Inheriting the Revolution*, 198–99, 204, was also broached in earlier historical works, such as Hatch, *The Democratization of American Christianity*, and Lewis, *The Pursuit of Happiness*. On post-Revolutionary reform predating the Second Great Awakening and in contrast to evangelicalism, see Ruffin, *A Paradise of Reason*.

38. Peterson, *The Jefferson Image in the American Mind*.

39. Burstein, *America's Jubilee*.

40. On political attacks against Jackson's anticlericalism, see Jortner, "Cholera, Christ, and Jackson." On the anti-Catholic rhetoric used against Al Smith in 1824,

see Slayton, *Empire Statesman*, ix–x, 299–317. Detailed accounts of anti-Catholic rhetoric leveled at Kennedy in 1960 and the ways it hurt and helped his presidential hopes are discussed in Casey, *The Making of a Catholic President*, and Carty, *A Catholic in the White House?*

Conclusion

1. Rush, Commonplace Book, August 8, 1811, in *The Autobiography of Benjamin Rush*, 339.

2. Anderson, *Imagined Communities*. The "Christian Nation" question has spawned a veritable cottage industry of scholarly publications. Works that treat this question as a viable historical construct include Noll, Hatch, and Marsden, *The Search for Christian America*, and Cornett, *Christian America?* Several historians have recently started to question the utility of the "Christian Nation" construct. John Fea, for instance, provides a summary of the present-day culture wars over America's past and argues that the history of America's founding era is far too complex to be confined to simple constructs such as the "Christian Nation" question. Yet Fea stops short of pushing for the historical community to abandon the "Christian Nation" paradigm altogether. See Fea, *Was America Founded as a Christian Nation?* David Sehat demonstrates the faultiness of histories and pieces of political commentary that emphasize the early United States as a country in which an exceptional level of religious freedom lay as the cornerstone of American liberty, as well as claims that the country has been in a steady state of religious decline from the alleged high religiosity of the founding era. See Sehat, *The Myth of American Religious Freedom*. Amanda Porterfield effectively challenges claims that Christianity—and evangelicalism in particular—was naturally intertwined in American concepts of republicanism and democracy. See Porterfield, *Conceived in Doubt*.

Researchers approaching the "Christian Nation" question from a quantitative study of church attendance include Stark and Finke, "American Religion in 1776." For a direct challenge to the claims of Stark and Finke, see Hutson, *Forgotten Features of the Founding*, 111–31. There are numerous works making arguments based upon the founders' religious beliefs. For examples of those arguing that the founders were by and large Christian, or at last sympathetic to Christianity in their respective worldviews, see Mapp, *The Faiths of Our Fathers*; and Hutson, *Religion and the Founding of the American Republic*. An example of those arguing that the founders were a more secularly minded group is the polemical Kramnick and Moore, *The Godless Constitution*. More balanced examinations of the founders and their religious beliefs include Holmes, *The Faiths of the Founding Fathers*; Frazier, *The Religious Beliefs of America's Founders*; and Waldman, *Founding Faith*.

Examples of scholarship focusing on a legal or institutional approach to the "Christian Nation" question abound. Daniel L. Dreisbach argues that it was not until the twentieth century that Jefferson's "wall" metaphor eclipsed and supplanted constitutional texts in church-state discourse. See Dreisbach, *Thomas Jefferson and the Wall of Separation between Church and State*. James H. Hutson contends that tradition and constitutional precedents of church-state relations in early America did not exclude religion from the operation of government but instead served to ensure liberty of conscience. See Hutson, *Church and State in America*. In Kramnick and Moore, *The Godless Constitution*, the authors insist that the framers of the Constitution willfully omitted any mention of God from the Constitution as a conscious statement that religion had no place in the functions of government. More recent and balanced approaches to the inclusion or exclusion of religion in America's legal, constitutional, and institutional history include Kabala, *Church-State Relations in the Early American Republic, 1787–1846*, Ragosta, *Religious Freedom*, and Meyerson, *Endowed by Our Creator*.

3. Thomas Jefferson to James Madison, September 6, 1789, *PTJ*, 15:392–97.

Bibliography

Manuscript Collections

Albert and Shirley Small Special Collections Library, University of Virginia, Charlottesville
  Joseph Carrington Cabel Papers
  Carter Family Papers
  Carter-Blackford Papers
  William Davis Personal Narrative
  Fitzhugh Family Collections
  William Fogg Letters
  David Griffith Papers
  Reverend John Hurt Address
  William Livingston Papers
  James Monroe Papers
  Thomas Nelson Letter
  Papers Pertaining to the Lebanon Presbyterian Church
  Edmund Pendleton Letter
American Antiquarian Society, Worcester, MA
  Jesse Appleton Letters
  Samuel Bixby Diary
  Ashley Bowen Diary
  Abner Brownell Diary
  Asa Dunbar Diary
  Thomas Fessenden Sermons
  Nathan Fiske Papers
  Justus Forward Diaries
  Lampi Collection of American Electoral Returns, 1788–1825
  Stephen Peabody Diaries
  Jonathan Sayward Diaries

Digital Collections and Archives, Tufts University, Medford, MA
    William Bentley Sermon Collection
Earl Gregg Swem Library Special Collections, College of William and Mary, Williamsburg, VA
    Tucker Coleman Papers
    Bishop James Madison Papers
    John Page Memorandum Book
General Theological Seminary, New York City
    Samuel Seabury Papers
Georgia Historical Society, Savannah
    Historic Augusta Incorporated Revolutionary and Early Republic Era Manuscripts
    Minutes of the Georgia Council of Safety
    George Walton Letters and Biography
    John J. Zubly Manuscripts and Letters, 1770–1781
Hargrett Special Collections and Rare Books, University of Georgia, Athens
    Samuel Edward Butler Diary
    William Manson Papers
    Reverend John Newton Diary
Historical Society of Pennsylvania, Philadelphia
    James Allen Diary
    Henry Laurens Papers
    Christopher Marshall Papers
Library Company of Philadelphia
    Rush Family Papers
Library of Virginia, Richmond
    Records of the General Assembly
Manuscript Division, Library of Congress, Washington, DC
    Breckinridge Family Papers
    Papers of the Continental Congress
    Society for the Propagation of the Gospel in Foreign Parts Manuscripts
    Thomas Jefferson Papers
Massachusetts Historical Society, Boston
    William Heath Papers
    Timothy Pickering Papers
South Carolina Department of Archives and History, Columbia
    Christ Church Parish, SC, Vestry Minutes, 1708–1759 and 1797–1847
    Journal of the Constitutional Convention of 1790
    Secona Baptist Church, Pickens, SC, Minutes, 1795–1945
    St. John's, Colleton Parish, South Carolina Vestry Minutes, 1734–1874
South Carolina Historical Society, Charleston
    St. Michael's Church Records

The First Consistory Book of the Germ. Evang. Lutheran Church of St. John the
    Baptist
South Caroliniana Library, University of South Carolina, Columbia
    Oliver Hart Papers
    St. Thomas and St. Denis Parish Records
    William Tennent Papers
Sterling Memorial Library, Yale University, New Haven, CT
    Dwight Family Papers
    Hillhouse Family Papers
Virginia Historical Society, Richmond
    Benjamin Bartholomew Diary
    William Bolling Diary
    Episcopal Church, Diocese of Virginia Papers, 1709–1792
    Robert Lewis Diary
    William Spencer Diary
    St. John's Church Vestry Book
    Wickham Family Papers

Newspapers

American Daily Advertiser (Philadelphia)
American Herald (Boston)
Aurora and General Advertiser (Philadelphia)
Columbian Mirror and Alexandria Gazette (Alexandria, VA)
Connecticut Courant (Hartford)
Gazette of the United States (New York City and Philadelphia)
Georgia Gazette (Savannah)
Minerva, & Mercantile Evening Advertiser (New York City)
National Intelligencer (Washington, DC)
New Jersey Gazette (Trenton)
Newport Mercury (Newport)
New-York Gazetteer (New York City)
Rivington's New-York Gazetteer (New York City)
South Carolina Gazette (Charleston)
The Temple of Reason (Philadelphia)
Western Star (Stockbridge, MA)

Published Diaries

Adams, John. *Diary and Autobiography of John Adams.* Edited by L. H. Butterfield.
    Cambridge, MA: Harvard University Press, 1961.

Beebe, Lewis. "Journal of Dr. Lewis Beebe." *Pennsylvania Magazine of History and Biography* 59, no. 4 (October 1935): 321–61.

Boardman, Benjamin. "Diary of Benjamin Boardman." *Proceedings of the Massachusetts Historical Society,* 2nd series, 7 (May 1892): 400–413.

Fitch, Jabez. "Diary of Jabez Fitch, Jr." *Proceedings of the Massachusetts Historical Society,* 2nd series, 9 (May 1894): 40–91.

———. *The New-York Diary of Lieutenant Jabez Fitch.* Edited by W. H. W. Sabine. New York: Colburn and Tegg, 1954.

Parkman, Ebenezer. *The Diary of Reverend Ebenezer Parkman, of Westborough, Massachusetts.* Edited by Harriette M. Forbes. Westborough, MA: Westborough Historical Society, 1899.

Stiles, Ezra. *The Literary Diary of Ezra Stiles, D.D., LL.D., President of Yale College.* Edited by Franklin Bowditch Dexter. 3 vols. New York: Charles Scribner's Sons, 1901.

Zubly, John J. *The Journal of the Reverend John Joachim Zubly, A.M., D.D., March 5, 1770 through June 22, 1781.* Edited by Lilla Mills Hawes. Savannah: Georgia Historical Society, 1989.

Published Document Collections

Adams Family Papers: An Electronic Archive. Massachusetts Historical Society, http://www.masshist.org/digitaladams.

Adams, John. *The Works of John Adams.* Edited by Charles Francis Adams. 10 vols. Boston: Little and Brown, 1950–1956.

Adams, John, and Thomas Jefferson. *The Adams-Jefferson Letters.* Edited by Lester Cappon. Chapel Hill: University of North Carolina Press, 1959.

Adams, Samuel. *The Writings of Samuel Adams.* Edited by Henry Alonzo Cushing. 4 vols. New York: Octagon Books, 1968.

Boucher, Jonathan. *Reminiscences of an American Loyalist, 1738–1789.* Edited by Jonathan Bouchier. Boston: Houghton Mifflin, 1925.

British Royal Proclamations Relating to America, 1603–1783. Edited by Clarence S. Brigham. Worcester, MA: American Antiquarian Society, 1911.

The Colonial Records of the State of Georgia. Edited by Allen D. Candler et al. 27 vols. Atlanta and Athens: State Printers, 1904–1916, and University of Georgia Press, 1976.

Davis, Robert Scott, ed. *Quaker Records in Georgia: Wrightsborough, 1772–1793, Friendsborough, 1776–1777.* Augusta, GA: Augusta Genealogical Society, 1986.

The Debates in the Several State Conventions on the Adoption of the Federal Constitution. Edited by Jonathan Elliot. 5 vols. Philadelphia: J. B. Lippincott, 1907.

The Documentary History of the Ratification of the Constitution. Edited by Merrill Jensen, John P. Kaminski, Gaspare J. Saladino, et al. 26 vols. to date. Madison: Wisconsin Historical Society, 1976–.

Franklin, Benjamin. *The Papers of Benjamin Franklin*. Edited by Leonard W. Labaree et al., 41 vols. to date. New Haven, CT: Yale University Press, 1959–.

Greene, Nathanael. *The Papers of General Nathanael Greene*. Edited by Richard K. Showman et al. 13 vols. Chapel Hill: University of North Carolina Press, 1976–2005.

Hamilton, Alexander. *The Papers of Alexander Hamilton*. Edited by Harold C. Synett. 27 vols. New York: Columbia University Press, 1961–1987.

Jefferson, Thomas. *The Autobiography of Thomas Jefferson*. Edited by Paul Leicester. New York: Knickerbocker, 1914.

———. *The Papers of Thomas Jefferson*. Edited by Julian P. Boyd et al. 39 vols. to date. Princeton, NJ: Princeton University Press, 1950–.

Journals of the Continental Congress, 1774–1789. Edited by Worthington C. Ford. 34 vols. Washington, DC: Library of Congress, 1904–37.

King, Rufus. *The Life and Correspondence of Rufus King*. Edited by Charles R. King. 6 vols. New York, 1894–1900.

Letters of Delegates to Congress, 1774–1789. Edited by Paul H. Smith et al. 25 vols. Washington, DC: Library of Congress, 1976–2000.

Madison, James. *The Papers of James Madison*. Edited by William T. Hutchinson et al. 37 vols. to date. Chicago and Charlottesville: University of Chicago Press, 1961–1977, and University Press of Virginia, 1977–.

Muhlenberg, Henry Melchior. *Journals of Henry Melchior Muhlenberg*. Translated and edited by Theodore G. Tappert and John W. Doberstein. 3 vols. Philadelphia, 1942.

New Hampshire Provincial Papers: Documents and Records Relating to the Province of New Hampshire, from 1774 to 1776. Edited by Nathaniel Bouton. 7 vols. Nashua, NH, 1873.

Official Letters of the Governors of the State of Virginia. Edited by H. R. McIlwaine. 3 vols. Richmond: Virginia State Library, 1926–1929.

Old Family Letters. Edited by Alexander Biddle. Philadelphia: J. P. Lippincott, 1892.

Paine, Thomas. *The Complete Writings of Thomas Paine*. Edited by Philip S. Foner. 2 vols. New York: Citadel, 1945.

———. *Selected Letters of Thomas Paine*. Edited by Ian Shapiro and Jane E. Calvert. New Haven, CT: Yale University Press, 2014.

Paltsits, Victor Hugo, ed. *Washington's Farewell Address, in Facsimile, with Transliterations of all the Drafts of Washington, Madison, & Hamilton : Together with Their Correspondence and Other Supporting Documents*. New York: New York Public Library, 1935.

Pennsylvania Archives: Selected and Arranged from Original Documents in the Office of the Secretary of the Commonwealth. 135 vols. Philadelphia: Joseph Severns, 1853–1935.

Political Sermons of the American Founding Era. Edited by Ellis Sandoz. 2 vols. Indianapolis: Liberty Fund, 1998.

The Pulpit of the American Revolution; or, the Political Sermons of the Period of 1776. Edited by John Wingate Thornton. Boston: Lothrop, 1876.

Records of the Presbyterian Church in the United States of America, 1706–1788. New York: Arno, 1969.

The Revolutionary Records of the State of Georgia. Edited by Allen D. Candler et al. 3 vols. Atlanta: Franklin and Turner Company, 1908.

Rush, Benjamin. *The Autobiography of Benjamin Rush: His "Travels Through Life" Together With His Commonplace Book for 1789–1813.* Edited by George Corner. Philadelphia: American Philosophical Society, 1948.

————. *Letters of Benjamin Rush.* Edited by L. H. Butterfield. 2 vols. Princeton, NJ: Princeton University Press, 1951.

Stiles, Ezra. *Extracts from the Itineraries and Miscellanies of Ezra Stiles, D.D., LL.D., 1775–1794: With a Selection from His Correspondence.* Edited by Franklin Bowditch Dexter. New Haven, CT: Yale University Press, 1916.

Trenchard, John, and Thomas Gordon. *The English Libertarian Heritage: From the Writings of John Trenchard and Thomas Gordon in "The Independent Whig" and "Cato's Letters."* Edited by David L. Jacobson. Indianapolis: Bobbs-Merrill, 1965.

Washington, George. *The Diaries of George Washington.* Edited by Donald Jackson and Dorothy Twohig. 6 vols. Charlottesville: University Press of Virginia, 1976–1979.

————. *The Papers of George Washington: Presidential Series.* Edited by Dorothy Twohig et al. 16 vols. to date. Charlottesville: University Press of Virginia, 1987–.

————. *The Papers of George Washington: Revolutionary War Series.* Edited by Philander D. Chase et al. 18 vols. Charlottesville: University Press of Virginia, 1985–2008.

Washington, George, and Jacob Duché. *The Washington-Duché Letters.* New York, 1890.

Zubly, John J. *"A Warm & Zealous Spirit": John J. Zubly and the American Revolution, A Selection of His Writings.* Edited by Randall M. Miller. Macon, GA: Mercer University Press, 1982.

Published Pamphlets

Address to the Citizens of Kent. Wilmington, DE, 1800.

Backus, Isaac. *The Kingdom of God, Described by His Word, With Its Infinite Benefits to Human Society.* Boston, 1792.

Beckley, John. *An Address to the People of the United States With An Epitome and Vindication of the Public Life and Character of Thomas Jefferson.* Richmond, 1800.

Belknap, Jeremy. *Dissertations on the Character, Death & Resurrection of Jesus Christ, and the Evidence of His Gospel.* Boston, 1795.

Bishop, Abraham. *An Oration on the Extent and Power of Political Delusion, Delivered in New Haven, On the Evening Preceding the Public Commencement*. Philadelphia, 1800.

Buel, John. *Reflections on the Inconsistency of Man, Particularly Exemplified in the Practice of Slavery in the United States*. New York, 1796.

Burke, Edmund. *Reflections on the Revolution in France*. London, 1790.

Chauncey, Charles. *A Discourse on "the Good News from a Far Country."* Boston, 1766.

Church, Benjamin. *Liberty and Property Vindicated*. Hartford, CT, 1765.

The Claims of Thomas Jefferson to the Presidency, Examined at the Bar of Christianity. Philadelphia, 1800.

Clinton, DeWitt. *A Vindication of Thomas Jefferson; Against the Charges Contained in a Pamphlet Entitled "Serious Considerations."* New York, 1800.

Committee of Inspection and Observance. *In Committee Chambers, May 16, 1776*. Philadelphia, 1776.

Deane, Samuel. *A Sermon Preached February 19th, 1795, Being a Day of National Thanksgiving, Appointed by the President of the United States*. Portland, ME, 1795.

DeSaussure, Henry W. *Answer to a Dialogue Between a Federalist and a Republican*. Charleston, SC, 1800.

———. *Citizens of South-Carolina on the Approaching Election of President and Vice-President of the United States*. Charleston, SC, 1800.

Duché, Jacob. *The American Vine*. Philadelphia, 1775.

Duffield, George. *A Sermon Preached in the Third Presbyterian Church, in the City of Philadelphia, on Thursday, December 11, 1783*. Philadelphia, 1783.

Dwight, Timothy. *The Duty of Americans, at the Present Crisis, Illustrated in a Discourse, Preached on the Fourth of July, 1798*. New Haven, CT, 1798.

———. *The Nature, and Danger, of Infidel Philosophy: Exhibited in Two Discourses, Addressed to the Candidates for the Baccalaureate, in Yale College*. New Haven, CT, 1798.

Edwards, Jonathan. *An Humble Attempt to Promote an Explicit Agreement and Visible Union of God's People thro' the World, in Extraordinary Prayer, for the Revival of Religion, and the Advancement of Christ's Kingdom on Earth, Pursuant to Scripture Promise and Prophesies Concerning the Last Time*. Boston, 1747.

Ely, Zebulon. *The Wisdom and Duty of Magistrates*. Hartford, CT, 1804.

Emerson, Joseph. *A Thanksgiving Sermon Preach'd at Pepperel*. Boston, 1776.

Evans, Israel. *A Discourse Delivered at Easton, On the 17th of October, 1779, to the Officers and Soldiers of the Western Army*. Philadelphia, 1779.

Green, Ashbel. *A Sermon Delivered in the Second Presbyterian Church in the City of Philadelphia, on the 19th of February, 1795, Being the Day of General Thanksgiving Throughout the United States*. Philadelphia, 1795.

Hamilton, Alexander. *The Farmer Refuted*. New York, 1775.

———. *A Full Vindication of the Measures of Congress*. New York, 1774.

Hitchcock, Gad. *A Sermon Preached at Plymouth December 22d, 1774*. Boston, 1775.

Hooker, Asahel. *The Moral Tendency of Man's Accountableness*. Hartford, CT, 1804.

Hopkins, Samuel. *A Dialogue Concerning the Slavery of Africans, Showing it to be the Duty and Interest of the American States to Emancipate All their African Slaves*. New York, 1776.

Hopkins, Stephen. *Rights of the Colonies Examined*. Providence, RI, 1765.

Huntington, Joseph. *A Discourse Adapted to the Present Day, on the Health and Happiness, or Misery and Ruin, of the Body Politic, in Similitude to that of the Natural Body*. Hartford, CT, 1781.

———. *God Ruling the Nations for the Most Glorious End*. Hartford, CT, 1784.

Jefferson, Thomas. *A Summary View of the Rights of British America*. Williamsburg, VA, 1774.

Langdon, Samuel. *The Republic of the Israelites and Example to the American States*. Exeter, NH, 1788.

Leland, John. *Politics Sermonized Exhibited in Ashfield on July 4, 1806*. Springfield, MA, 1806.

Linn, William. *Serious Considerations on the Election of a President*. New York, 1800.

Madison, Rev. James. *A Form of Prayers to be Used by the Ministers of the Protestant Episcopal Church, in Virginia on the 9th of May, 1798, Recommended to be Observed as a Day of Solemn Humiliation, Fasting and Prayer*. Richmond, 1798.

———. *A Nation Mourns: Bishop James Madison's Memorial Eulogy on the Death of George Washington, Delivered February 22, 1800 in Burton Parish Church, Williamsburg, Virginia*. Mount Vernon, VA: Mount Vernon Ladies Association, 1999.

———. *An Oration, in Commemoration of the Founders of William and Mary College*. Williamsburg, VA, 1772.

Minutes of the Baptist Association Held at New York, October 1787. New York, 1787.

Morse, Jedediah. *A Sermon, Exhibiting the Present Dangers, and Consequent Duties of the Citizens of the United States of America, Delivered in Charleston, April 25, 1799, the Day of the National Fast*. Hartford, CT, 1799.

Murray, John. *Jerubbaal, or Tyranny's Grove Destroyed, and the Alter of Liberty Finished*. Newburyport, MA, 1783.

Palmer, Elihu. *The Examiners Examined: Being a Defence of the Age of Reason*. New York, 1794.

Pollard, Benjamin. *Serious Facts, Opposed to "Serious Considerations"; or, The Voice of Warning to Religious Republicans*. N.p., 1800.

Prince, John. *A Discourse, Delivered at Salem, on the Day of the National Fast, May 9, 1798*. Salem, MA, 1798.

Russell, Jonathan. *To the Free Men of Rhode-Island*. Providence, RI, 1800.

Seabury, Samuel. *The Congress Canvassed; or, an examination into the conduct of the Delegates, at Their Grand Convention, Held in Philadelphia, Sept. 1, 1774*. New York, 1775.

———. *Free Thoughts on the Proceedings of the Continental Congress*. Early American Imprints, series 1. New York, 1774.

————. *A View of the Controversy Between Great Britain and Her Colonies.* Early American Imprints, series 1. New York, 1775.

Skinner, John. *The Nature and Extent of the Apostolic Commission, A Sermon Preached at the Consecration of the Right Reverend Samuel Seabury.* Aberdeen, Scotland, 1785.

Smith, Robert. *The Obligations of the Confederate States of North America to Praise God.* Philadelphia, 1781.

Smith, William Loughton. *The Pretensions of Thomas Jefferson to the Presidency Examined.* Philadelphia, 1796.

Stiles, Ezra. *The United States Elevated to Honor and Glory.* New Haven, CT, 1783.

A Test of the Religious Principles, of Mr. Jefferson; Extracted (Verbatim) From His Writings. Easton, MD, 1800.

Throop, Benjamin. *A Thanksgiving Sermon, Upon the Occasion, of the Glorious News of the Repeal of the Stamp Act.* New London, CT, 1766.

Weld, Ludovicus. *A Sermon, Delivered on the Day of the Annual Fast.* Windham, CT, 1804.

West, Samuel. *A Sermon Preached Before the Honorable Council, and the Honorable House of Representatives, of the Colony of the Massachusetts-Bay, May 29th, 1776.* Boston, 1776.

White, William. *The Case of the Episcopal Churches in the United States Considered.* Philadelphia, 1782.

Wortman, Tunis. *A Solemn Address to Christians and Patriots.* New York, 1800.

Zubly, John Joachim. *Calm and Respectful Thoughts on the Negative of the Crown on a Speaker Chosen and Presented by the Representatives of the People.* Savannah, GA, 1772.

————. *An Humble Enquiry into the Nature of the Dependency of the American Colonies Upon the Parliament of Great-Britain.* Savannah, GA, 1769.

————. *The Law of Liberty: A Sermon on American Affairs.* Savannah, GA, 1775.

————. *The Stamp Act Repealed; A Sermon, Preached in the Meeting at Savannah in Georgia, June 25th, 1766.* Savannah, GA, 1766.

Published Articles and Books

Abbot, W. W. *Royal Governors of Georgia, 1754–1775.* Chapel Hill: University of North Carolina Press, 1959.

Adams, Thomas Randolph. *American Independence: The Growth of an Idea.* Providence, RI: Brown University Press, 1965.

Allen, Carolos R., Jr. "David Barrow's *Circular Letter* of 1798." *William and Mary Quarterly,* 3rd series, 20, no. 20 (July 1963): 448–50.

Alter, Robert, and Frank Kermode, eds. *The Literary Guide to the Bible.* Cambridge, MA: Harvard University Press, 1987.

Anderson, Benedict. *Imagined Communities: Reflections on the Origins and Spread of Nationalism.* London: Verso, 1983.

Anderson, Fred. *A People's Army: Massachusetts Soldiers and Society in the Seven Years' War*. Chapel Hill: University of North Carolina Press, 1984.

Andrews, Dee E. *The Methodists and Revolutionary America, 1760–1800: The Shaping of an Evangelical Culture*. Princeton, NJ: Princeton University Press, 2000.

Applebee, Joyce. *Inheriting the Revolution: The First Generation of Americans*. Cambridge, MA: Harvard University Press, 2000.

Armitage, David. *The Declaration of Independence: A Global History*. Cambridge, MA: Harvard University Press, 2007.

Austin, Allen. *African Muslims in Antebellum America: A Sourcebook*. New York: Garland, 1984.

Ayers, Edward L., et al. *All Over the Map: Rethinking American Regions*. Baltimore: Johns Hopkins University Press, 1996.

Bailyn, Bernard. *The Ideological Origins of the American Revolution*. Cambridge, MA: Harvard University Press, 1967.

Bailyn, Bernard, et al. *The Great Republic: A History of the American People*. 2 vols. 2nd edition. Lexington, MA: D. C. Heath, 1981.

Baldwin, Alice E. *The New England Clergy and the American Revolution*. Durham, NC: Duke University Press, 1928.

Beard, Charles A. *An Economic Interpretation of the Constitution of the United States*. New York: Macmillan, 1913.

Beardsley, E. E. *Life and Correspondence of the Right Reverend Samuel Seabury, D.D.* Boston, 1881.

Beasley, James R. "Emerging Republicanism and the Standing Order: The Appropriation Act Controversy in Connecticut, 1793 to 1795," *William and Mary Quarterly*, 3rd series, 29, no. 4 (October 1972): 587–610.

Beeman, Richard. *Plain and Honest Men: The Making of the American Constitution*. New York: Random House, 2009.

Bell, James D. *A War of Religion: Dissenters, Anglicans, and the American Revolution*. New York: Palgrave Macmillan, 2008.

Bellah, Robert N. *The Broken Covenant: American Civil Religion in Time of Trial*. 2nd edition. Chicago: University of Chicago Press, 1993.

Bellah, Robert N., and Phillip E. Hammond. *Varieties of Civil Religion*. New York: Harper and Row, 1980.

Berens, John F. *Providence and Patriotism in Early America, 1640–1815*. Charlottesville: University Press of Virginia, 1978.

Berkin, Carol. *A Brilliant Solution: Inventing the American Constitution*. New York: Houghton Mifflin Harcourt, 2002.

Berkus, Catherine A. *Sarah Osborne's World: The Rise of Evangelical Christianity in Early America*. New Haven, CT: Yale University Press, 2013.

Bloch, Ruth. *Visionary Republic: Millennial Themes in American Thought, 1756–1800*. New York: Cambridge University Press, 1985.

Bonomi, Patricia U. *Under the Cope of Heaven: Religion, Society, and Politics in Colonial America.* New York: Oxford University Press, 1986.

The Book of Common Prayer. London, 1662.

Boorstin, Daniel. *The Genius of American Politics.* Chicago: University of Chicago Press, 1953.

Boyd, Julian P. "The Disputed Authorship of the Declaration on the Causes and Necessity of Taking up Arms, 1775." *Pennsylvania Magazine of History and Biography* 74, no. 1 (January 1950): 51–73.

Bradburn, Douglas. *The Citizenship Revolution: Politics and the Creation of the American Union, 1774–1804.* Charlottesville: University of Virginia Press, 2009.

Bradley, Gerard V. "The No Religious Test Clause and the Constitution of Religious Liberty: A Machine That Has Gone of Itself." *Case Western Reserve Law Review* 37 (1987): 674–747.

Brown, Richard D. *Knowledge Is Power: The Diffusion of Information in Early America, 1775–1800.* New York: Oxford University Press, 1989.

Brydon, G. MacLaren. "The Clergy of the Established Church in Virginia and the Revolution." *Virginia Magazine of History and Biography* 41 (1933): 11–23.

———. "Revision of the Prayer Book by an American Civil Legislature." *Historical Magazine of the Protestant Episcopal Church* 19, no. 2 (June 1950): 133–38.

———. *Virginia's Mother Church and the Political Conditions under Which It Grew.* 2 vols. Philadelphia: Church History Society, 1952.

Buel, Richard, Jr. *America on the Brink: How the Political Struggle over the War of 1812 Almost Destroyed the Young Republic.* New York: Palgrave Macmillan, 2005.

Burnett, Edmund Cody. *The Continental Congress: A Definitive History of the Continental Congress from Its Inception in 1774 to March 1789.* New York: Macmillan, 1941.

Burstein, Andrew. *America's Jubilee: How in 1826 a Generation Remembered Fifty Years of Independence.* New York: Knopf, 2001.

———. *Democracy's Muse: How Thomas Jefferson Became an FDR Liberal, a Reagan Republican, and a Tea Party Fanatic, All the While Being Dead.* Charlottesville: University of Virginia Press, 2015.

———. *Jefferson's Secrets: Death and Desire at Monticello.* New York: Basic Books, 2005.

———. *Sentimental Democracy: The Evolution of America's Romantic Self-Image.* New York: Hill and Wang, 1999.

Burstein, Andrew, and Nancy Isenberg. *Madison and Jefferson.* New York: Random House, 2010.

Bushman, Richard L. *From Puritan to Yankee: Character and the Social Order in Connecticut, 1690–1765.* Cambridge, MA: Harvard University Press, 1967.

Butler, Jon. *Awash in a Sea of Faith: Christianizing the American People.* Cambridge, MA: Harvard University Press, 1990.

———. "Enthusiasm Described and Decried: The Great Awakening as an Interpretive Fiction." *Journal of American History* 69 (1982): 302–25.

Butterfield, L. H. "Elder John Leland, Jeffersonian Itinerant." *Proceedings of the American Antiquarian Society* 62 (October 1952): 142–252.

Byrd, James P. *Sacred Scripture, Sacred War: The Bible and the American Revolution.* New York: Oxford University Press, 2013.

Calvert, Jane E. *Quaker Constitutionalism and the Political Thought of John Dickinson.* New York: Cambridge University Press, 2009.

Carey, Patrick W. *Catholics in America: A History.* Westport, CT: Greenwood, 2004.

Carp, Benjamin L. *Defiance of the Patriots: The Boston Tea Party and the Making of America.* New Haven, CT: Yale University Press, 2011.

———. *Rebels Rising: Cities and the American Revolution.* New York: Oxford University Press, 2007.

Carty, Thomas. *A Catholic in the White House? Religion, Politics, and John F. Kennedy's Presidential Campaign.* New York: Palgrave Macmillan, 2004.

Casey, Shaun. *The Making of a Catholic President: Kennedy vs. Nixon 1960.* New York: Oxford University Press, 2009.

Chernow, Ron. *Alexander Hamilton.* New York: Penguin, 2004.

———. *Washington: A Life.* New York: Penguin, 2010.

Cleves, Rachel Hope. *The Reign of Terror in America: Visions of Violence from Anti-Jacobinism to Antislavery.* New York: Cambridge University Press, 2009.

Cogliano, Francis D. *No King, No Popery: Anti-Catholicism in Revolutionary New England.* Westport, CT: Greenwood, 1995.

Cohen, Hennig, ed. *South Carolina Gazette, 1732–1775.* Columbia: University of South Carolina Press, 1953.

Colley, Linda. *Britons: Forging the Nation, 1707–1837.* New Haven, CT: Yale University Press, 2009.

Conrad, Sebastian. "The Enlightenment in Global History: A Historiographical Critique." *American Historical Review* 117, no. 4 (October 2012): 999–1027.

Cordle, Charles G. "The Will of John Zubly." *Georgia Historical Quarterly* 22 (December 1938): 384–90.

Cornell, Saul. *The Other Founders: Anti-Federalism and the Dissenting Tradition in America, 1788–1828.* Chapel Hill: University of North Carolina Press, 1999.

Cornett, Daryl C., ed. *Christian America? Perspectives on Our Religious Heritage.* Nashville: B&H Academic, 2011.

Cotlar, Seth. *Tom Paine's America: The Rise and Fall of Transatlantic Radicalism in the Early Republic.* Charlottesville: University of Virginia Press, 2011.

Crabtree, Sarah. "Holy Nation: The Quaker Itinerant Ministry in an Age of Revolution, 1750–1820." PhD diss., University of Minnesota, 2007.

Crowe, Charles. "Bishop James Madison and the Republic of Virtue." *Journal of Southern History* 20, no. 1 (February 1964): 58–70.

Cunningham, Charles E. *Timothy Dwight, 1752–1817: A Biography.* New York: Macmillan, 1942.

Cunningham, Noble E., Jr. *The Jeffersonian Republicans: The Formation of Party Organization, 1789–1801.* Chapel Hill: University of North Carolina Press, 1959.

———. "John Beckley: An Early American Party Manager." *William and Mary Quarterly,* 3rd series, 13, no. 1 (January 1956): 40–52.

Dabney, William M., and Marion Dargan. *William Henry Drayton and the American Revolution.* Albuquerque: University of New Mexico Press, 1962.

Daniel, Marjorie. "John Joachim Zubly—Georgia Pamphleteer of the Revolution." *Georgia Historical Quarterly* 19 (March 1935): 1–16.

Davis, Derek H. *Religion and the Continental Congress, 1774–1789: Contributions to Original Intent.* New York: Oxford University Press, 2000.

Dellape, Kevin J. *America's First Chaplain: The Life and Times of the Reverend Jacob Duché.* Bethlehem, PA: Lehigh University Press, 2013.

Dennis, Matthew. *Red, White, and Blue Letter Days: An American Calendar.* Ithaca, NY: Cornell University Press, 2002.

Diouf, Sylvia A. *Servants of Allah: African Muslims Enslaved in the Americas.* New York: New York University Press, 1998.

Doll, Peter M. *Revolution, Religion, and National Identity: Imperial Anglicanism in British North America, 1745–1795.* Madison, NJ: Farleigh Dickinson University Press, 2000.

Dorsey, Peter A. *Common Bondage: Slavery as Metaphor in Revolutionary America.* Knoxville: University of Tennessee Press, 2009.

Doyle, William. *The Oxford History of the French Revolution.* New York: Oxford University Press, 1989.

Dreisbach, Daniel L. *Thomas Jefferson and the Wall of Separation between Church and State.* New York: New York University Press, 2003.

Dreisbach, Daniel L., and Mark David Hall. *Faith and the Founders of the American Republic.* New York: Oxford University Press, 2014.

Edmonson, James H. "Desertion in the American Army during the Revolutionary War." PhD diss., Louisiana State University, 1971.

Einhorn, Robin L. "Patrick Henry's Case against the Constitution: The Structural Problem with Slavery." *Journal of the Early Republic* 22, no. 4 (Winter 2002): 549–73.

Elkins, Stanley, and Eric McKitrick. *The Age of Federalism: The Early American Republic, 1788–1800.* New York: Oxford University Press, 1995.

Ellis, Joseph J. *American Sphinx: The Character of Thomas Jefferson.* New York: Knopf, 1998.

Ericson, David F. *The Shaping of American Liberalism: The Debates over Ratification, Nullification, and Slavery.* Chicago: University of Chicago Press, 1993.

Farrell, James M. "John Adams and the Rhetoric of Conspiracy." *Proceedings of the Massachusetts Historical Society* 104 (1992): 55–72.

Farrelly, Maura Jane. *Papist Patriots: The Making of an American Catholic Identity.* New York: Oxford University Press, 2012.

Fea, John. *Was America Founded as a Christian Nation? A Historical Introduction.* Louisville: Westminster John Knox Press, 2011.

Federici, Michael P. *The Political Philosophy of Alexander Hamilton.* Baltimore: Johns Hopkins University Press, 2012.

Ferguson, Robert A. *The American Enlightenment, 1750–1820.* New York: Cambridge University Press, 1994.

Ferling, John. *Adams vs. Jefferson: The Tumultuous Election of 1800.* New York: Oxford University Press, 2005.

Field, Peter S. *The Crisis of the Standing Order: Clerical Intellectuals and Cultural Authority in Massachusetts.* Amherst: University of Massachusetts Press, 1998.

Fitzmier, John R. *New England's Moral Legislator: Timothy Dwight, 1752–1817.* Bloomington: Indiana University Press, 1998.

Flavell, Julie, and Stephen Conway, eds. *Britain and America Go to War: The Impact of War and Warfare in Anglo-America, 1754–1815.* Gainesville: University Press of Florida, 2004.

Fliegelman, Jay. *Declaring Independence: Jefferson, Natural Language, and the Culture of Performance.* Stanford, CA: Stanford University Press, 1993.

———. *Prodigals and Pilgrims: The American Revolution against Patriarchal Authority, 1750–1800.* New York: Cambridge University Press, 1985.

Foner, Eric. *Tom Paine and Revolutionary America.* New York: Oxford University Press, 1976.

Fox-Genovese, Elizabeth, and Eugene Genovese. *The Mind of the Master Class: History and Faith in the Southern Slaveholder's Worldview.* New York: Cambridge University Press, 2005.

Frazier, Gregg L. *The Religious Beliefs of America's Founders: Reason, Revelation, Revolution.* Lawrence: University Press of Kansas, 2012.

Freeman, Joanne. "The Election of 1800: A Study in the Logic of Political Change." *Yale Law Journal* 108, no. 8 (June 1999): 1969–74.

Gaustad, Edwin S. *Sworn on the Altar of God: A Religious Biography of Thomas Jefferson.* Grand Rapids, MI: Eerdmans, 1996.

Gleckner, Robert F., and Gerald E. Enscoe, eds. *Romanticism: Points of View.* Englewood Cliffs, NJ: Prentice-Hall, 1962.

Gomez, Michael A. *Black Crescent: The Experience and Legacy of African Muslims in the Americas.* New York: Cambridge University Press, 2005.

Goodman, Paul. *The Democratic-Republicans of Massachusetts: Politics in a Young Republic.* Cambridge, MA: Harvard University Press, 1964.

Gould, Eliga H. *Among the Powers of the Earth: The American Revolution and the Making of a New World Empire.* Cambridge, MA: Harvard University Press, 2012.

———. *The Persistence of Empire: British Political Culture in the Age of the American Revolution.* Chapel Hill: University of North Carolina Press, 2000.

————. "A Virtual Nation: Greater Britain and the Imperial Legacy of the American Revolution." *American Historical Review* 104, no. 2 (April 1999): 476–89.

Gould, Philip. "Wit and Politics in Revolutionary British America: The Case of Samuel Seabury and Alexander Hamilton." *Eighteenth-Century Studies* 41, no. 3 (Spring 2008): 383–403.

Green, Steven K. *Inventing a Christian Nation: The Myth of the Religious Founding.* New York: Oxford University Press, 2015.

Greer, Donald. *The Incidence of the Terror during the French Revolution: A Statistical Interpretation.* Cambridge, MA: Harvard University Press, 1935.

Guyatt, Nicholas. *Providence and the Invention of the United States, 1607–1876.* New York: Cambridge University Press, 2007.

Gwaltney, Mary S. "Bishop James Madison's Letters on Politics, 1787–1809." Honors thesis, College of William and Mary, 1983.

Hall, Charles S. *Life and Letters of Samuel Holden Parsons.* Binghamton, NY, 1905.

Hall, David D. *Worlds of Wonder, Days of Judgment: Popular Religious Belief in Early New England.* New York: Knopf, 1989.

Hammond, John Craig, and Matthew Mason, eds. *Contesting Slavery: The Politics of Bondage and Freedom in the New American Nations.* Charlottesville: University Press of Virginia, 1981.

Hanna, William S. *Benjamin Franklin and Pennsylvania Politics.* Stanford, CA: Stanford University Press, 1964.

Harrell, Isaac Samuel. *Loyalism in Virginia: Chapters in the Economic History of the Revolution.* Durham, NC: Duke University Press, 1926.

Haselby, Sam. *The Origins of American Religious Nationalism.* New York: Oxford University Press, 2015.

Hatch, Nathan O. *The Democratization of American Christianity.* New Haven, CT: Yale University Press, 1989.

————. *The Sacred Cause of Liberty: Republican Thought and the Millennium in Revolutionary New England.* New Haven, CT: Yale University Press, 1977.

Hawke, David Freeman. *Benjamin Rush: Revolutionary Gadfly.* Indianapolis: Bobbs-Merrill, 1971.

Hazelton, John H. *The Declaration of Independence: Its History.* New York: Dodd, Mead, 1906.

Heimert, Alan. *Religion and the American Mind: From the Great Awakening to the Revolution.* Cambridge, MA: Harvard University Press, 1966.

High, J. Walter. "Thomas Coombe, Loyalist." *Pennsylvania History* 62, no. 3 (July 1995): 272–92.

Hobbes, Thomas. *De Cive.* London, 1642.

————. *Leviathan; or the Matter, Forme and Power of a Common Wealth Ecclessiasticall and Civil.* London, 1651.

Hoeveler, J. David. *Creating the American Mind: Intellect and Politics in the Colonial Colleges.* Lanham, MD: Rowman and Littlefield, 2002.

Hoffman, Ronald, and Peter J. Albert, eds. *Religion in a Revolutionary Age*. Charlottesville: University Press of Virginia, 1994.

———, eds. *Sovereign States in an Age of Uncertainty*. Charlottesville: University Press of Virginia, 1981.

Hoffman, Ronald, Thad Tate, and Peter J. Albert, eds. *An Uncivil War: The Southern Backcountry during the American Revolution*. Charlottesville: University Press of Virginia, 1985.

Holbach, Baron de. *The System of Nature; or, Laws of the Moral and Physical World*. Amsterdam, 1770.

Holmes, David L. *The Faiths of the Founding Fathers*. New York: Oxford University Press, 2006.

Holmes, Richard. *Redcoat: The British Soldier in the Age of Horse and Musket*. New York: HarperCollins, 2001.

Horn, James, Jan Ellen Lewis, and Peter S. Onuf, eds. *The Revolution of 1800: Democracy, Race, and the New Republic*. Charlottesville: University of Virginia Press, 2002.

Hull, N. E. H., Peter C. Hoffer, and Steven L. Allen. "Choosing Sides: A Quantitative Study of the Personality Determinants of Loyalist and Revolutionary Political Affiliation in New York." *Journal of American History* 65, no. 2 (1978): 344–66.

Hume, David. *A Treatise on Human Nature*. London, 1748.

Hutson, James H. *Church and State in America: The First Two Centuries*. New York: Cambridge University Press, 2007.

———. *Forgotten Features of the Founding: The Recovery of Religious Themes in the Early American Republic*. Lanham, MD: Lexington Books, 2003.

———. *Religion and the Founding of the American Republic*. Washington, DC: Library of Congress, 1998.

"Intercommunion of the American and Scottish Churches." *Scottish Ecclesiastical Journal* 1 (October 1851): 215.

Ireland, Owen S. "The Ethnic-Religious Dimension of Pennsylvania Politics, 1778–1779." *William and Mary Quarterly*, 3rd series, 30, no. 3 (July 1973): 423–48.

Irvin, Benjamin H. *Clothed in the Robes of Sovereignty: The Continental Congress and the People Out of Doors*. New York: Oxford University Press, 2011.

———. "Tar, Feathers, and the Enemies of American Liberties, 1768–1776." *New England Quarterly* 76, no. 2 (June 2003): 197–238.

Isaac, Rhys. *The Transformation of Virginia, 1740–1790*. Chapel Hill: University of North Carolina Press, 1982.

Isenberg, Nancy. *Fallen Founder: The Life of Aaron Burr*. New York: Viking, 2007.

Israel, Jonathan. *Radical Enlightenment: Philosophy and the Making of Modernity, 1650–1750*. New York: Oxford University Press, 2002.

Jasanoff, Maya. *Liberty's Exiles: American Loyalists in the Revolutionary World*. New York: Knopf, 2011.

Jefferson, Thomas. *The Life and Morals of Jesus of Nazareth*. Washington, DC: National Museum, 1895.

———. *Notes on the State of Virginia*. Edited by William Penden. Chapel Hill: University of North Carolina Press, 1954.

Jortner, Adam. "Cholera, Christ, and Jackson: The Epidemic of 1832 and the Origins of Christian Politics in Antebellum America." *Journal of the Early Republic* 27, no. 2 (Summer 2007): 233–64.

Kabala, James S. *Church-State Relations in the Early American Republic, 1787–1846*. London: Pickering and Chatto, 2013.

Kaminski, John, ed. *A Necessary Evil? Slavery and the Debate of the Constitution*. Lanham, MD: Rowman and Littlefield, 1995.

Kidd, Thomas S. *God of Liberty: A Religious History of the American Revolution*. New York: Basic Books, 2010.

———. *The Great Awakening: A Brief History with Documents*. New York: Bedford/St. Martin's, 2007.

———. *Patrick Henry: First among Patriots*. New York: Basic Books, 2011.

Klein, Rachel N. *Unification of a Slave State: The Rise of the Planter Class in the South Carolina Backcountry, 1700–1789*. Chapel Hill: University of North Carolina Press, 1990.

Kowalski, Gary. *Revolutionary Spirits: The Enlightened Faith of America's Founding Fathers*. New York: Blue Bridge, 2008.

Kramnick, Isaac, and R. Laurence Moore. *The Godless Constitution: A Moral Defense of the Secular State*. New York: W. W. Norton, 2005.

Kranish, Michael. *Flight from Monticello: Thomas Jefferson at War*. New York: Oxford University Press, 2011.

Krawczynski, Keith. *William Henry Drayton: South Carolina Revolutionary Patriot*. Baton Rouge: Louisiana State University Press, 2001.

Lambert, Frank. *The Founding Fathers and the Place of Religion in America*. Princeton, NJ: Princeton University Press, 2006.

———. "'God—and a Religious President . . . [or] Thomas Jefferson and No God': Campaigning for a Voter-Imposed Religious Test in 1800." *Journal of Church and State* 39 (1997): 769–89.

———. *Inventing the "Great Awakening."* Princeton, NJ: Princeton University Press, 1999.

———. *Religion in American Politics: A Short History*. Princeton, NJ: Princeton University Press, 2010.

Larsen, Edward J. *A Magnificent Catastrophe: The Tumultuous Election of 1800, America's First Presidential Campaign*. New York: Free Press, 2007.

Leamon, James S. *The Reverend Jacob Bailey, Maine Loyalist: For God, King, Country, and for Self*. Amherst: University of Massachusetts Press, 2012.

Lewis, Gwynne. *Life in Revolutionary France*. New York: G. P. Putnam's Sons, 1972.

Lewis, Jan. *The Pursuit of Happiness: Family and Values in Jefferson's Virginia*. New York: Cambridge University Press, 1983.

Locke, John. *Letter Concerning Toleration*. London, 1689.

———. *Two Treatises of Government*. London, 1689.

Lohrenz, Otto. "The Advantage of Rank and Status: Thomas Price, A Loyalist Parson of Revolutionary Virginia." *Historian* 60, no. 3 (Spring 1998): 561–77.

———. "A Dedicated Clergyman and Local Revolutionary Leader: Samuel Smith McCroskey of Virginia's Lancaster County and Eastern Shore." *Northern Neck of Virginia Historical Magazine* 60, no. 1 (December 2010): 7278–97.

———. "Impassioned Virginia Loyalist and New Brunswick Pioneer: The Reverend John Agnew." *Anglican and Episcopal History* 76, no. 1 (March 2007): 29–60.

———. "The Life and Career of Christopher MacRae: A Nonjuring and Physically Abused Anglican Clergyman of Revolutionary Virginia." *Southern Studies* 13, no. 3/4 (Fall/Winter 2006): 117–35.

———. "The Reverend Thomas Smith of Revolutionary Virginia: A Case Study in Social Rank." *Northern Neck of Virginia Historical Magazine* 54, no.1 (December 2004): 6458–75.

———. "Thomas Price: A Loyalist Parson of Revolutionary Virginia." *Historian* 60, no. 3 (Spring 1998): 561–77.

Lossing, Benjamin J. "Great Seal of the United States." *Harper's New Monthly Magazine*, July 1856, 178–86.

Love, W. DeLoss, Jr. *Fast and Thanksgiving Days of New England*. Boston: Houghton Mifflin, 1895.

Lund, Christopher C. "The Congressional Chaplaincies." *William and Mary Bill of Rights Journal* 17, no. 4 (2009): 1177–87.

Maier, Pauline. *American Scripture: Making the Declaration of Independence*. New York: Knopf, 1997.

———. *Ratification: The People Debate the Constitution, 1787–1789*. New York: Simon and Schuster, 2010.

Mann, Bruce H. *Republic of Debtors: Bankruptcy in the Age of American Independence*. Cambridge, MA: Harvard University Press, 2002.

Mapp, Alf. *The Faiths of Our Fathers: What America's Founders Really Believed*. Lanham, MD: Rowman and Littlefield, 2005.

Marston, Jerrilyn Greene. *King and Congress: The Transfer of Political Legitimacy, 1774–1776*. Princeton, NJ: Princeton University Press, 1987.

Martin, Roger A. "John J. Zubly Comes to America." *Georgia Historical Quarterly* 19 (Summer 1977): 125–39.

———. *John J. Zubly: Preacher, Planter, Politician*. New York: Arno, 1982.

Martis, Kenneth C. *The Historical Atlas of Political Parties in the United States Congress, 1789–1989*. New York: Macmillan, 1989.

Mason, Henry. *Christian Humiliation; or, A Treatise of Fasting*. London, 1625.

May, Henry F. *The Enlightenment in America.* New York: Oxford University Press, 1976.

Mays, David John. *Edmund Pendleton, 1721–1803: A Biography.* 2 vols. Cambridge, MA: Harvard University Press, 1952.

McBride, Spencer W. "A 'Masterly Stroke of Policy': The American Revolution and the Politics of Congressional Prayer." *Journal of Religion, Identity, and Politics* (April 2013): 1–22.

McDonnell, Michael A. *The Politics of War: Race, Class, and Conflict in Revolutionary Virginia.* Chapel Hill: University of North Carolina Press, 2007.

McCullough, David. *1776.* New York: Simon and Schuster, 2005.

McGauhy, J. Kent. *Richard Henry Lee of Virginia: A Portrait of an American Revolutionary.* Lanham, MD: Rowman and Littlefield, 2003.

McLoughlin, William G. *Isaac Backus and the American Pietistic Tradition.* Edited by Oscar Handlin. Boston: Little, Brown, 1967.

———, ed. *Isaac Backus on Church, State, and Calvinism: Pamphlets, 1754–1789.* Cambridge, MA: Belknap Press of Harvard University Press, 1968.

Meade, William. *Old Churches, Ministers and Families of Virginia.* 2 vols. Philadelphia: J. B. Lippincott, 1861.

Menendez, Albert J. *The Religious Factor in the 1960 Presidential Election: An Analysis of the Kennedy Victory over Anti-Catholic Prejudice.* Jefferson, NC: McFarland, 2011.

Mews, Stuart, ed. *Religion and National Identity.* Oxford: Blackwell, 1982.

Meyerson, Michael I. *Endowed by Our Creator: The Birth of Religious Freedom in America.* New Haven, CT: Yale University Press, 2012.

Middlekauf, Robert. *The Glorious Cause: The American Revolution, 1763–1789.* New York: Oxford University Press, 1982.

Miller, Perry. *The Puritans.* New York: American Book, 1938.

Minkema, Kenneth P., and Harry S. Stout. "The Edwardsean Tradition and the Anti-Slavery Debate, 1740–1865." *Journal of American History* 92, no. 1 (June 2005): 47–74.

Moore, James P., Jr. *Prayer in America: A Spiritual History of Our Nation.* New York: Doubleday, 2005.

Murastin, Bennet. "Benjamin Nones: Profile of a Jewish Jeffersonian." *American Jewish History* 83, no. 4 (December 1995): 381–85.

Nathans, Heather. "A Much Maligned People: Jews on and off Stage in the Early American Republic." *Early American Studies* 2, no. 2 (Fall 2004): 310–42.

Neill, Edward Duffield. "Rev. Jacob Duché: The First Chaplain of Congress." *Pennsylvania Magazine of History and Biography* 2, no. 1 (1878): 66–67.

Noll. Mark A. *America's God: From Jonathan Edwards to Abraham Lincoln.* New York: Oxford University Press, 2002.

Noll, Mark A., Nathan Hatch, and George Marsden. *The Search for Christian America.* Colorado Springs: Helmers and Howard, 1989.

Obolensky, Dimitri. "Nationalism in Eastern Europe in the Middle Ages." *Transactions of the Royal Historical Society,* 5th series, 22 (1972): 1–16.

Oechsli, Wilhelm. *History of Switzerland, 1499–1914.* New York: Cambridge University Press, 1922.

Onuf, Peter S. *Jefferson's Empire: The Language of American Nationhood.* Charlottesville: University Press of Virginia, 2000.

Paine, Thomas. *The Age of Reason.* Paris, 1794.

Pasley, Jeffrey L. *The First Presidential Contest: 1796 and the Founding of American Democracy.* Lawrence: University Press of Kansas, 2013.

———. "'A Journeyman, Either in Law or Politics': John Beckley and the Social Origins of Political Campaigning." *Journal of the Early Republic* 16, no. 4 (Winter 1996): 531–69.

———. *"The Tyranny of Printers": Newspaper Politics in the Early American Republic.* Charlottesville: University Press of Virginia, 2001.

Pasley, Jeffrey L., Andrew W. Robertson, and David Waldstreicher, eds. *Beyond the Founders: New Approaches to the Political History of the Early American Republic.* Chapel Hill: University of North Carolina Press, 2004.

Pencak, William. *Jews and Gentiles in Early America, 1654–1800.* Ann Arbor, MI: University of Michigan Press, 2005.

———, ed. *Pennsylvania's Revolution.* University Park: Pennsylvania State University Press, 2010.

Perkins, Eunice Ross. "John Joachim Zubly: Georgia's Conscientious Objector." *Georgia Historical Quarterly* 15 (December 1931): 313–23.

Perkins, William. *A Godly and Learned Exposition of Christ's Sermon in the Mount.* Cambridge, 1608.

Perry, Lewis. *Radical Abolitionism: Anarchy and the Government of God in Antislavery Thought.* Ithaca, NY: Cornell University Press, 1973.

Peterson, Merrill D. *The Jefferson Image in the American Mind.* New York: Oxford University Press, 1960.

Peterson, Merrill D., and Robert C. Vaughan, eds. *The Virginia Statute for Religious Freedom: Its Evolution and Consequences in American History.* New York: Cambridge University Press, 1988.

Polf, William A. *Garrison Town: The British Occupation of New York City, 1776–1783.* New York: Bicentennial Commission, 1976.

Porter, Roy. *Flesh in the Age of Reason: The Modern Foundations of Body and Soul.* New York: W. W. Norton, 2003.

Porter, Roy, and Mikuláš Teich, eds. *The Enlightenment in National Context.* Cambridge, MA: Harvard University Press, 1982.

Porterfield, Amanda. *Conceived in Doubt: Religion and Politics in the New American Nation.* Chicago: University of Chicago Press, 2013.

Prestwich, Menna, ed. *International Calvinism, 1541–1715.* Oxford: Clarendon, 1985.

Ragosta, John A. *Religious Freedom: Jefferson's Legacy, America's Creed.* Charlottesville: University of Virginia Press, 2013.

———. *Wellspring of Liberty: How Virginia's Religious Dissenters Helped Win the American Revolution and Secured Religious Liberty.* New York: Oxford University Press, 2010.

Rakove, Jack N. *The Beginnings of National Politics: An Interpretive History of the Continental Congress.* New York: Knopf, 1979.

———. *James Madison and the Creation of the American Republic.* New York: Harper-Collins, 1990.

———. *Original Meanings: Politics and Ideas in the Making of the Constitution.* New York: Knopf, 1996.

Randall, William Sterne. *Alexander Hamilton: A Life.* New York: HarperCollins, 2003.

Robson, David W. *Educating Republicans: The College in the Era of the American Revolution, 1750–1800.* Westport, CT: Greenwood, 1985.

Roche, Daniel. *France in the Enlightenment.* Translated by Arthur Goldhammer. Cambridge, MA: Harvard University Press, 1998.

Roche, John F. *The Colonial Colleges in the War for American Independence.* Millwood, NY: Associated Faculty, 1986.

Rock, Howard B. *Haven of Liberty: New York Jews in the New World, 1654–1865.* New York: New York University Press, 2012.

Rounes, Leroy S., ed. *Civil Religion and Political Theology.* Notre Dame, IN: University of Notre Dame Press, 1986.

Rousseau, Jean-Jacques. *Emile; or on Education.* Amsterdam, 1762.

———. *The Social Contract.* Amsterdam, 1762.

Royster, Charles. *A Revolutionary People at War: The Continental Army and American Character, 1775–1783.* Chapel Hill: University of North Carolina Press, 1979.

Ruddiman, John A. *Becoming Men of Some Consequence: Youth and Military Service in the Revolutionary War.* Charlottesville: University of Virginia Press, 2014.

Ruffin, J. Rixey. *A Paradise of Reason: William Bentley and Enlightenment Christianity in the Early Republic.* New York: Oxford University Press, 2008.

Sabine, Lorenzo. *Biographical Sketches of Loyalists of the American Revolution.* 2 vols. Boston: Little, Brown, 1864.

Said, Edward. *Orientalism.* New York: Random House, 1978.

Sassi, Jonathan D. *A Republic of Righteousness: The Public Christianity of the Post-Revolutionary New England Clergy.* New York: Oxford University Press, 2001.

Schlereth, Eric. *An Age of Infidels: The Politics of Religious Controversy in the Early United States.* Philadelphia: University of Pennsylvania Press, 2013.

Sehat, David. *The Jefferson Rule: How the Founding Fathers Became Infallible and Our Politics Inflexible.* New York: Simon and Schuster, 2015.

———. *The Myth of American Religious Freedom.* New York: Oxford University Press, 2011.

Siemers, David J. *Ratifying the Republic: Antifederalists and Federalists in Constitutional Time.* Stanford, CA: Stanford University Press, 2002.

Shalev, Eran. *American Zion: The Old Testament as a Political Text from the Revolution to the Civil War.* New Haven, CT: Yale University Press, 2013.

———. *Rome Reborn on Western Shores: Historical Imagination and the Creation of the American Republic.* Charlottesville: University of Virginia Press, 2009.

Sharp, James Roger. *American Politics in the Early Republic: The New Nation in Crisis.* 2nd edition. New Haven, CT: Yale University Press, 1993.

———. *The Deadlocked Election of 1800: Jefferson, Burr, and the Union in the Balance.* Lawrence: University Press of Kansas, 2010.

Shaw, Peter. *American Patriots and the Ritual of Revolution.* Cambridge, MA: Harvard University Press, 1981.

———. *The Character of John Adams.* Chapel Hill: University of North Carolina Press, 1976.

Sheldon, Garret, and Daniel L. Dreisbach, eds. *Religion and Politics in Jefferson's Virginia.* Lanham: Rowman and Littlefield, 2000.

Shepard, E. Lee. "Sketches of the Old Richmond Bar: Andrew Ronald." *Richmond Quarterly* 3, no. 3 (Winter 1980): 38–41.

———. "Sketches of the Old Richmond Bar: John Warden." *Richmond Quarterly* 7, no. 1 (Summer 1984): 35–41.

Skemp, Sheila L. *William Franklin: Son of a Patriot, Servant of a King.* New York: Oxford University Press, 1990.

Slauter, Eric. *The State as a Work of Art: The Cultural Origins of the Constitution.* Chicago: University of Chicago Press, 2009.

Slayton, Robert A. *Empire Statesman: The Rise and Redemption of Al Smith.* New York: Free Press, 2001.

Smith, Anthony D. *Chosen Peoples.* New York: Oxford University Press, 2007.

Smith, Henry A. M. "Purrysburg." *South Carolina Historical and Genealogical Magazine* 10, no. 4 (October 1909): 187–219.

Sorkin, David. *The Religious Enlightenment: Protestants, Jews, and Catholics from London to Vienna.* Princeton, NJ: Princeton University Press, 2008.

Spellberg, D. A. "Could a Muslim Be President? An Eighteenth-Century Constitutional Debate." *Eighteenth-Century Studies* 39, no. 4 (Summer 2006): 485–506.

———. *Thomas Jefferson's Qur'an: Islam and the Founders.* New York: Knopf, 2013.

Stark, Rodney, and Roger Finke. "American Religion in 1776: A Statistical Portrait." *Sociological Analysis* 49, no. 1 (Spring 1988): 39–51.

Steiner, Bruce E. *Connecticut Anglicans in the Revolutionary Era: A Study in Communal Tensions.* Hartford, CT: Bicentennial Commission of Connecticut, 1978.

———. *Samuel Seabury, 1729–1796: A Study in the High Church Tradition.* Athens: Ohio University Press, 1971.

Stoll, Ira. *Samuel Adams: A Life.* New York: Free Press, 2008.

Stout, Harry S., and D. G. Hart, eds. *New Directions in American Religious History.* New York: Oxford University Press, 1997.

Strauch, Tara. "Open for Business: Philadelphia Quakers, Thanksgiving, and the Limits of Revolutionary Religious Freedom." *Church History* 85, no. 1 (March 2016): 133–39.

Thomas, Herbert. *Samuel Seabury: Priest and Physician, Bishop of Connecticut.* Hamden, CT: Shoestring, 1963.

Thompson, Mary V. *"In the Hands of Good Providence": Religion in the Life of George Washington.* Charlottesville: University of Virginia Press, 2008.

Thomson, Charles. *The Holy Bible, Containing the Old and New Covenant, Commonly Called the Old and New Testament, Translated from the Greek.* Philadelphia, 1808.

Thornton, John Wingate, ed. *The Pulpit of the American Revolution; or, The Political Sermons of the Period of 1776.* New York: B. Franklin, 1970.

Thürer, Georg. *Free and Swiss: The Story of Switzerland.* Translated by R. P. Heller and E. Long. Coral Gables, FL: University of Miami Press, 1970.

Tiedemann, Joseph S. *Reluctant Revolutionaries: New York City and the Road to Independence, 1763–1776.* Ithaca, NY: Cornell University Press, 1997.

Tocqueville, Alexis de. *Democracy in America.* Translated by Harvey C. Mansfield and Debra Winthrop. Chicago: University of Chicago Press, 2000.

Trevor-Roper, H. R., ed. *Essays in British History.* London: Macmillan, 1965.

Tuckness, Alex. "Discourses of Resistance in the American Revolution." *Journal of the History of Ideas* 64, no. 4 (October 2003): 547–63.

Tuveson, Ernest Lee. *Redeemer Nation: The Idea of America's Millennial Role.* Chicago: University of Chicago Press, 1968.

Tyler, Lyon Gardiner. *The College of William and Mary in Virginia: Its History and Work, 1693–1907.* Richmond: Whittet and Shepperson, 1907.

Voltaire, François-Marie Arquet de. *Dictionnaire philosophique.* Geneva, 1764.

Wakelyn, Jon L. *Birth of the Bill of Rights: Encyclopedia of the Antifederalists.* 2 vols. Westport, CT: Greenwood, 2004.

Waldman, Steven. *Founding Faith: How Our Founding Fathers Forged a Radical New Approach to Religious Liberty.* New York: Random House, 2008.

Waldstreicher, David. *In the Midst of Perpetual Fetes: The Making of American Nationalism.* Chapel Hill: University of North Carolina Press, 1997.

———. *Runaway America: Benjamin Franklin, Slavery, and the American Revolution.* New York: Hill and Wang, 2004.

———. *Slavery's Constitution: From Revolution to Ratification.* New York: Hill and Wang, 2010.

Walters, Kerry S. *The American Deists: Voices of Reason and Dissent in the Early Republic.* Lawrence: University Press of Kansas, 1992.

Westminster Confession of Faith. London, 1646.

Wickwire, Franklin B. *British Subministers and Colonial America, 1763–1783.* Princeton, NJ: Princeton University Press, 1966.

Wilkinson, James. *Memoirs of My Own Time.* 3 vols. Philadelphia, 1816.

Wilson, Bird. *Memoir of the Life of the Right Reverend William White, D.D., Bishop of the Protestant Episcopal Church in the State of Pennsylvania.* Philadelphia, 1839.

Wilson, Douglas L. "The Evolution of Jefferson's 'Notes on the State of Virginia.'" *Virginia Magazine of History and Biography* 112 (2004): 98–133.

Wood, Gordon S. *The American Revolution: A History.* New York: Modern Library, 2002.

———. *The Creation of the American Republic.* Chapel Hill: University of North Carolina Press, 1969.

———. *The Radicalism of the American Revolution.* New York: Knopf, 1991.

Yokota, Kariann Akemi. *Unbecoming British: How Revolutionary America Became a Postcolonial Nation.* New York: Oxford University Press, 2011.

Index

Recent Books in the Jeffersonian America Series

Maurizio Valsania
Nature's Man: Thomas Jefferson's Philosophical Anthropology

John Ragosta
Religious Freedom: Jefferson's Legacy, America's Creed

Robert M. S. McDonald, editor
Sons of the Father: George Washington and His Protégés

Simon P. Newman and Peter S. Onuf, editors
Paine and Jefferson in the Age of Revolutions

Daniel Peart
Era of Experimentation: American Political Practices in the Early Republic

Margaret Sumner
Collegiate Republic: Cultivating an Ideal Society in Early America

Christa Dierksheide
Amelioration and Empire: Progress and Slavery in the Plantation Americas

John A. Ruddiman
Becoming Men of Some Consequence: Youth and Military Service in the Revolutionary War

Jonathan J. Den Hartog
Patriotism and Piety: Federalist Politics and Religious Struggle in the New American Nation

Patrick Griffin, Robert G. Ingram, Peter S. Onuf, and Brian Schoen, editors
Between Sovereignty and Anarchy: The Politics of Violence in the American Revolutionary Era

Armin Mattes
Citizens of a Common Intellectual Homeland: The Transatlantic Origins of American Democracy and Nationhood

Julia Gaffield, editor
The Haitian Declaration of Independence: Creation, Context, and Legacy

Robert M. S. McDonald
Confounding Father: Thomas Jefferson's Image in His Own Time

Adam Jortner
Blood from the Sky: Miracles and Politics in the Early American Republic

Spencer W. McBride
Pulpit and Nation: Clergymen and the Politics of Revolutionary America

CPSIA information can be obtained
at www.ICGtesting.com
Printed in the USA
FSHW011256091219
64898FS